BOTSWANA
Vryburg
BOPHUTHATSWANA
Kuruman River
Kuruman
Reivilo
SCHWEIZER-RENEKE
BOPHUTHATSWANA
Taung
Hartswater
TVL.
Kathu
KURUMAN HILLS
Lohatlha
Glosam
Manganore
Owendale
Danielskuil
Postmasburg
Lime Acres
Boetsap
WOLMARANSSTAD
Vaal River
Vaal River
Barkly West
Schmidtsdrif
Griquatown
Campbell
ASBESTOS MOUNTAINS
BLOEMFONTEIN
KIMBERLEY
BLOEMFONTEIN
Douglas
Modder River
Orange River
O.F.S.
Koffiefontein
Orange River
PROVINCE
PORT ELIZABETH
DE AAR
COLESBERG
SPRINGFONTEIN
GW01606842

KAIAS & COCOPANS

Kaias & Cocopans

The Story of Mining
in South Africa's Northern Cape

ANTHONY HOCKING
Illustrations by Dave Gaskill

Hollards
JOHANNESBURG

PUBLISHED BY HOLLARDS PUBLISHERS
75 8TH AVENUE, PARKTOWN NORTH
JOHANNESBURG, SOUTH AFRICA

THE NORTHERN CAPE MINE MANAGERS ASSOCIATION IS GRATEFUL
TO JOE VERMAAK OF SAMANCOR, WHO DREW THE MAP THAT APPEARS
ON THE ENDPAPERS

ISBN 0 620 06442 0

Set in 10½ on 12 pt Bembo

Printed and bound in South Africa
by the Rustica Press (Pty) Ltd, Wynberg, Cape

To the Memory of the Pioneers

AND TO GORDON JARMAN.

THIS IS A SMALL GIFT TO REMIND YOU AND RUTH WHERE NANNA AND I GREW UP AND WHERE BOTH OF YOU HAD THE OPPERTUNITY TO SHARE IN.

THIS BOOK IS TO SAY THANK YOU BOTH FOR YOUR KINDNESS WE HOPE YOU TWO WILL ENJOY RETIREMENT.

REGARDS

PHILIP AND NANNA BOTHA.

1991.09.28.

Contents

List of Illustrations

INTRODUCTION

Kaias & Cocopans

KAIAS ARE one-roomed huts and cocopans are tiptrucks on rails. Both terms are as South African as boeresport yet have earned places in dictionaries published far away. The American *Webster's International Dictionary* defines 'cocopan' as 'a mining tipcart' and the British *Oxford English Dictionary* says it is derived from '*nqukumbana*', the Zulu for 'stumpy cart'. The *OED* says 'kaia' or 'kya' is 'an African's hut; also quarters of an African servant', but the definition is too narrow. In today's Northern Cape, a kaia may well be a miner's office and blasting shelter.

The Northern Cape is a vast region of South Africa's Cape Province, and *Kaias & Cocopans* tells the story of its mining industry from the earliest times to the present. Parts of the region fall within the Karoo sheep country, parts within the cattle ranges of the Kalahari thirstland. To the north is Botswana, to the west are South West Africa/Namibia and Namaqualand, to the east lie the Transvaal and Orange Free State. The southern boundary is not so easy to define, but the southernmost mine is at Copperton which lies 65 km south-west of Prieska on the Orange River.

Geologists see the Northern Cape as a hotchpotch of systems that have each made their mark on the landscape. Precambrian lava spilled across the basal rock more than 1 500 million years ago. Seas came and went, and in their passage laid thick beds of sediment and then exposed them to the forces of erosion. Movements of the earth tipped the sediments, forced up ranges of hills and mountains and interrupted the neat strata with faults and volcanic dykes that thrust from below. Successive Ice Ages purged the surface formations and left beds of debris in their wake.

Today, much of the Northern Cape is buried in a deep layer of Kalahari sand and the terrain is predominantly flat. Two ranges of high ground curl through the region from south to north. The eastern range contains the Asbestos Mountains and Kuruman Hills and consists largely of banded ironstone. To the west are the Langeberg and Koranna mountains which hold jasper and quartzite. Between these ranges lies a basin of manganese and haematite iron ore, and associated with them are vast beds of dolomite and limestone that to the south-east form the Ghaap Plateau.

Towards the south, the plateau ends in spectacular cliffs that overlook a plain stretching to the south. Crossing the plain from east to west is the Orange River, which for much of its length carries the water of the Vaal River from the north-west. The rivers meet in 'Griqualand West', which before joining the Cape Colony in 1879 was a territory with its own administration. The same went for 'British Bechuanaland' to the north, which joined the Cape Colony in 1895. The south-western portion of the region has been known as 'Bushmanland' and the north-west as 'Gordonia'.

The Northern Cape was inhabited long before black or white men put in an appearance. Archaeologists have found evidence of man that stretches back hundreds of thousands of years and today's Khoisan Bushmen provide links with the cultures that have disappeared. Hottentots whose forbears were from East Africa have lived in the Northern Cape for at least 3 000 years and dominated the region until the eighteenth century when the Tswana (or Bechuana) arrived from the west. Early in the nineteenth century Griqua frontiersmen of the old Cape Colony crossed the Orange River from the south.

The Griquas were half white and half Hottentot. They were a product of Africa yet they dressed like Europeans and lived aboard wagons like the taal-speaking white trekboers who were on the move all through South Africa. Before long, isolated trekboer families tested the Northern Cape for themselves but were discouraged by the scarcity of surface water. The first Europeans to make the Northern Cape their home were missionaries, but during the 1860s and 1870s there was an influx of white men after the discovery of diamonds in Griqualand.

It was 'diamond fever' that infected the Northern Cape with kaias and cocopans. White diggers first lived in tents, but as soon as materials became available many invested in one-roomed shacks of wood or iron that their black labourers soon dubbed 'kaias'. The 'cocopans' were probably introduced by former copper miners who had worked in Namaqualand. Photographs show that Namaqualand copper mines had rudimentary cocopans at least as early as the middle 1860s, really no more than little flatbed trucks mounted on four flanged wheels and pushed or pulled on narrow gauge rails.

The diggers improved the cocopans by replacing the flat platforms with detachable side-tipping pans that had high walls and rounded bottoms. Cocopans came in various sizes, but the most popular held one ton of kimberlite 'blue ground' and to this day diamond men calculate tonnages in cocopan 'loads'. The cocopans were so useful that during the 1880s they were introduced to the Transvaal's gold and coal mines, and later to asbestos and base metals mines opened in the Northern Cape. Some were pushed by hand, some pulled by donkeys, some hauled by locomotives or hoisted by winches.

The design of the cocopan was established at an early stage and changed little in a century. The kaia, meanwhile, was running through endless permutations. Asbestos 'tributors' lived in the veld with their families and built rectangular stone kaias close to their workings. Prospectors looking for diamonds, iron ore and other minerals lived in prefabricated huts made of corrugated iron. Tswana accustomed to lands with little stone built rondavels of brushwood faced with mud. Koranna Hottentots opted for beehive domes that were admirably cool during summer.

In older mines of the manganese basin, miners traditionally use kaias as homes from home. Each miner is allocated a section of the mine and a gang to help work it, and he assigns several men to build him a kaia from whatever materials are available. In some cases kaias have been built of oil drums, though these are draughty in winter. At least one has a roof consisting of four upturned cocopans. But a typical kaia is built of blocks of stone cut locally, a rectangular structure with a doorway and a window or two and a strong roof held up by thick beams.

Beside the kaia there is a drum of water replenished from a water cart, and almost certainly a cooking place where the miner's 'piccanin' brews coffee. Inside, there may be a stone couch cushioned with long grass where the miner takes his ease after lunch. There may be a chair and perhaps a table but in many kaias the only pieces of furniture are two red boxes, one for new explosives and the other for old charges that have misfired. Papers are 'filed' on a convenient nail. Awaiting a blast, the miner shelters in his kaia and catches up on his paperwork.

'Leading hands' or 'bossboys' in a miner's gang have a kaia of their own, and the rank and file crawl into a large blasting shelter that in most cases consists of a square of oil drums with a solid roof thrown over them. Until 1979 the manganese gangs of older mines used cocopans to carry ore from the working face to the sorting floors, but now the work is mechanised. The cocopans have been retired and many have been sold as metal scrap. Only in the asbestos mines is the cocopan more than a memory, and even there its days may be numbered.

In Barkly West on the Vaal River there is a café named The Cocopan, and on the pavement outside are two cocopans painted bright red and used as rubbish bins. That is a less than romantic finale to a long career, and nobody regrets it more than Piet Ludick who since the 1940s has been working at the Ulco limestone complex some 30 km north-west of Barkly West. 'When I started here, the great treat on Sundays was to go to the quarry and ride in the cocopans,' he says. 'I remember it well because that's how I courted the most beautiful girl I've known. Today she's my wife.'[1]

CHAPTER ONE BEFORE 1869

Banded Ironstone

KATHU FOREST is a prickly wilderness of withaak and camelthorn on the fringe of the Kalahari thirstland. The thick vegetation is fed by large reserves of underground water that in places used to bubble to the surface. The springs attracted nomadic trekboers as early as the 1840s, and more recently they have served prospectors and miners working on the rich iron ore deposits of Sishen farm. The miners' presence is appropriate, for they are heirs to a great tradition. For hundreds of thousands of years the fountains of Kathu have attracted men who work with stone.

Not far from the springs there is a circular outcrop of red-brown banded ironstone, a superhard laminate made up of thin strata of iron and silica that from the side look like layers of plywood. The outcrop is about 200 metres in diameter and at first sight it seems like scores of similar formations elsewhere in the Northern Cape. But this one is special, a Stone Age quarry where workers patiently chiselled flakes from lumps of rock to make hand tools. Modern generations have little affection for banded ironstone, but in ages long forgotten it was a mineral of the first rank.

The banded ironstone quarry was first noticed by a local farmer, Naas Viljoen, who is an enthusiastic amateur historian. Flakes lie thick on the ground but the outcrop has lain naked to the elements for thousands of years. To date Stone Age finds an archaeologist has to rely on organic evidence like animal or human remains or peat that preserves pollen. There is no such evidence at Kathu, so archaeologists say it is impossible to say when the banded ironstone was quarried or who was responsible.

During 1974 Naas Viljoen noticed several deep sinkholes on his farm, apparently formed through the collapse of cavities hollowed out by underground streams. When they first appeared the sinkholes were flooded, but gradually they emptied as water from nearby boreholes was pumped to Sishen mine. One day the farmer's sons were playing near the sinkholes and noticed some unusual stones at the bottom. They climbed down a soil ramp for a closer look, and when they showed the stones to their father he immediately recognised them as almond-shaped hand-axes from the Stone Age.

Most of the hand-axes had been made from banded ironstone but some had been chiselled from white quartzite or black chert and a few from relatively soft sandstone. The largest pieces were about 20 cm long and up to 10 cm wide, and many were coated in a mysterious natural glaze that made them appear brand-new. Naas Viljoen found many more hand-axes in the sinkholes, and several samples reached the McGregor Memorial Museum in Kimberley along with enamel tooth-cappings also found in the holes, the only remains of long-dead elephants.

At the museum the hand-axes and tooth-cappings were examined by Peter Beaumont, the resident archaeologist. Beaumont was a disciple of the famous Professor Raymond Dart of Johannesburg's University of the Witwatersrand, who in the 1920s had upset the world of anthropology when he identified the man-ape *Australopithecus* from a fossil skull found in the Northern Cape. In the 1930s Dart had similarly outraged archaeologists when he claimed that Stone Age man had been a miner—a theory vindicated in the 1960s when a pigment mine in Swaziland was shown to be more than 40 000 years old.

The archaeologists concerned in the Swaziland discovery included Peter Beaumont, and he and a colleague dramatically revised notions of the antiquity of the Stone and Iron Ages in Southern Africa. In the Northern Cape, Beaumont became interested in the Kathu sinkholes because of the elephants' teeth. 'It's most unusual to find animal remains associated with an ancient hand-axe site,' he says. 'From evidence in East Africa we knew the elephants' teeth were from a species that became extinct 500 000 years ago. It meant that the hand-axes were at least that old and possibly much older.'[1]

Beaumont visited the sinkholes with Naas Viljoen and found that the hand-axes covered an area several hundred metres long. The find cried out for excavation, but the archaeologist was brought up short when he realised that to reach the Stone Age strata he would have to burrow through three metres of surface deposits. That was beyond the museum's resources but there was help close at hand. Sishen's mine management provided a large mechanical shovel that cleared many tons

1. A miner's kaia, still in daily use at the Lohatlha manganese mine north of Postmasburg.

Humphry Clinker

2. A miner's tools—pick, shovel and cocopan.

Humphry Clinker

3. Archaeologist Peter Beaumont displays one of the banded ironstone hand-axes found at Kathu Springs, close to Sishen.

McGregor Memorial Museum

4. Gatkoppies near Postmasburg, an ancient specularite mine visited by many early travellers.

Humphry Clinker

of sand and earth and gave Beaumont a flying start.

Late in 1979 the archaeologist and a team of helpers gingerly opened a window into the Stone Age, a hole not much more than two metres square. Before long they were unearthing scores of hand-axes and other artefacts. Normally archaeologists store their finds in small sample bags like those used by geologists, but at Kathu Beaumont's helpers collected so many that they had to resort to grain sacks. By the time they reached the lowest strata they had uncovered half a million separate items and had dug through a sequence of levels more than 3,5 metres deep.

From an early stage of the dig Beaumont realised that near the top strata there was a sharp break in the sequence of hand-axes. The tools towards the bottom had been made by *homo erectus*, a forerunner of modern *homo sapiens sapiens* who lived between 300 000 and 1,6 million years ago. Those at the top were relics of *homo sapiens* Neanderthals dating back 120 000 years. Ironically, Kathu's earlier residents had been far more painstaking than those who came later. *Homo erectus's* hand-axes were near-perfectly symmetrical and many remain razor-sharp. His grandson's tools were no more than crude bludgeons with a point.

For Beaumont, the chief interest in finding the younger tools was that with them were lumps of specularite and red ochre of the sort that Southern Africa's peoples have long prized as cosmetics. Specularite or '*blinkklip*' (shining stone) is black iron ore with a brilliant glitter that can be rubbed into hair to make it sparkle. Red ochre is haematite or 'blood-stone' and ancient man commonly used it to represent strength and vitality, smearing it over his own body or sprinkling it on corpses in vain hopes that they would rise from the dead. Some authorities see haematite as the direct ancestor of rouge and lipstick.

Where it was available, ancient man favoured a soft variety of haematite known as limonite that feels like shoe polish. Limonite was comparatively scarce but if necessary those needing red ochre could pound haematite rock into powder and mix it with fat. Specularite, however, was much more difficult to come by and therefore more valuable. The richest sources were underground caverns in the Northern Cape, and the most extensive workings so far discovered were on the farm Doornfontein which lies north-west of Postmasburg and belongs to the Associated Manganese Mines of South Africa.

During the 1960s an Associated Manganese board member contacted Adrian Boshier, one of the archaeologists concerned in the Swaziland pigment mine excavation, and asked him to examine Doornfontein and other ancient mines on Associated Manganese properties. Boshier recruited two Postmasburg high school students, Rudolf and Louis Vertue, to guide him to local caves that might have been mines. That way two new sites were identified, and in 1969 Boshier brought in Peter Beaumont to take part in a lightning dig.

Boshier had found that the Doornfontein workings consisted of at least four separate chambers that together stretched more than 100 metres. In two of the chambers the roof or 'hanging wall' had collapsed. He and Beaumont decided to concentrate on just one chamber and as a first step had to smoke out thousands of bats. In the past the bats had proved a valuable source of guano and local farmers had dug it out to serve as nitrate fertiliser. Now the archaeologists probed beneath the guano and cut twin trial trenches across the selected chamber, each just short of a metre wide and in places excavated right down to bedrock.

In less than two weeks at Doornfontein the archaeologists and their helpers removed nearly a ton of earth and recovered nearly two thousand stone mining tools including hammers, choppers, chisels, and wedges. They also found animal and human remains, including the skull and bones of a man apparently crushed in an ancient rockfall. The remains date from about AD 800 and are now in Kimberley. Peter Beaumont notes that the bones are slightly charred and show signs of cut marks, which suggests insult was added to injury and the victim of the disaster was cannibalised.

After sifting through all the evidence collected at Doornfontein, Boshier and Beaumont reached what seems a modest conclusion: 'The findings show that a portion of its specularite content was being extracted immediately subsequent to AD 800, by tall, robust, and perhaps Khoikhoi-speaking Khoisan miners who made degenerate Late Stone Age artefacts and "Hottentot" pottery, and who were apparently hunters and gatherers only.'[2] Even so, the mine was the oldest so far discovered in South Africa and the archaeologists tentatively dated it back to 2 000 BC or even earlier.

Hills with a Hole

Doornfontein was not the only source of pigment in the Northern Cape. There used to be evidence of old workings at Sishen but modern mining operations swallowed them years ago. At least three more ancient mines survive on Associated Manganese farms, and the most famous of all overshadows the Groenwater River close to Postmasburg. Today known as Gatkoppies or 'Hills with a Hole', the site was visited by white men at least as early as 1801 and probably before that. Indeed, the ancient mine is described in a number of early travel books.

All the early visitors complained of the difficulty of climbing into Gatkoppies' deep 'caves'. The modern tourist finds it much easier. The central chamber collapsed decades ago and one can clamber up the hillside and walk straight into the cavity. Clearly visible on the walls are gouges and scrape marks left by the tools of the ancient miners, who in Gatkoppies' recorded history included Tswana as well as Hottentots. Adrian Boshier visited the old mine as early as 1968, but it was not until 1979 that Peter Beaumont supervised a trial 'dig' like the one at Doornfontein.

'Again we found vast quantities of artefacts,' he says. 'The strata went down nearly three metres and included metal trading goods and amber-coloured beads that were almost certainly brought in from the north. They're an indication of the site's importance as an economic centre, for specularite from the Northern Cape was carried all over Southern Africa. We also found Hottentot pottery and sheep bones that helped us establish who the ancient miners were. And in the unconsolidated layers at the top there was evidence of the Tswana who eventually began mining specularite for themselves and cut out the need for Hottentot middlemen.'[1]

The first white travellers to record a visit to Gatkoppies were members of the Somerville–Truter expedition of 1801, sent north from the Cape Colony to buy cattle from the Tswana. William Somerville is probably best known as the husband of Mary Somerville, who gave her name to one of Oxford University's most illustrious colleges. Somerville's *Narrative* records that on the journey north a man who knew the region took him to see the hill 'at which Koras (*Koranna Hottentots*) are said to dig the metallic ore with which they besmear their bodies'.[3]

A fuller account was provided by a youngster accompanying the expedition, Petrus Borcherds, in a letter to his father: 'We went there (*to Gatkoppies*) and found that in a pointed hill was a cave, dug to an unbelievably deep depth and width. To see the furthest parts a candle was needed. Filled with dark-red earths, mixed with iron parts, greasy or very slippery to the touch and in weight about the same as iron, between which were spread streaks or veins of yellowish hard matter, this cave was inhabited by wood pigeons and filled with their nests, in several of which we found eggs—by the remains of fires, bones etc we concluded that people had visited not long ago.'[4]

Four years after the Somerville–Truter party, a second expedition was sent north to make peace with warring Bushmen and gain information about the Koranna and Tswana. One of its members was a young German physician named Hinrich Lichtenstein whose task was to make scientific observations. Lichtenstein's *Travels in Southern Africa* names Gatkoppies as 'the most southern point to which the wanderings of the Beetjuan (*Tswana*) people extend'.[5] Members of the party entered the mine with lanterns and after thirty paces came upon an archway only 50 cm high.

'Through this we were obliged to crawl,' wrote Lichtenstein, 'when we entered a sort of passage, running in a horizontal direction, by which we soon arrived at a spacious lofty-arched room, whence issued six or eight other caverns. All about the arched sides and roof, the chrystals sparkled with the reflection of our lights, and our hands and cloaths had acquired, from the soft and greasy nature of the stone, quite a shining brown appearance. Large pieces of the stone were broke off with a little exertion, and great masses about the roof seemed ready to be shaken down with any convulsion.'[5]

Each of the early travellers tried to explain how Gatkoppies 'blinkklip' was used, none better than the naturalist William Burchell in *Travels in the Interior of Southern Africa*. Burchell made a private journey through the region in 1812 and reported that Tswana knew specularite as *sibilo*, 'soft and greasy to the touch. . . . The mode of preparing it and using it is simply grinding it together with grease, and smearing it generally over the body, but chiefly on the head; and the hair is often so much loaded and clotted with an accumulation of it, that the clots exhibit the appearance of lumps of mineral.'[6]

Mining methods at Gatkoppies were haphazard, and both Lichtenstein and Burchell recorded recent disasters when miners had been killed by cave-ins. Burchell commented: 'The place being open to every one without restriction or regulations, each person had dug away the quantity he wanted, from that part where it was found of the best quality; and no one appears to have reflected on the necessity, in such excavations especially when the rock is in parts of a loose nature, of leaving pillars at proper distances to support the roof.'[6]

Peter Beaumont says that Gatkoppies is the best documented archaeological site in Southern Africa, even though none of the early travellers saw it in operation. A clearer picture of early mining methods comes from E J Dunn, who in 1872 visited an open-pit working 40 km north-west of Prieska. Beaumont went looking for the site and eventually located an old mine on the farm Nauwka. But he cannot be sure it is the same one, for in his mine the mineral was specularite whereas in Dunn's it was haematite.

'Shortly after leaving the spring at Naugat,' wrote Dunn, 'on the road to Steerman's Pits, little beacons are to be seen on the road-side, formed of a few stones. Leading away from the road up the hill side. They are placed at every few yards, while alongside runs a footpath. At the end, in the hill side, is a great excavation. Here is the famous locality at which that indispensable toilet requisite to all good tribesmen, red paint, is obtained. With this they smear not only their person, but their clothes and utensils. In fact, it is quite respectable to daub this unctuous red haematite over everything, and therefore every one does it.

'Taking off our coats, we descend. The precaution is very necessary, for if this fine oxide of iron but touches anything, it can only be removed with difficulty. How many pilgrims must have visited this spot to dig out such a large hole, and that too with such implements! Half an old axe head, with a piece of stick thrust through for a handle, the edge of another broken axe, and an old koodoo horn are left on the premises for the use of visitors. By the way, there is no book to sign names in. The soft portion has been followed. All around are huge blocks of hard haematite, black, hard, tough, and heavy.'[7]

The Philosophers

Travellers like Hinrich Lichtenstein and William Burchell were trained observers. Their books brim with fascinating sidelights covering everything that caught their fancy, from flora and fauna to rock art and rainfall. In the language of their time they were true 'philosophers', lovers of wisdom for its own sake. Their deductions were not always correct but their anecdotes were colourful and rich in detail. There was, for instance, Lichtenstein's account of a salt pan he visited not far south of the Orange River.

'We arrived at a perfect plain,' Lichtenstein wrote, 'of some hours in circumference, which, in very heavy rains, is filled entirely with water, and resembles a lake. When it dries again, after having been thus overflowed, it is covered with a thick crust of natron. In this situation the valley so entirely resembles a frozen lake, that even in going over it, from the glitter of the natron, and the crackling of the salt under the feet, any one might easily be deceived into the belief that they were actually going on ice.

'The crust was in many places, particularly about the middle, where the moisture had continued the longest, from two or three lines thick, and might be broke off in large lumps. On every side the footsteps of game of various kinds were perfectly traced in the salt, so that I had to regret the brittleness of the crystals, which would not resist impressions. This place is generally called the Chalk Fountain, the base of one of the hills consisting entirely of a white chalk, while higher up it is composed of a variety of minerals running one into another.'[5] A century later, mining men began extracting the salt from such pans, and some are still being worked today.

Lichtenstein and his companions forded the Orange River at a place the Koranna called Priskab, which later developed as the town of Prieska. 'The river here makes a curve in the form of an S,' wrote Lichtenstein, 'so that in the first day's journey we did not entirely quit its banks, but remained always upon, or at a short distance from them. The most northern part of this curve is four hours distant from the ford: but as we loitered a long time upon the road, and a part of our company did not return from the chase till late, we only reached it as the sun was fast declining.'[5]

From Lichtenstein's description and particularly in view of what he found there, we may guess that he camped close to the site of Koegas. Directly before him was the river, and directly behind was a steep wall of rock. There was another cliff opposite. Lichtenstein wrote: 'The steep walls, indeed, which compel the river to take this extraordinary turn are extremely picturesque. They rear their heads to a vast height, often curving like arches over the willows and mimosas which ornament the banks: vast blocks which have fallen, and between which these trees slowly and sparingly shoot up, display forcibly the vast power of the waters when they rise to a considerable height.'[5]

At this point of his narrative, Lichtenstein sprang a surprise and described a substance until then unknown to science: 'The stone of which the rock consists stretches in strata of a sort of slate deep into the river; it is of a fine blue colour, and is esteemed by the colonists extremely durable; they use it therefore very much, where it can be procured, for rubbing over their houses and walls, first oiling it well. Farther within the valley the rocks are covered with a sort of crust of red yellow ochre, which proves that they contain a great quantity.'[5]

That is all Lichtenstein had to say about his discovery, but a footnote accompanying his text is more helpful. According to the footnote a physicist named Klaproth later examined Lichtenstein's blue rock in Berlin 'and pronounced it a new species of mountain, and gave it the name of *Blue-iron-stone* (Blau Eisenstein). Its particular hardness, and the durability of the blue colour, which resists fire, are very marked characters of it.'[5] But even Klaproth's report is less than clear, and neither he nor Lichtenstein commented on the rock's most curious quality. It consisted of crystallised fibres that could be rubbed off like cotton. Lichtenstein had stumbled on a new form of asbestos, and within a decade scientists would dub it 'crocidolite' from Greek words meaning 'woolly stone'.

Perhaps Lichtenstein can be forgiven for his vague description because even the 'chrysotile' asbestos found in Europe had been neglected for centuries. Even so, it had a long history. Asbestos was an ancient Greek word meaning 'inextinguishable', and Greeks had employed asbestos fibres as everlasting wicks in ceremonial lamps. There is a record of the great sculptor Callimachus using such a wick in 436 BC when he made a golden lamp for the temple of Pallas Athene in Athens, where it was to be kept lighted for eternity. The Romans valued asbestos fibre too, both as an everlasting wick and as a source of thread spun to weave cloth that would never catch fire.

Fragments of asbestos cloth were found in the ruins of Pompeii, which was destroyed in AD 79. The Emperor Charlemagne is said to have used an asbestos tablecloth that could be dry-cleaned—rather than have it washed, he ordered his servants to hold it over flames. The use of asbestos seems to have died away during the Middle Ages, but not long before Lichtenstein arrived in the Northern Cape, Napoleon Bonaparte had been encouraging asbestos research in Italy. Lichtenstein's rather cryptic account suggests that Northern Cape settlers were already using asbestos fibres as a building sealer, presumably mixed with mud.

Mining men usually champion Lichtenstein as the discoverer of blue asbestos, but it was apparently William Burchell who first recognised it for what it was. Burchell came upon it in the country of the Griquas, a frontier race living north of the Orange River that had resulted from alliances between whites and Hottentots. Griquas customarily dressed in the European style—according to Burchell that meant they possessed handkerchiefs. Burchell's asbestos was located near the site of Griquatown and so was 'Eland's Fountain' which would one day be mined.

'Little notice as the Hottentots, in general, take of mineralogical objects,' began the former schoolmaster, 'their attention has been attracted by a production of these mountains, which, observing to have the singular property of becoming, on being rubbed between the fingers, a soft cotton-like substance, resembling that which they made from their old handkerchiefs for the purpose of tinder, they have named *Doeksteen*, (Handkerchief-stone, or Cloth-stone). They pointed out a particular part of the mountains where it might be found; and I made an excursion for the purpose of examining it, and at the same time to explore the *Kloof-Valley* and its productions.

'The *Doeksteen* is a kind of *Asbestos*, of a blue color. Having found the spot, I made a drawing of the remarkable laminated rocks, between the thin horizontal layers of which it is found. These veins of asbestos are of various thickness, from the tenth of an inch to half an inch, and consequently their fibre, which is always transverse, is very short. But, in the mountains, at a place called *Eland's Fountain*, about five and twenty miles north-eastward, some is found, the fibres of which are above two inches long. This is, in fact, another species, and differs not only in the length, but in the more compact, perfectly straight and glossy fibre, and in its deeper color.'[6]

On this last spot Burchell went astray, but he was on target when he identified a hardened form of asbestos today known as tiger's eye, which is found only in the Northern Cape. He described it in these terms: 'Between these laminae (*of banded ironstone*) a beautiful kind of stone is found, sometimes of a blue and sometimes of a silky golden color, from the twentieth part of an inch to three inches thick. It is a *species of asbestos* in a less motive and flaxen state, with compact fibres of a flinty hardness, either transverse or oblique, straight or wavy. The fracture of these laminae is generally according to the direction of the fibres. When cut and polished, the stone exhibits a very beautiful appearance.'[6]

Burchell noticed deposits of another gemstone that has served the Northern Cape well: 'a handsome kind of jasper, brown, striped with black.'[6] But it was not only travel writers who explored the region's treasures. At about the time of Burchell's journey the name 'Asbestos Mountains' was added to the map of Southern Africa, and the range was a familiar landmark when the missionary John Campbell reached the area in 1814. The frontispiece of Campbell's *Travels* depicts him striding about the Northern Cape under the shade of a huge parasol. He struck the Asbestos Mountains at a Griqua outpost named Hardcastle, near the site of Niekerkshoop.

'Some of us walked after breakfast to examine the asbestos rocks,' wrote Campbell, 'where we found plenty of that rare material, between strata of rocks. That which becomes, by a little beating, soft as cotton, is all of Prussian blue. When ascending a mountain alone, I found some of the colour of gold, but not soft, or of cotton texture like the blue: some I found white, and brown, and green, etc.'[8] Like Burchell he had found tiger's eye, and Niekerkshoop is an even richer source than Griquatown.

Campbell was the first to appreciate the economic significance of the Northern Cape's blue asbestos. 'Had this land been known to the ancients in the days of imperial Rome,' intoned the missionary, 'many a mercantile pilgrimage would have been made to the Asbestos Mountains in Griqualand. Were the ladies' gowns in England woven of this substance, many lives would annually be saved, that are lost by their dress catching fire; for cloth made from it endures the fire, and the ancients burned their dead in such cloth to retain their ashes.'[8] In spite of Campbell's enthusiasm, it would be a long time before the world's fire brigades invested in asbestos suiting.

Like Burchell and Lichtenstein, Campbell commented on the vast reserves of iron ore in the Northern Cape. But they had been preceded by the Somerville–Truter expedition of 1801. As Petrus Borcherds wrote to his father: 'Our supposition was confirmed that the country must be rich in iron ore when we arrived at a spring the next day situated amongst many rocky hills, which we found to be so abundant in iron that the removal of the compass from one stone to another, brought about a different indication of the north point every time, so that the spring also known by the name *Haggara* was named Yzerbergs Fontein by us.'[4]

In spite of this abundance, there is no evidence that any of the Northern Cape's peoples tried to smelt iron ore like their cousins of the Transvaal. Against that, Lichtenstein found that at any rate the Tswana were skilled blacksmiths. When his party needed urgent repairs to their wagons, 'two of these people were hired, for wages agreed upon, and performed their work with a celerity which appeared scarcely credible to our people, considering the imperfect nature of their tools.

'The most essential part of their work was to shorten the iron bands of the wheels, which from the drying of the wood had become too large, and were very loose. For this purpose they made a sort of pile of wood embers, and to keep them alive used bellows made of a couple of goat-skins, very similar to those used by the Koassas (*Xhosa*); they had heavy iron hammers, which had a sharpened side that served as an axe; instead of tongs, they had only two thick pieces of stick, with which they took up the hot iron, and for an anvil they used a large block of stone. Notwithstanding such impediments, the work was finished by evening.'[5]

Lichtenstein found that the Tswana could also work copper and brass, but in each case their raw materials came from the north. Burchell felt that Tswana's knowledge of metals was 'very imperfect; and they were totally ignorant of their relative value according to the estimation of civilised nations. The word *tsupi* or *tsipi* (tseepy), used alone, signifies iron; *tsipi e kubilu*, literally "red iron", expresses copper; *tsipi e tseka*, "yellow iron", was the name for gold as well as brass; and silver was called *tsipi e chu* (or *shu*) or "white iron". It seems, therefore, that the word *tsipi* may be taken as equivalent to that of "metal".'[5]

Enter Robert Moffat

Banded ironstone, red ochre, blinkklip, salt, blue asbestos, tiger's eye, jasper, iron ore—and limestone. The missionary Robert Moffat arrived in the Northern Cape in 1920 and soon drew attention to the most plentiful mineral of all, though he understandably confused it with less valuable dolomite that looks very similar. Years later he described the mission buildings of Kuruman as constructed 'of blue or dove-coloured limestone' when today we see they are dolomite plain and simple. As a man of science Moffat was not in the same league as Lichtenstein and Burchell.

'The substratum of the whole of the country,' wrote Moffat in *Missionary Labours and Scenes in Southern Africa*, 'as far as the Orange River, is compact limestone, which in some of the Hamhanna hills rises considerably above the neighbouring plain; but these only form the basis of argillaceous hills and iron schist, on the top of which the compass moves at random, or according to the position in which it is placed. The strata of these schistose formations are often found to bend and curve into all shapes, frequently with an appearance of golden asbestos, but extremely hard.

'The common blue asbestos is to be found at Gamopeti, in the neighbourhood (*of Kuruman*), the same as that found near the Orange River. The limestone extends to Old Lithako (*the former capital of the Batlapin Tswana*) where there are hills of basalt and primitive limestone; among which masses of serpentine rock, of various colours, usually called pipe stone, are to be met with. Beyond the Batlapi dominions, towards the Molopo (*River*), there is abundance of granite, green stone, etc, while the limestone formation, towards the west, terminates among the sandy wilds of the southern Zahara'[9]—a quaint name for the Kalahari thirstland.

That was all Moffat had to say about the Northern Cape's geology, for he reserved most of his curiosity for people and agriculture. Even so he is worth a close look because more than anyone he helped to make the Northern Cape what it is today. Born in Scotland in 1795, he volunteered for service with the London Missionary Society and in 1817 began a short ministry in Namaqualand. During a visit to Cape Town he married Mary Smith, the daughter of a market gardener who had employed him before he left Britain and who had sown the seeds of his interest in plants.

On the same trip, Moffat met John Campbell who was in South Africa again to sort out problems affecting a mission to the Tswana. Campbell was impressed by Moffat's results in Namaqualand and asked him for help. Moffat agreed, and he and his bride spent their honeymoon trekking towards Bechuanaland. They were brought up short when the governor of the Cape Colony refused to let them travel further than Klaarwater, a mission station founded early in the century to serve the Griquas.

Klaarwater was soon to be renamed Griquatown, the first European-style settlement north of the Orange River. But when the Moffats arrived it was little more than an outspan sited to take advantage of three natural springs. At heart the Griquas were trekboers and they lived aboard their wagons, men of the frontier who prized freedom to go where they wanted. Already many of those who had crossed the Orange to join the mission settlement had grown disenchanted and moved on to new 'independent republics' of their own, Campbell and Danielskuil.

Not far from Danielskuil there is a fascinating group of Bushman engravings that must date from this period. The engravings show men on horseback, half-covered wagons, women with long dresses and even ostriches penned in a kraal—perhaps the Danielskuil 'republic's' first citizens. In charge there was an old Griqua leader named Barend Barends who employed a deep sinkhole as a prison. According to tradition there were poisonous snakes at the bottom, and a prisoner who survived a night with them was hauled up and released. That was how 'Daniel's Kuil' got its name, a reference to the Old Testament story of Daniel in the Lion's Den.

Returning to the Moffats, we find they had to spend half a year in Klaarwater. The administration was holding them up because it could not justify more 'English' missions beyond the frontier when 'Dutch' colonists were strictly forbidden to settle there. Then came a change of heart. The Moffats pressed forward and in 1821 they reached the Kuruman River where they met the Batlapin Tswana.

The name 'Kuruman' is said to recall 'Khuduma', an aggressive Bushman leader who lived near the river towards the end of the eighteenth century. The Batlapin Tswana arrived in the region at about that time, pushed westwards from the Transvaal by more powerful rivals. The Bushmen preyed on Tswana cattle, and the Tswana took revenge with an ambush in which Khuduma was killed. According to tradition he was buried on the hill Gamohaan which overlooks the town of Kuruman. His followers were forced to flee to the parched regions to the west.

In spite of their success against the Bushmen the Batlapin Tswana were ill-equipped as warriors and were still threatened by tribes to the east. They were at the end of a line that led all the way to the expanding empire of Shaka of the Zulu. During 1823 Moffat learnt that an army led by a fierce prophetess named Mantatee was on the warpath and heading towards Batlapin territory. He immediately went to Klaarwater and raised a force of 100 mounted Griquas who rode against Mantatee's followers and routed them. Moffat became a hero to the Tswana, and the stage was set for a ministry that was to last for nearly half a century.

Waiting for the political situation to return to normal, the Moffats lived at Klaarwater during 1824 and produced their only child, a Mary like her mother. Moffat took a hand in building a new mission residence from blocks of stone now known as griqualandite, a form of hardened asbestos that represents a halfway stage between blue fibre and tiger's eye. The residence included a large hall to serve as chapel and meeting-room and two other rooms for missionaries and their families. It still stands, the oldest stone building in the Northern Cape.

The stone for the Klaarwater mission was probably gathered from surrounding kopjes, for there is no record of any quarrying. Before the building was finished the Moffats had returned to Bechuanaland, where the chief of the Batlapin Tswana granted them a piece of land on the Kuruman River. Moffat had chosen the site for its agricultural potential and planned to dig an irrigation furrow to bring water from Kuruman's 'Eye', a spring that produces water every day in millions of litres. Moffat's irrigation system was the first of its kind in Southern Africa.

In Kuruman, Moffat joined forces with a fellow missionary named William Hamilton, and the two men constructed a series of buildings including the beautiful mission church that has been described as 'Africa's Canterbury' and which opened for worship in 1838. The church and three of the other buildings have been proclaimed as national monuments. In serving his congregation, Moffat insisted on high standards. Converts were not baptised until they had renounced polygamy, and worshippers were not admitted to the church unless dressed in the European fashion.

For years, Moffat had been working on a written version of the Tswana language and had produced a Sechuana translation of the whole New Testament. In 1839 he travelled to Britain in hopes of finding a publisher, and while he was away a young medical missionary from Scotland arrived in South Africa and was told to report to Kuruman. The newcomer was David Livingstone, who after the Moffats' return fell in love with their daughter Mary and proposed to her at the mission under an almond tree. Its stump still stands. In 1845 the couple was married in the mission church.

As Kuruman developed, new missions were launched. In 1832 a French mission to the Tswana had been founded at Motito, about 60 km north of Kuruman. In 1845 the Berlin Mission bought land on the Vaal River from the Griquas and founded Pniel as a mission to the Koranna. The move was approved by the government of the Cape Colony and was to prove important when diamonds were discovered. Later the Berlin Mission founded a second station upstream and named it Hebron, today's Windsorton.

The Koranna of Pniel and Hebron were docile enough, but down the Orange far to the west the Koranna bands were more lively. The bands lived on densely-wooded islands in the middle of the river, from where they raided cattle and sheep belonging to Griquas and white trekboers who were moving into the area. In 1868 the Cape administration sent a force of police to patrol the frontier. The police were based at Koegas, one day to become an important centre of the asbestos industry.

The police had to watch an operational front stretching for 330 km, and they were no match for the Koranna who had faster horses and better weapons. Besides, the Koranna knew the country. By 1869 their raids were becoming so serious that the Cape administration sent in troops, who scattered the bandits but could not pin them down. Peace was not restored until one of the Koranna leaders treacherously captured his colleagues and handed them over to the troops.

The Koranna were subdued and those at Pniel and Hebron were learning German; the Griquas were settling down and Griquatown, Campbell and Danielskuil looked like villages; the Tswana were learning about agriculture from Robert Moffat and were spreading south down the Harts River valley. White missionaries, trekboers, traders and even 'smous' pedlars were entering the region—but as yet no mining men. That was about to change.

CHAPTER TWO 1869–1914

The Diggings

LATE IN 1868 a Griqua shepherd picked up a heavy white stone on the banks of the Orange River. The stone had a magical glitter and the man wondered if it was a '*blinkklip*' of the sort that white men prized. A relative of his contacted a trader who was buying such *blinkklippe* and it was agreed that the stone should change hands for 500 sheep. The trader hurried south to sell the stone, which brought him £11 500. He had stumbled on a prime quality diamond of 83,5 carats, the beautiful stone that became famous as the 'Star of South Africa'.

The fortunate trader was named Schalk van Niekerk, and a year previously he had spotted a diamond on a farm south of the Orange River. At the time nobody believed that diamonds could be found outside India and Brazil, but the stone was sent for analysis and was pronounced the real thing. Since then about 20 more diamonds had come to light, most of them picked up on the banks of the Vaal. Each of these finds received modest publicity, but the sale of the 'Star' was hailed as a major event and the search for diamonds began in earnest.

As yet only a few white settlers had penetrated the region close to the Orange and Vaal, so most of the work was done by Griquas and Koranna. 'These natives would form themselves into long lines, joined hand in hand,' wrote an early authority, 'and walk slowly over the ground and look for diamonds, especially after rain; and if they found one they would take it to a trader, and offer it to him at a most exorbitant price. If the trader were to make an offer he would never get the diamond, but by leaving the native to make the offer, he would gradually fall by about 1 000 per cent from his former demand.'[1]

The first white men to try prospecting for diamonds were in two independent parties drawn from King William's Town in 'British Kaffraria' and Pietermaritzburg in Natal. The first group was led by a Mr McIntosh, the second by an army officer named Paddy Rolleston, and they apparently met at Hebron mission station late in 1869. At first the two parties were mutually suspicious, but they soon became better acquainted and agreed to co-operate. As they were in Griqua territory they had to obey the dictates of their hosts, who forbade them to prospect with picks and shovels.

The Griquas were on shaky ground, for their authority was being challenged by local Koranna and indeed by Tswana spreading from the north. To raise funds they had sold farmland to the young Orange Free State to the east of them, and that caused complications later. As it was, the white prospectors patrolled the west bank of the Vaal equipped with sharp sticks which they poked at the gravel. Nothing was found at Hebron, so the McIntosh party moved downstream to a ford named Klipdrift.

Klipdrift—today's Barkly West—was sited close to the Pniel mission station or 'Peeneel' as the diggers called it. The prospectors were not keen to tangle with the missionaries so concentrated on the opposite bank. There they persuaded a Koranna to show them a kopje where he had found diamonds. To their surprise it was 1 000 metres back from the river, but McIntosh used his stick to turn soil at the roots of a camelthorn tree. He found a small diamond and immediately sent word to the Natalians. In spite of the Griquas the two parties brought in picks and shovels and began digging on the kopje.

One of Rolleston's men was a Frenchman with experience of diamond mines in Brazil. At least one of the others had knowledge of alluvial gold-washing in Australia. The expertise was pooled, and the two parties hauled a load of gravel from the kopje to the river-bank. There they erected an Australian-style 'cradle', a rectangular washing sieve in which gravel could be cleaned. Ground or 'stuff' was poured into a drawer or tray, then jerked back and forth as water was poured in. The gravel was rinsed in an ordinary lime sieve, then turned up on a board where it could be sorted with a flat metal scraper.

There was success from the beginning. The very first load produced several diamonds, and on subsequent days the two parties recovered many more. They found that diamonds lay in a triangular piece of ground about 60 metres long. The rich gravel was from 17 cm to a metre deep. Days went by and the prospectors worked hard, so much so that although they kept their finds secret, both Griquas and white traders kept a close watch on them. One day Paddy Rolleston clumsily dropped a five carat stone in front of one of the traders and the game was up.

'This discovery caused great excitement,' wrote the early authority, 'and all the traders immediately took up claims on the Old Kopie.'[1] From this time the Natal and King William's Town men kept their finds separate. In less than two months 300 diamonds were taken from the small triangle of gravel, among them a 40 carat stone found by the Natalians. At this point local Koranna decided the white men were stealing wealth that was theirs by right. A force 60 strong arrived at Klipdrift and told the diggers to go back where they had come from.

At first the diggers took no notice of the Koranna, though they were outnumbered two to one. Then the Koranna's leader told his men to kick gravel back into the diggers' pits as fast as they shovelled it out. That was too much. The white men drove off the Koranna and prepared to defend themselves. A laager was established on the site of Barkly West and the diggers slept in it and posted sentries. The diggers were better armed than their opponents and the Koranna knew it, so there was no more trouble. Even so the white men knew they were in a weak position.

So it was that a colourful trader named Stafford Parker wrote to newspapers in the Cape Colony and issued a general invitation to the diamond fields. There were fortunes for all, he promised, and the response was immediate. Hundreds of men from the Cape and from the Boer republics too converged on the Vaal. Some were in wagons, some in carts, many were on foot. The first arrivals went straight to Klipdrift and the Old Kopie and began digging next to the famous triangle. Two more kopjes were found to contain diamonds and diggers swarmed on them like bees.

As yet there was no form of authority on the diamond fields, so it was decided to set up a diggers' council to draw up suitable rules and regulations. The council was elected at a rowdy public meeting—Stafford Parker as president and four councillors to assist him. In draughting rules the council drew freely on regulations tested on the goldfields of California and Australia. A committee of seven was appointed to administer the rules and all diggers would be required to sign them. If they refused, they were not entitled to protection and others were welcome to jump their claims.

According to the rules, each digger was entitled to a single claim measuring 20 feet square—just short of 44 square metres. Any digger working or taking such a claim had to pay the committee 2/6d, the equivalent of 25 cents, 'this sum to be expended for local purposes'.[2] Anyone claiming more ground than allowed was liable to lose the surplus. Anyone wanting to erect business premises had to pay the committee £1 (R2,00) per month. All thoroughfares were to be left free and uninterrupted. Dead animals had to be removed from camp, nobody could sell liquor to natives on Sundays, and nobody was to discharge firearms in camp.

The problem with the Koranna convinced President Parker that his diggers had to be ready for all emergencies. Soon he organised a volunteer commando like those raised in the Boer republics. Its value became apparent later in 1870 when the Transvaal volksraad decided its authority extended to the diamond fields, or at least to the camps north of the river. The Transvaal's boundaries had always been vague, and given the chance the little republic's volksraad would probably have extended its territory to the Atlantic. As it was, two men were granted a long-term mining lease covering the banks of the Harts River, a major tributary of the Vaal.

The two men were named Webb and Posno. During July 1870 they arrived in Klipdrift and announced that they intended to charge diggers a monthly fee if they wanted to look for diamonds in the concession area. A public meeting was called and 500 diggers attended. President Parker told them of the young men's plan and asked them what they intended to do. The diggers replied that 'they were not going to pay one penny to any one for the privilege of mining; that they were not going to recognise the authority of the Transvaal Republic over the mines; and that, if Messrs Posno and Webb did not sign the rules, and recognise the president and council of the mines, they would put them through the river'.[1]

Webb and Posno signed as required, and no more was heard of their plan to charge fees. Two weeks later, however, President Marthinus Pretorius of the Transvaal arrived on the diggings in person. A digger noted in his diary that Pretorius had 'taken up a claim on the Klip Drift side, and works at it himself like a navvy. He is on a visit to the fields for the purpose of proving the claims of the Transvaal Republic to them.'[1] A week later he was to discuss these claims with President Parker, President J H Brand of the Orange Free State and also three native chiefs.

The diggers treated President Pretorius well. 'The miners made arrangements for a subscription ball' in his honour, noted the digger diarist. 'It was successfully arranged, and was held in President Parker's tent. There were about one hundred and fifty gentlemen, in all conceivable costumes, from the swallow-tail to a clean mining suit. Sixteen ladies graced the ball with their presence. There was no roof to the tent; the floor was washed gravel from the mines. A few tallow candles dimly illuminated this festive scene, and the moon had to do the balance. . . . The music consisted of an accordeon, fiddle, flute and bass drum.'[1]

The Transvaal leader seems to have taken a genuine interest in how the diggers worked. President Parker took him to meet the most colourful of all, an American named Jerome Babe who had dug for gold in California and had fought for the Confederation in the American Civil War. Babe had come to South Africa in search of gold and for a time worked as an agent of the Winchester rifle company. He had arrived on

5. The Northern Cape's Langeberg in the 1830s. A watercolour by Charles Davidson Bell.

Africana Museum

6. Washing for diamonds at Klipdrift on the Vaal River, the forerunner of Barkly West.

McGregor Memorial Museum

7. Windlasses top shafts at alluvial diggings in Griqualand West. In the foreground, labourers sieve diamond-bearing gravel and prepare it for the sorting-table.

Cape Archives

8. Windsorton in the 1880s: a digger and his labourers comb the gravel of an ancient river-bed.

De Beers Consolidated Mines

the diamond fields soon after Parker had publicised them, and brought with him a sifting machine of his own invention.

Babe's fellow diggers dubbed his machine the 'Yankee Baby' and versions of it are still used today. Babe tried to describe it in a little book he wrote on his experiences, but more is revealed by an accompanying diagram. The chief elements of a Baby were two sloping screens mounted on four strong poles. The upper screen consisted of wide mesh, the lower of very fine mesh, and the former sloped backwards while the latter tilted towards the front. Gravel was shovelled on to the top screen, which allowed all but the largest pebbles to filter through to the screen below.

The large pebbles were soon nicknamed 'bantams' as a corruption of the Afrikaans expression '*band oms*' or 'stripe-arounds', a reference to distinctive black lines that many carried. These 'bantams' were quickly scanned for diamonds and gently trickled down the slope until they fell on to a heap behind the machine. The gravel that had fallen through to the lower screen was resifted and all sand dropped through the fine mesh. The gravel that was left trickled forwards until it fell on to a heap gathering in front. That left the digger with three separate heaps—bantams, fine sand, and gravel to be washed for diamonds.

Most diggers kept Babys on their claims, which might well be located several hundred metres from the river. The next step was to wash the gravel, and the procedure was well described by Charles Payton who visited the river diggings in 1872. Some diggers carted water to the gravel, most carted gravel to the water where they erected a 'cradle' and sorting table. From an early stage all land along the water's edge was reserved for washing equipment and nobody tried to dig ground. Payton noted that most diggers had invested in a cart and a couple of mules or oxen.

'When a cartload of gravel or "stuff" has been dug out of the claim,' he wrote, 'it is carted down to the river, and emptied into a large trough made in the ground, with smooth bottom and sides, or merely on to a smooth floor. A proper quantity of it is put into the "cradle", which is a strong wooden framework, holding two or three sieves of perforated iron or zinc, or wire meshing, one over the other, the top having large holes, and the bottom one very small ones—the whole framework resting on two strong rockers.

'While the stuff is being rocked in this cradle, one of the diggers pours bucketfuls of water into it. The gravel being thus thoroughly cleansed by this double process of sifting and washing, the large stones in the top sieve are hastily glanced over, to see if perchance any *big* diamond be amongst them, and the other sieve or sieves are taken out, and the contents emptied on to the "sorting-table", which is an ordinary table of deal, with or without legs, or a smooth sheet of iron or other inexpensive metal. At this table the digger either sits or lies, according as it has legs or rests on the ground, and quickly sorts over the stuff with the aid of an iron or wooden scraper.'[3]

Jerome Babe has left a picture of the daily programme on the diggings. 'The miners generally rise at break of day,' he wrote, 'and dig, and sift, and cart till 9 am, when they have breakfast. At 10 am they convene to wash and sort at the river or at the mine; one person rocks the cradle, while another pours in water that he dips with a pail from the river. The rocker then sorts the stones in the upper sieve, and empties the pebbles from the middle and bottom sieves on a common table, where they are carefully sorted. . . .

'With our machines, pump, and hose, two white men and five boys, we could get through fifteen cart-loads a day. About six feet of frontage is allowed at the river for each cradle or machine. The sorting is the most monotonous part of the work, and five boys will wash enough in four hours to keep three men sorting for ten hours. At 1 o'clock the work is knocked off for tiffin or lunch. At 4 o'clock the washers cease, and go to mining for next day's washing. Some of the miners cart their "cascalho" (*ground*) during moonlight nights to the river ready for washing next day. . . .

'At 6 pm the miners knock off work and dine, after which some would write, some would make their purchases of provisions, and others would go to the main camp and play billiards, black-pool, or unlimited, loo; others would hunt up the diamond merchants and sell their finds, or go to the store where they had diamond scales and weigh them, if they intended to keep them for the European market.'[1] That was the pattern six days a week, but on Sundays most diggers rested and socialised or went to church or fished or washed their clothes. The lifestyle was captured in *Digger's Song:*

Six months ago to the Fields I came,
I was a heavy swell,
My clothes were brushed, my boots the same,
My coat it fitted well;
I wore a collar then, of course,
Alas! that day's gone past;
And stockings too my feet did grace,
Oh dear! I've seen my last.

Chorus—*Rocking at the cradle, sifting all the day,*
That's the life we diggers lead,
Rocking at the cradle, sifting all the day,
That's the life for me!

Now straying cattle and wayward 'boys',
And diamonds never handy,
Have brought me down, and all my joys
Are centred in Cape Brandy;
I wear a shirt and trousers now,
And smoke a dirty clay;
My feet are cased just anyhow;
This hat I 'jumped' today.

Chorus—*Rocking at the cradle, &c*

Bad luck, however, cannot last,
A turn must come some day,
A ninety-carat would change the past,
And make the future gay.
May every digger's luck be this
Who to these Fields has come,
And take back health, and wealth, and bliss,
To those he's left at home.

Chorus—*Rocking at the cradle, &c*[3]

The story goes that one 'new chum' from Cape Town was thinking of those he'd left at home when he sat down to write a letter to his wife. Since arriving on the fields he had been busy building a sifting machine like those used by other diggers. He told his wife he was having a wonderful time and was trying to make a Baby. He was most surprised when she wrote back and said she wanted a divorce.

Griqualand West

By late 1870 diggers had spread to Pniel across the river from Klipdrift, to Hebron upstream, and to many new camps with names like Gong Gong, Webster's Koppie and Waldeck's Plant. At Pniel, diggers had to pay the missionary for claims. Others were at work on 'dry diggings' located 30 km south of the Vaal—the first of the diamond 'pipes' that were to develop into the big holes of Kimberley. But Klipdrift was still the centre of the diggings, and that was where the Transvaal, Orange Free State and the diggers themselves wrangled for control of the whole district.

The 'summit conference' of August 1870 had failed. In the next month President Pretorius and a force of burghers sent by the Transvaal *volksraad* tried to raise the republic's flag over the diggings. Stafford Parker and his council firmly resisted the move. The Orange Free State stationed a magistrate in Pniel. Most diggers accepted Free State rule over the land south of the Vaal, but the north bank was a different matter. Parker organised a 'diggers' mutual protection association' pledged to defend the camps against aggression from outside or indeed from within.

The British in the Cape watched these developments and quietly persuaded the Griquas living north of the Vaal to accept British protection. From there it was only a short step to the annexation of the whole area as a British colony, soon named 'Griqualand West' as disenchanted Griquas had formed a new Griqualand in what is now Natal. At first Griqualand West was said to contain only diggings that lay north of the Vaal, but soon the British insisted that the 'dry diggings' of Kimberley were included too. To its anger the Orange Free State was forced to redraw its western border.

Most river diggers accepted the British annexation and President Parker graciously relinquished his authority to a British magistrate. Klipdrift was renamed 'Barkly West' in honour of the British high commissioner. The community had official status, but already it was being eclipsed by a sprawling tent town on the dry diggings. The discovery of new 'pipes' was attracting thousands more fortune-hunters who came from all over the world. 'New Rush', the tent town serving mines discovered on De Beers farm, was renamed Kimberley after the British colonial secretary.

As yet diggers on the dry claims had no understanding of the pipes they were working. They had no idea that the pipes were virtually bottomless, stretching deep into the earth as cones of rock-hard kimberlite that had been formed through volcanic activity. Workings were like those on the rivers, except that they went deeper and deeper. Even the most entrenched river diggers were tempted to join in. But diamonds were not everything, and enterprising prospectors to the west planned to mine tiger's eye and sell it in Europe.

William Burchell had reported finding 'hardened asbestos' as early as 1812 and had taken samples to Britain. There its mysterious golden sheen had suggested the name tiger's eye though in South Africa prospectors wrongly called it crocidolite. The most abundant source was an area north of Prieska, and in 1872 the administration of Griqualand West granted mining leases covering two farms there. Tiger's eye was to be marketed by local traders with experience of diamonds, and there is evidence that they deliberately limited supplies to increase their value.

In this same year of 1872 the British high commissioner commissioned George Stow to report on Griqualand West's potential. Stow was a Fellow of the Royal Geographical Society and he began his researches at the confluence of the Vaal and the Orange. From there he could see the edge of the Ghaap Plateau to the north, stretching 'like a vast cliff-like coast line' parallel to the course of the rivers. Spilling down the cliff-face Stow found 'stalactitic limestone of very great thickness'[4]—deposits that the Union Lime Company has long quarried for lime and cement.

Mounting the plateau, Stow travelled into the Asbestos Mountains, 'amongst the most remarkable in Griqualand. They are composed principally of a series of fine jaspers of a yellowish brown colour, and abound with magnificent iron ores, haematite and magnetite. The latter is in such immense quantities, that in a number of parts of these hills, and some of the outliers connected with them, the compass is perfectly useless, veering round to every point according to the position of the nearest rocks. Near Klipfontein, masses of the purest iron I have ever seen are frequent, and could fuel be but procured, this place would become a mine of unsurpassed richness.'[4]

Curiously, Stow's report made only a passing reference to the asbestos after which the mountains were named, though in other passages he talked enthusiastically of lesser minerals like slate and marble. When he came to the Langeberg he had to rely largely on hearsay—'I was informed by a trader that indications of copper have been found in the Langeberg, much further to the north, but not having seen specimens I cannot speak with certainty upon the subject; but I have fragments of galena (*a prime source of lead*) that were found in some *debris* near the summit of the mountains, although want of time prevented me from discovering the spot where it was "in situ".

'A vein of lead-ore is known to traverse the rocks that form the continuance of the Campbell Randt (*Ghaap Plateau*), near the spot where they cross the bed of the Orange River, but, for the want of a proper guide and the shortness of the time I could appropriate to it, I did not succeed in striking the exact locality, although I rode a great number of miles to visit it. Fortunately, however, in this case, I secured one or two specimens of what will prove to be an excellent ore, should the lode be found to be sufficiently large to ensure a profitable return for the labour required.'[4]

When Stow reached the district of the old Gatkoppies specularite workings he was told of a deposit of 'steatite' that local Griquas used to make stone pipes—'the only species of industry that I was able to notice among them, but so jealous were they lest we should discover its true position, that they constantly pointed out to us the wrong direction whenever we inquired about it, to prevent our discovering it.'[4] Such behaviour did little to enhance Stow's already low opinion of the Griquas—'one of the most insolent and degraded of all the races in the southern part of Africa'[4]—though to be fair he laid the blame on missionaries who had taught them about equality but not about work.

Other whites shared Stow's view of the Griquas and thought the same of the Koranna, so it was a shock when in 1878 the two races rose in rebellion. The Koranna were back at their old tricks, raiding cattle and sheep along the Orange. A military expedition was sent against them and after the 'second Koranna War' a buffer colony of Cape coloureds was established at what became Upington. The Griqua rebellion began when several hundred frustrated Griquas began looting trading stores around Griquatown and murdered several whites. They threatened to ride in and capture Griquatown itself if the 150 whites living there did not surrender voluntarily.

The whites of Griquatown prepared to defend themselves, together with a handful of friendly Griquas. Word was sent to the Diamond Fields Horse, a voluntary regiment composed mainly of diggers living in Kimberley and Barkly West. The regiment had only just returned from fighting in the Gaika–Gcaleka War of British Kaffraria and soon 120 mounted men were riding to relieve Griquatown. They reached the settlement before the rebels advanced and next day were joined by a contingent of Frontier Mounted Police from Koegas. That afternoon the Griquas attacked.

The diggers and police were in strong positions on a kopje and their strong fire took the Griquas by surprise. The attackers retired in confusion but several hundred of them took refuge in sunken kraals on a hill. The diggers delayed their attack until after dark, and in the 'Battle of Driefontein' that night they rushed the kraals and killed or captured all they found inside. The Griquas lost 48 dead and 100 wounded, but compatriots of theirs carried on fighting for another year before British troops ended their resistance. In August 1879 Griqualand West became part of the Cape Colony.

With the excitement over, the warlike diggers returned to their claims. For some the lure of diamonds was beginning to pall, and there was great glee when it was reported that gold and cinnabar had been found in the Vaal River. Cinnabar is valuable as the source of vermilion dye. The administrator of Griqualand West asked a geologist, Thomas Kitto, to investigate. Kitto found the 'cinnabar' was really bantams of haematite and the 'gold' was iron pyrites, but he took the opportunity of re-examining river diggings that had been relatively neglected since the spotlight moved on to Kimberley. Most authorities had been saying the alluvial diggings were worked out but Kitto found they still held many diamonds.

'Before going to Barkly,' reported Kitto, 'the description given to me of people on the river diggings was anything but flattering; but after spending a fortnight among them, I have no hesitation in saying that a more obliging and gentlemanly class of man I have never seen.'[5] An encounter near Delportshoop spoilt the good impression: 'I met a man at this place, who conceived the idea that everybody went out of their way to injure him. He told me he had been on the diggings over six months and had found only three diamonds, consequently he was leaving, disgusted with the diggings and things in general. . . . It is generally people of this kind who give places a bad name when they do not deserve it.'[5]

Diamonds there might be, but Kitto was quite sure there was no gold in the Vaal or its tributaries. Even so tales of great discoveries in the Eastern Transvaal kept hopes alive. Gold had been found there in 1873, and among those panning gravel and quarrying quartz from the hillsides were several alumni of the river diggings. One was Stafford Parker, ex-president of the Klipdrift 'diggers' state'. Meanwhile, the farmers of Griqualand West kept their eyes peeled for precious metals and in 1884 a Kimberley newspaper reported finds near Danielskuil. It was said that a farmer named J J Roux 'some time ago washed gravel, washed by rain from a quartz reef, and succeeded in finding eleven small nuggets'.[6]

Nothing came of farmer Roux's effort, though a neighbour later found a 'speck of gold embedded in a piece of quartz picked up on the surface'.[6] The newspaper's correspondent was quite sure that 'gold exists, but whether in payable quantities remains to be seen'.[6] Two years later the scene shifted to a farm 30 km from Griquatown, where 'several specks of the precious metal and one or two small nuggets were said to have been found by parties who had started prospecting there'.[7] It was rumoured that the farmer had been offered £10 000 for his property but had turned it down.

Several shafts were being sunk on Willis's farm, one by a Griquatown firm, one by Willis himself and one by 'an old Australian digger named Johnson'.[8] A party of Kimberley speculators went out to inspect the workings and afterwards reported: 'Willis's shaft; which is on the side of one of the kopjes, about half way to the top, was being sunk through a substance believed to be gold-bearing alluvium. This is surrounded by jasper, which exists in great quantity all about these kopjes. The intention of Mr. Willis is, after going a certain distance, to strike into the jasper and find out whether a reef exists or not.'[7]

Unfortunately for farmer Willis, none was to be found. Experienced diggers advised the Kimberley speculators to proceed on to the Langeberg where 'indications presented themselves which showed the region to be gold-bearing. . . . The party broke off several specimens of quartz, and brought them with them on their return to Kimberley. They have since been examined by old gold diggers here, who pronounce them to be pieces of genuine quartz, though without any gold in them.'[7]

No more was heard of gold in the Langeberg, though local farmers were 'said to be extremely anxious to encourage prospecting on their farms, and promise every assistance to the furtherance of that object'.[7] In the next year Transvaal prospectors uncovered the great gold-bearing reef of the Witwatersrand and many diggers left for the bustling new tent town that became Johannesburg. In 1889 there was a brief flurry of excitement when specks of gold were found on Barkly West commonage, but they too were flashes in the pan. The only gold in Griqualand was the gold in tiger's eye.

In the 1880s even tiger's eye was glistering less brightly following the breakdown of a trading monopoly. For ten years the firm Lilienveld Brothers had been sending small quantities of tiger's eye to selected cutters in Britain. They continued to limit supplies and refused to deal with cutters in other countries. All that changed when Griqua guides led a visitor from Cape Town to a new deposit of tiger's eye, claiming it was gold. Far from being disappointed, the visitor was delighted. He arranged to quarry the mineral and transport it to Cape Town by the cartload.

Within a short time the new speculator sent samples of the tiger's eye to cutters at Idar–Oberstein in Germany, the centre of the European gem industry. German dealers had little knowledge of tiger's eye and assumed it was scarce. They immediately wrote to Cape Town offering to buy tiger's eye by the carat at prices that would have delighted the diamond diggers. The Cape Town man stood to make a fortune, but in the meantime he had written to Idar–Oberstein pointing out that he could supply tiger's eye in whatever quantities were wanted.

The letters crossed in the post and great confusion was caused. In the end the German cutters agreed to buy tiger's eye by the kilogram rather than the carat and the mineral's value slumped all over Europe. From being a rare gem it became relatively common and was frequently to be seen in rings, necklaces and hatpins. The cutters of Idar–Oberstein thought out many new uses for it, and as a final indignity tiger's eye was used to make umbrella handles and doorknobs.

The Woolly Stone

Two events of 1884 had far-reaching consequences for the lands north of the Orange River. In August a small naval detachment raised the flag of Germany over South West Africa. In November a British military expedition annexed Bechuanaland in the name of Queen Victoria. Ostensibly the British moved into the region at the request of people living there, among them the burghers of two tiny Boer republics that had splintered from the Transvaal. Perhaps the real intention was to prevent Germany or indeed the Transvaal from taking possession. Whatever the motivation, the Union Jack was raised and the land north of Griqualand West became a Crown colony.

'British Bechuanaland' stretched to the Molopo River, and soon the British would create a 'Bechuanaland Protectorate' over the country beyond. Before that happened, a Kimberley newspaper drew attention to a new mineral. Prospectors had found crocidolite or 'woolly stone' all through the Kuruman Hills, also known as the Asbestos Mountains. The newspaper commented: 'It is to be hoped that too much of this valuable article will not be discovered and thus glut the market.'[6]

The first report on crocidolite was published in 1884. Three years later a Kimberley speculator named Cohen inspected asbestos samples from the Prieska area, brought to the diamond fields by labourers. Cohen showed the samples to one of the most knowledgeable mining

9. A makeshift screen helps asbestos miners to prepare crocidolite asbestos for the market.

Africana Museum

10. Freelance tributors use small hammers to 'cob' and 'stamp' asbestos fibre ready to sell to the mine.

Africana Museum

11. Crocidolite or blue asbestos.
Humphry Clinker

12. Gefco's Harold Pascoe, mine manager at Elandsfontein in the 1930s.
Harold Pascoe

13. Dawie and Suzann Voges, pioneers of South Africa's tiger's eye industry.
Humphry Clinker

men in Kimberley, Francis Oats. Years earlier Oats had been Griqualand West's government mining engineer. He had resigned to manage a diamond company later swallowed by the De Beers colossus run by Cecil Rhodes and Alfred Beit. Now he was a director of De Beers and rubbed shoulders with South Africa's leading financiers.

Oats was interested in Cohen's samples but in 1887 he would have been even more interested in news from the Transvaal, where gold had been found on the Witwatersrand. Oats eventually visited Prieska to examine the asbestos deposits on the spot, but it was 1891 before he and others created the 'Cape Mineral Syndicate' to buy farms and mine them. Among members of the syndicate were Cohen the speculator, a Mr Weingarten of Griquatown and Ludwig Breitmeyer, a close associate of Alfred Beit's. The syndicate prepared to buy or lease farms near Koegas and begin exporting to Europe.

At this time European asbestos manufacturers worked with chrysotile, a white fibre much softer than the hard blue crocidolite. An article published in the *Cape Times* in 1926 shows that the syndicate's early progress was less than smooth: 'Mining a new material in an almost unknown area presented many awkward problems, but they were as nothing compared with the trouble experienced in marketing the fibre. The producers of white asbestos opposed its introduction in every way and manufacturers looked askance at it. One firm that took a trial consignment put in a claim for thousands of pounds for the damage they asserted it had done to their machinery, and at least two cargoes of blue asbestos were dumped into the sea because no purchaser could be found.'[9]

In spite of these discouragements, by the end of 1895 the syndicate had bought three farms on the north bank of the Orange, among them Koegas, and had obtained mining rights on a fourth farm across the river. The fledgling mines were producing bags of cleaned fibre ready for milling, so Ludwig Breitmeyer suggested the syndicate should start mills of its own and become an asbestos manufacturer. That would need capital, so it was decided to float a new public company registered in Britain rather than South Africa because its mills and factories would be located in Britain.

So it was that the Cape Asbestos Company was launched in December 1893. One John J Borthwick was managing the mines at Koegas and with him was a small corps of white miners. Asbestos 'cobs' the size of fists were recovered from the banded ironstone formations and 'stamped' to fluff the fibre which was then bagged and carted to the nearest railhead. That meant an ox-wagon journey of more than 250 kilometres, for there was no station nearer than De Aar. The fibre was railed to the coast, shipped to Europe, and delivered to the mills that spun it into asbestos thread.

Cape Asbestos's early history is being pieced together by Allen Robinson, who worked at Koegas for many years and today lives in Johannesburg. After the first year's operations, says Robinson, Ludwig Breitmeyer told the shareholders that their directors stood before them 'in debt and without a dividend'.[10] Francis Oats was more encouraging when he announced: 'I visited the property as a mining expert and although I hadn't then the slightest idea as to whether the article was of any use in the asbestos market, it seemed to me that unlimited quantities could be obtained.'[10]

From what Oats said it seems that Koegas crocidolite was already being woven into cloth and there were prospects of using it to make fishing nets. Should demand increase as Oats hoped it would, he was sure that Koegas would be able to match it. 'The veins are very regular and run for miles,' he told the shareholders. 'They are just like the Johannesburg reefs, and for that reason I do not suppose they will give out at any reasonable depth.'[10] Unfortunately supply soon outstripped orders and during 1895 Koegas closed and remained shut for two years before things improved.

The Cape Asbestos Company was a Kimberley enterprise. Johannesburg financiers were not far behind when they founded a company to mine saltpetre in Griqualand West. Saltpetre is potassium nitrate and its main use was as a constituent of gunpowder. The South African Saltpetre Company was launched in 1895 with a distinguished chairman —Fred Struben, now regarded as the father of Witwatersrand goldmining. During the early 1880s Struben and his brother worked hard to find payable gold on the Rand, though it was left to others to discover the all-important main reef.

The South African Saltpetre Company was the direct ancestor of Gefco, the Griqualand Exploration and Finance Company today based in Kuruman. Unfortunately its early career was a fiasco. At the shareholders' meeting of 1897 Struben confessed that the company had been formed on the strength of 'salted samples' and large amounts of money had been wasted. One story is that the 'saltpetre' was really dried dassie urine or 'klipsweet' that had accumulated over many centuries. All was not lost, for the chairman volunteered to travel to Griqualand West and see what could be done.

The company had bought two or three farms near Griquatown. Fred Struben left Kimberley in a two-wheeled Cape cart and reached the farms in three days. By chance the farms included Elandsfontein, the 'Eland's Fountain' mentioned by William Burchell as a source of long asbestos fibre and tiger's eye. Struben was impressed as Burchell had been and saw a way out of the company's difficulties. He returned to Johannesburg and suggested to his fellow directors that they should forget saltpetre and mine asbestos instead.

Several years went by before any mining started at Elandsfontein, first because a rinderpest epidemic was killing off transport oxen and then because the South African War broke out. The same difficulties played havoc with operations at Koegas and with a private venture launched on a farm south of Prieska. Information about this third site is sketchy, but some is contained in a letter written by Captain Thomas Shone of Postmasburg in 1943. We shall be meeting Shone again later, but on this occasion he was writing to an investment house in Johannesburg.

'Are you interested in Copper?' he asked. 'If so I have some Copper Prospects, in this District one on the Orange River, that was worked before the Boer War, and the Ore transported by Ox and Donkey Wagon over 200 miles to De Aar, and railed from there, and shipped to Germany. . . . I am informed the main shaft is still there, but during the Boer War the mine got waterlogged and the then Owner a Mr Weingarten never worked it again.'[11]

A 'Mr Weingarten' had been a member of Francis Oats's Cape Mineral Syndicate and had connections with Germany. Otherwise we know little about him, and it may be that his forgotten mine holds a fortune to this day.

War and Peace

In 1895 British Bechuanaland became part of the Cape Colony, just in time for the national rinderpest epidemic that played havoc with farm stock and the transport system. The veld was littered with the bones of dead oxen and fledgling mining operations were forced to a halt. To add to the misery there was a political crisis. The British high commissioner, Sir Alfred Milner, was on a collision course with President Paul Kruger of the Transvaal. The Orange Free State sided with its sister republic. War broke out in October 1899 when Boer commandos invaded both Natal and the Cape Colony.

Burghers of the Free State had long resented Britain's high-handed annexation of Griqualand West and quickly entered diamond country. There was a strong British military force in Kimberley and several commandos surrounded the city and besieged it. Many of the river diggers took refuge in Barkly West. The Boers had no quarrel with them and allowed them the run of the town so long as they did not attempt to leave. They had plentiful supplies of food but were short of fuel. Some of the more enterprising dug into a small pocket of low-grade coal located on Barkly West commonage.

During the early stages of the war Boer forces had things their own way. Several times they defeated superior British forces sent to relieve Kimberley and had similar success in Natal and the Cape Midlands. The tables were turned when Lord Roberts of Kandahar was sent to South Africa with reinforcements. Like a juggernaut Roberts's army rolled northwards to relieve Kimberley, annex the Free State and overwhelm the Transvaal. After capturing Pretoria Roberts returned to Britain and left Horatio Kitchener, his second-in-command, to sort out the details. Unfortunately for Kitchener, many of the Boer commandos saw no reason to lay down their arms and simply carried on fighting.

Griqualand West and British Bechuanaland were to be the main battlegrounds of this second stage of the war—ironic, as neither of them had anything to do with it. Boer commandos took refuge among the wild kopjes of Bushmanland and the sandy wastes of the Kalahari. British patrols were sent to flush them out. Many farmers of the region sympathised with the burghers and helped them whenever possible. If the British caught them they were branded 'rebels' and sent to Cape Town to be interned. When Kitchener initiated a 'scorched earth' policy to bring the burghers to their knees, many of the farmers' women and children were sent to concentration camps.

For nearly two years, commandos and British patrols tusselled for advantage all across the countryside. The commandos knew their way about, the British had the advantage of superior numbers and ready supplies. Often commandos ambushed patrols to obtain food, clothing and ammunition and many a British soldier was left naked on the veld while a burgher rode off with his uniform. Commandos quickly learnt to avoid skirmishes which resulted in unnecessary casualties and instead concentrated on sabotage. A favourite target was the railway line between Kimberley and Vryburg, which the British eventually protected with blockhouses and armoured trains.

By 1902 the stubborn British and elusive Boers were fighting themselves to a standstill. The Boer leaders met Kitchener at Vereeniging and peace was signed. The 'rebels' of Griqualand West and Bechuanaland were released from internment and rejoined their wives and children. Many found their farms devastated but the British provided each family with food, tools and livestock ready to make a fresh start. Some families had no farms to go to, and for them the only possibility was to try their luck on the river diggings.

One veteran digger with memories of those days is Daniel Ludick who has long since retired and now lives in Delportshoop. 'We were a family of 16 children and I was third from last,' he says. 'I was born in 1897, and during the war my father was interned as a rebel. We lived at Douglas while he was away, and when he came back he decided to start diamond digging with my elder brothers. He didn't know anything about diamonds but people said that in some places if you pulled up a bush you'd find them clinging to the roots. Of course he quickly found it wasn't quite like that.

'After the war there was a terrible shortage of labourers—there just weren't any left, they'd all gone. So white men did all the work themselves, just them and their sons. One of the other diggers showed my father how to gravitate a sieve—shake it so that the diamonds ended up in the middle. My father picked out a lot of stones and said, Yes, these are diamonds. But then one of my brothers picked out a very bright one, a four-carat stone. My father realised the ones he'd been saving were only crystals so he threw them all away.'[12]

All over the diggings it was noticeable that men were thinking deep. Perhaps it was the influence of the mines of Kimberley, but even modestly-equipped diggers seemed to think nothing of sinking a shaft of 10 or 20 metres in hopes of finding payable gravel from an old streambed. If they found a payable deposit they tunnelled into the gravel and worked their way around in a circle or rather a horseshoe until they re-entered the shaft. That left a pillar supporting the 'hanging wall', and they probably extended the stope before starting a similar horseshoe on the other side.

Even today, prospectors stumble on old 'figure-of-eight' stopes at the bottom of shafts that were long ago filled in and forgotten. By modern standards they seem dangerous, yet judging from old Barkly West mining commissioners' reports, mishaps were rare. In 1904, for instance, there were only five accidents in the whole region, whether on alluvial workings or in kimberlite mines like the newly-discovered Leicester mine near Barkly West and the dumb-bell-shaped Frank Smith mine near Boetsap, 60 km to the north, where more than 300 men were at work.

In 1908 there were three accidents, one of them especially tragic: 'A digger, W L Gamie by name, put down a shaft in what was thought Maiden ground; at a depth of 15 to 20 feet a Native working at the bottom called out that he had broken through to an old underground drive, the existence of which was unknown. Gamie called him to the surface, and he and the deceased (an old experienced digger) went down the shaft to inspect the reported old drive. The deceased got off the rope, and Gamie himself was in the act of doing so when the whole bottom of the shaft "caved in", and the deceased was caught by the foot between two large boulders.

'The old excavation below acted the part of an hour glass, and the sides of the new shaft started trickling away. Some half-dozen European diggers and a large number of Native labourers came to the rescue, and all that was humanly possible was done to extricate the unfortunate man from his perilous position, but, after an hour's work, the whole shaft suddenly collapsed, completely burying the man, and, as afterwards appeared, breaking his neck. No blame could be attached to the Claimholder, but the accident goes to show the great danger of putting down shafts in diggings where underground burrowings have been going on for the last 37 years.'[13]

Half of the accidents reported in these years were at the Frank Smith mine, a reflection of its large workforce. In 1904 the mine had gone underground when twin shafts were sunk to 100 metres and then connected by underground drives. In the same year a farmer named Ben Peiser sank a borehole near Griquatown and to his surprise struck kimberlite. The pipe contained diamonds, and soon the discovery was proclaimed a public diamond mine of 148 claims of which many went to Peiser as owner and discoverer.

Peiser's mine came into production at about the time the South African Saltpetre Company began mining asbestos. As we have seen, Fred Struben had advised his directors not to sell the farms they owned near Griquatown. Unfortunately the company's luck was little better than it had been in the 1890s. A fire destroyed buildings erected at Elandsfontein and it was decided to lease the mine to a private syndicate which paid a royalty on the asbestos produced. The syndicate soon employed a new source of labour—Herero refugees from South West Africa, who had fled to escape German retribution after an unsuccessful rebellion.

At Koegas, the Cape Asbestos Company was feeling the effects of a grave drought. Rundle Olds, Francis Oats's nephew by marriage, had been appointed mine manager and was trying to find a transport contractor to carry asbestos to De Aar. He drew a blank, for drought had ended what rinderpest and the war had begun. In the whole district there were no oxen or indeed stock of any kind. There had been little rain for three years and the country was arid and parched.

Production had restarted at Koegas, even though there was no means of transporting the ore. Oats was touched by the poverty of Koegas miners, all of them self-employed tributors from whom the company bought fibre. 'As Christmas was coming,' he wrote, 'and as very many of them had not tasted meat for a long time, we instructed Olds to go so far as £20 for an ox from Griquatown or somewhere where they have had rains, and bring it down and slaughter it for Christmas, dividing it equally amongst the work-people with compliments, good will and best wishes of the company.'[10]

Olds's difficulties were partially overcome when a new railway was built between De Aar and Prieska, cutting the necessary wagon trip by two-thirds. The railway was ready for use in 1905 and Olds celebrated by opening two new mines. One was at Kliphuis, across the river from Prieska and only 15 km from the railhead. The other was Westerberg, across the river from Koegas and working the same ore body from the other end of a syncline. At Westerberg Olds sank a shaft or rather a vertical winze in a bid to 'mine' asbestos instead of scratching at it from the surface.

Allen Robinson has unravelled the story of the shaft and finds that by the end of 1907 it was 100 metres deep. It was circular rather than square and 'was brick lined where it went through bad ground. The cleaning kibble was raised and lowered by means of a whim, powered by donkeys.'[10] During 1908 a crosscut was made into the asbestos horizon but 'the intersections made were of poor value, and in the hard blue, fresh, zone'.[10] On the surface miners were used to oxidised formations in which the asbestos remained blue but the banded ironstone layers were red and brown and relatively easy to drill. Here they were unoxidised. With the equipment of the day 'drilling blastholes was almost impossible, very little reef development was done'.[10]

The Westerberg shaft was closed. On workings in other areas, Cape Asbestos was mining more fibre than it could sell, and in 1910 Olds ordered drastic production cutbacks. Elsewhere the Elandsfontein syndicate was still in business and at least two other producers were active. One was a syndicate mining at Carn Brea farm near Koegas and selling its production to Cape Asbestos. The other was Mr Weingarten, formerly of the Cape Mineral Syndicate and now mining on his own account on a farm near the hamlet of Niekerkshoop, 43 km north of Prieska.

Before the South African War Weingarten had mined copper south of the Orange River. In 1906 an unknown prospector came upon copper on Vogelstruisbult, a farm of 7 000 hectares located 60 km south-west of Prieska. Vogelstruisbult was being farmed by Charles Marais, who had acquired it in 1890. During the South African War he had been interned as a rebel but on his release he and his wife soon produced Charlie junior who in due course took over the farm and still lives there today. In recent years Vogelstruisbult has blossomed as the site of Prieska Copper Mines, but in 1906 all it contained were flocks of merino sheep.

'I was too young to take it in, but I heard about the prospector from my mother,' recalls Charlie Marais. 'She said the man was like a tramp and carried all his prospecting equipment on a donkey. He asked my father if there were any signs of minerals on the farm. My father said, as far as he knew there weren't, but there were a few places where meerkats had dug holes and when it rained the stone turned blue. That was limestone. He'd also noticed there were places where the stones had green spots.

'My father told the tramp all this and he started digging holes. Then he went away and tried to interest a man called Samowit. Mr Samowit came here in—my mother told me 1908. Mr Samowit talked to my mother and said there might be a reef of copper, and he went away and wrote a report.'[14] Perhaps Samowit was not impressed, perhaps he was unable to interest investors. Copper prices were well down. Even so, the copper mines of Namaqualand were still in business and a group of speculators opened a new mine at Areachap, not 40 km north of Upington.

Areachap came into being at a time of great excitement in South Africa. Since the South African War the British had administered the region as four separate colonies—the Cape, Natal, Transvaal and 'Orange River Colony'. Then in 1909 delegates from the four colonies met at a National Convention to discuss federation or union. They reached agreement, and during 1910 the 'Union of South Africa' came into being with General Louis Botha as prime minister. The old Cape Colony became the new Cape Province, but not in time to save Areachap which closed in the same year.

Soon after Areachap's closure a diamond prospector named Fred Cornell visited the area and wrote of 'the sad sight of a beautifully equipped and rich little mine being beaten in its struggle for existence by the heavy handicap of being situated 170 miles or so (*c 270 km*) from the nearest railway. Rich heaps of ore lay there ready to be carted away, there was much valuable machinery going to rack and ruin, and the buildings must have cost a large sum to erect; and here it stood, alone and deserted in the midst of the solitary waste of the veldt. . . .

'The tall yellow shaft was visible hours after we had left it,' Cornell continued, 'a most incongruous landmark in the wide expanse of desert.'[15] Areachap had gone underground but at Vogelstruisbult the copper was close to the surface. As Charlie Marais remembers it—he was nine years old—'round about 1912 some people came here and took options on the farm for mineral rights. They started digging holes, quite a few though they didn't go deeper than a few metres. They brought out stones and then sent them away for analysis.'[14] The stones were gossan, and it was copper oxide.

'The man in charge of the prospecting was called Bleloch and he drilled several boreholes. Parts of the old drill were found here years later and also an old drilling bit with the diamonds removed. Bleloch's men sent the stones to Prieska station on donkey wagons, on the worst roads you can imagine. We don't know where they sent the ore. They were German people and before World War I broke out they suddenly quit. They left everything—their spades, holes, dynamite, the men who worked for them. We never saw them again.'[14]

CHAPTER THREE 1914–1926

Hit and Turn

THE YEARS LEADING up to World War I saw an arms race among the powers of Europe. Nowhere was it more evident than in the navy of Imperial Germany, which commissioned new battleships in scores and many other vessels too. The Germans tested various materials in protective cladding for ships' boilers and found South African crocidolite was far superior to the chrysotile used previously. From then on blue asbestos's future was assured. But it was ironic that when war broke out, German warships equipped with South African asbestos tried to prevent fresh supplies from reaching Europe.

South Africa was a long way from the main theatres of the war, but Generals Louis Botha and Jan Smuts committed the new country to fight. Soon the government sent an expeditionary force to secure ports along the coast of South West Africa, and a second force crossed the Kalahari to fight the Germans on their own ground. To support the troops the westbound railway was extended beyond Prieska to Upington. Marydale was on the route and from then on Cape Asbestos's Koegas operations were only 28 km from a railhead.

Many farmers of the Northern Cape openly resented the government's war effort on the grounds that it helped the British. One such was Daan Schoeman who was homesteading on a farm about 60 km west of Kuruman. Farms like his had never been properly surveyed, but that was put right between 1915 and 1917. Two government surveyors were sent to cover a large area stretching from south of Postmasburg to north of the Kuruman River. One was named Wessels and surveyed farms in the south. The other was Dirk Roos and he was made responsible for the north.

Roos is remembered as a workaholic with a mop of red hair that seldom saw a comb and shirts and shorts that he liked to wear until they fell to pieces. He took great pains over his survey and often worked far into the night, yet still found time for fierce political arguments with Daan Schoeman and others who opposed the government. Schoeman made a special request that his farm be registered as 'Eerstegat' because he had drilled the district's first borehole. He was less than delighted when the survey was published and he found his farm named 'Botha'.

But then, Schoeman was aware that Roos had an unusual sense of humour. One lonely kopje in the sandy Kalahari appeared on his survey as 'Paradise Island'. Not far away was a farm that Roos named 'Hotazel'. Other names he registered included 'Mamatwan' (meaning 'bats'), 'Middelplaats', 'Devon', 'Smartt', 'Gloria', 'Nchwaning' and even 'Wessels' in honour of his brother surveyor—all of which would one day flourish as manganese mines. So for that matter would many of Wessels's farms in the south, but that lay in the future. For the present the growth of the Northern Cape's mining industry depended not on manganese but on asbestos.

A government survey of the Cape asbestos industry in 1917 divided it into two sections, northern and southern. Dealing first with the southern section, it reported: 'During 1917 recovery of crocidolite was carried on by the *Cape Asbestos Co* on eight farms; by the *Carn Brea Syndicate* on Keikams Poort, some twenty miles south of Prieska; by the *Good Hope Syndicate* on Kliphuis and adjoining ground. . . . A certain amount of fibre was also produced on *Blackridge* and *Elandsfontein*. By far the largest share in the combined operation of these concerns falls to the Cape Asbestos Co.'[1]

In the northern section, the report continued, 'a number of smaller companies and syndicates have been prospecting and developing crocidolite for about ten years. Among these may be mentioned the Northern Asbestos Co, Messrs Gillanders and Campbell's Syndicate, the Crown Lands Syndicate, and Harris's Syndicate; of these the first named is next in importance to the Cape Asbestos Co.'[1] Northern Asbestos was producing on two farms that were still being worked in 1981—Warrendale and Owendale, near Danielskuil. Gillanders and Campbell were two Scotsmen who had acquired neighbouring farms.

The government survey provides an interesting glimpse of mining methods in use at the time. Rather than employ white miners, the producers preferred to buy fibre from self-employed 'contractors' who included Tswana, 'mixed races' (apparently all brown people including Griquas, Cape coloureds and even Bushmen) and Herero from South West Africa (who were wrongly described as 'Damaras'). The asbestos-bearing ground was laid out in blocks of uniform size and handed over to the contractors who were paid by footage or production or both. 'All necessary tools and mining materials, except candles and dynamite, are supplied.'[1]

A more detailed account was published in the *Cape Times* during 1926. Written by 'a government official', the article explained that 'the problem is to get the asbestos out without excessive cost in labour or supervision'. As a result mining was often a family affair. 'The men do the drilling, blasting and breaking out of the rock while the women and children "stamp" the asbestos, that is, they break up the asbestos-bearing fragments with light hammers, reject the waste rock, and throw the now partially separated fibres into sacks, according to length.

'A bag of properly stamped asbestos is not so soft as a feather pillow, perhaps, but it is strange to think that this mass of woolly threads came out of an intensely hard rock, wherein it was formed by some natural process. At the end of each month the bags of asbestos are collected, taken to the mine store and weighed, each man being credited with his own output; after deducting debts to the store for clothes, food and explosives, the fortunate ones obtain a larger or smaller amount of cash.

'This system has many drawbacks, but it appears as if it were the only method of running the industry with any chance of success. Under it a steady worker, with his "stampers", can make a good living, according to native standards—accumulate goats and donkeys, buy a cart or wagon, and even save enough to purchase a small farm. The lazy and thriftless, of whom there are plenty, need not starve, though they are always in debt and are the bugbear of the manager's life.'[2]

By modern standards, even the 'lazy and thriftless' had to work hard if they were to produce fibre. As yet there were no jackhammer drills to bore blasting holes in the rock. Such holes were made by hand with a 'jumper', a long steel chisel which when blunted could be sharpened by a blacksmith. Miners had to 'hit and turn'—'hit' the end of the chisel with a square hammer held in one hand, then with the other hand 'turn' the jumper ready for the next blow. If the rock was hard it might take all day to drill a single hole 30 cm deep, but most men went faster than that.

The stamping was a manual process too, and the only machine used on the mines was a rotating 'trommel' used to sift out sand and grit. The trommel was a cylindrical screen of fine mesh, bolted on to iron hoops. It was about two metres long and set on a slight incline. The trommel was rotated with a handle and asbestos cobs were tipped in at the top. As they tumbled over and over, the sand and grit were rubbed off and fell through holes in the screen. Cleaned cobs inched forwards towards the bottom and were collected in bags. At Koegas, there was a trommel driven by an engine.

'The visitor to a blue asbestos mine must not, therefore, expect to see tall headgears stretching tower-like to the sky, or extensive buildings full of engines or machinery,' continued the *Cape Times* article. 'What he will see will be a few buildings of brick, stone, or iron, set in a fairly level spot among the hills; the manager's house, stores, and so on; a few clusters of native huts, generally placed convenient to a water supply; probably goats, donkeys and cattle peacefully grazing, and a ring of rugged hills, silent and seemingly unoccupied.

'The only visible evidence of the mine is scattered heaps of debris on the face of the hills, their raw colour showing their comparative newness. Presently a series of explosions issues from behind one of these heaps, accompanied by clouds of dust, proof that work is going on. If one climbs the hill by the stony native path, one comes across, first a group of women and children busy "stamping", keeping time with their hammers as likely as not to some oft-repeated native chant, or to a hymn-tune.

'Higher up still, over the heaps of waste rock, a couple or so of "asbestos boys" will be found busy with pick and shovel clearing away the rock broken by the blasting, picking out every piece containing the precious "garen", or "cotton", as they called it, and throwing the rubbish on the ever-increasing pile behind. They will show one the narrow bands of bluish asbestos threading through the rock, and though they can work in a burrow, not much larger than a jackal's hole, one sees that they have to remove about 20 tons of rock to get a ton of asbestos. Two "boys" working well in an average place can get out about a ton of asbestos in a month which will bring them in £10 to £14 according to quality.

'In places where the deposits are consistent regular tunnels have been made with trolley-lines laid, and "coco-pans" pushed by hand or hauled by donkeys to bring out the rock from the interior. Some of the best reefs dip nearly vertically and have to be worked by shafts fitted with bucket and windlass—hand-labour again. Looking down one may see the natives working 60 or 80 feet, perhaps, below; the adventurous visitor can descend in the bucket to watch them in the half-light of candles.

'Drilling and blasting have to be done here also, and after the fuses are lit, the miner must be hauled up by the bucket out of harm's way. These native miners are very careful in their work, and blasting accidents are practically unknown. The deepest workings are some 300 feet, reached by two or even three windlasses and ropes in succession; asbestos, for some reason, probably connected with pressure, does not seem to occur more than 300 feet from the surface'[2]—a naïve conclusion that amuses miners today.

The official ended his article with a swift look at the economics of blue asbestos: 'There are no certain figures available as to the number of persons engaged in the industry, but one would not be far wrong in saying that about 10 000 natives, men, women and children depend on the asbestos work for their livelihood. The number of whites who are fully occupied with it are small, but a further number, including a good many farmers, derive benefit from the industry in the form of rent and royalties. Next to diamonds blue asbestos is the chief mineral product of the Cape Province.'[2]

Diggers' Luck

There were more than a few Northern Cape men in the expeditionary force that invaded South West Africa in 1915. Many had volunteered but others were conscripts aged 16 and up. One of the 16-year-olds was Daniel Ludick, who when the campaign ended decided to go diamond digging. He was no stranger to diamonds as his father and brothers were diggers too, but he was not yet old enough to apply for a digger's certificate. Without a certificate he could not hold a claim on public diggings, so like many in his position he went to work at Vaal Estates.

'Over on Vaal Estates it was as if there was only one licence,' he recalls. 'They were a private company and they held mining rights over a whole area south of the Vaal River. You worked claims on their land and they let you have 90 per cent of the value of the stones you found.'[3] It was the result of a curious anomaly. Vaal Estates were owned on 'Free State title' dating back to the time when the area south of the Vaal had been administered by the Orange Free State. Those who bought land there had been granted not only surface rights but all the mineral rights too.

Each Friday diggers like Daniel Ludick first had to register their week's finds with the Vaal Estates' evaluator who put a price on them. Then they offered their stones to independent diamond buyers from Barkly West. If an independent buyer offered more money than the evaluator the digger was in luck. If not, he had to sell to the evaluator at the basic price. In either case the company deducted 10 per cent before any money changed hands. Ludick and others lived in ramshackle zinc kaias close to their claims and made enough money to live, though chances of making a fortune at Vaal Estates were remote.

Daniel Ludick remained at Vaal Estates until he turned 21 and could apply for his digger's certificate, which entitled him to peg claims on proclaimed public diggings and go prospecting for new deposits. There were rumours of finds on farms near Douglas on the Orange River, so Ludick went to a farm named Brakfontein where prospectors were at work. 'As often happened, the farmer had taken out a prospecting licence covering his whole farm and he allowed prospectors to wash gravel,' he says. 'The prospectors paid him a commission on any stones found.'[3]

The mining commissioner at Barkly West kept an eye on such farms, and was on the point of proclaiming Brakfontein a public diggings. That meant a 'rush' was in the offing, and diggers from all over the diamond fields converged on Brakfontein in hopes of a stroke of luck. Each would be allowed to peg a single claim on the day of the rush and five more a week later. Before that happened, the farmer would be entitled to peg 50 owner's claims and—assuming he held the prospecting licence—50 discoverer's claims as well. His farm was being plunged into chaos but he would be well compensated.

Cape 'rushes' were much tamer than those organised in the Transvaal, where diggers were marshalled on a starting line and raced off at the drop of a flag. In the Cape, diggers wanting to take part notified the mining commissioner in advance and were given a number. The mining commissioner stood on a lorry with diggers gathered around him and read out the proclamation, then dipped into a raffle box and pulled out slips of paper. As a digger's number was called he stepped forward to receive a licence, then began walking or running to the part of the diggings that attracted him.

Each digger carried four wooden or metal pegs and when he reached his chosen spot drove them into the ground to make a square with sides of roughly 15 metres. Officials and police were stationed at strategic points to settle disputes when diggers pegged overlapping claims. In such a case the verdict went to the first to hammer in two pegs. Diggers were to be numbered in scores rather than the hundreds and indeed thousands who figured in the Transvaal Lichtenburg rushes of the later 1920s, so competition was not unduly strong.

That was the pattern at Brakfontein and at other farms of the region that were proclaimed as public diggings. Always some diggers preferred to keep one step ahead of their fellows and moved further and further afield in search of new deposits. A few went east into the Orange Free State or north into the Transvaal. Others preferred the west, among them a German-born prospector named Henry Samuel Richter whose nose for diamonds was second to none. Time and again Richter was to play a part in the discovery of major deposits, and in 1919 he was at work in Postmasburg.

At this time Postmasburg was a snug village serving surrounding farms. There was a handsome stone church, a school, hotel, police station, a store or two and a few houses of sun-dried brick overlooking the Groenwater River. The first residents had been Doppers, members of a strict sect within the Gereformeerde Kerk, and in 1891 they had won the Cape government's approval to name the village after the revered church leader, Ds Dirk Postma of Rustenburg in the Transvaal. Postma had died a year earlier and the little village he had never visited was his memorial.

Each Sunday farmers from all over the Postmasburg district drove to church in two-wheeled Cape carts or perhaps four-wheeled 'spiders'.

During the service their horses were outspanned to graze. One day in 1918 a farmer named Casper Venter came out of church to find his horses had strayed and went to look for them. Walking across the village commonage he noticed a shining stone at the top of a meerkat hole. Bending down to investigate, he found it was a diamond. Next day he brought in a labourer named Plaatjie to dig a prospecting hole and found a second stone.

Casper Venter knew nothing about prospecting, but soon he joined forces with men who had more experience, among them H S Richter. The syndicate was given permission to prospect on public land, but before much work had been done its rights were taken over by Johannesburg interests that prepared to start mining. The Johannesburgers named their operation the 'West End', perhaps in imitation of the suburb of that name in Kimberley. It was six months before any diamonds were produced.

The mine was still young when it was bought by the Abe Bailey mining group of Johannesburg, until then better known for its gold-mining interests than for any involvement with diamonds. A few kilometres east of the West End, prospectors had found a group of kimberlite fissures lying between Postmasburg and Gatkoppies. Here the men responsible were a James West who had permission to prospect and Captain Thomas Shone who had earlier worked on diamond diggings at Bloemhof on the Free State–Transvaal boundary.

During World War I Shone had joined the South African Army and had fought in Tanganyika, today's Tanzania. He was invalided home with malarial fever but ever afterwards he was known as 'Captain' —even 'Skipper'—Shone. According to Postmasburg's village board minutes Shone had found diamonds on land near Postmasburg during 1919 and asked for permission to erect buildings on the site. The modest 'Postmas Mine' came into being with Shone as manager and a Johannesburg attorney named Reggie Saner as a sleeping partner.

Yet another new mine was floating north of Postmasburg on a farm named Makganyene. According to certificates issued, the owner's claims went to the New Makganyene Mining Company but the discoverer's claims went to H S Richter. Almost immediately Richter sold his claims to the company. Perhaps he was short of cash, perhaps he was less than confident that the mine would make his fortune—but the most likely explanation is that he was keen to move on to fresh fields.

Three new mines had come into production in a single year, but not all prospecting yielded such happy results. Thomas Shone investigated kimberlite fissures near Danielskuil and found them less than worthwhile. Far more sobering, a prospector who apparently worked by himself sank a deep shaft on the farm Goold which lies north of Sishen. The shaft caved in on him and by the time it was realised he was missing it was too late to pull him out. The shaft became his grave, and his remains are probably there to this day.

Carrot Holes

Van der Merwe admirers tell stories of a holiday their hero took in Europe. One day he made friends with an Australian and a Canadian and somehow the conversation turned to vegetables. The Australian was boasting that where he came from, cabbages grew as tall as trees. The Canadian said that was nothing special. His country grew melons the size of elephants. Not to be outdone, Van der Merwe told them that South Africa produced the world's biggest carrots. 'Of course, we soon eat them and only the holes are left,' he said. 'We call them diamond pipes.'

There are several giant 'carrot-holes' in and around Kimberley, the gaping cavities left behind when diggers and miners have removed millions of tons of kimberlite. There are similar, but less famous, 'carrot-holes' at the Frank Smith mine near Windsorton and at the old West End mine in Postmasburg. A diamond pipe is indeed shaped like a carrot-hole extending deep into the earth's crust, but the carrot it contains is blue rather than orange except right at the top where the oxidised 'yellow ground' is much easier to work than the hard blue ground below.

The miners who opened Postmasburg's West End mine in 1921 first scooped yellow ground from the top of the pipe as if from a Stilton cheese. So long as the pit was shallow it was easy to reach the working level and haul kimberlite to the crushers and washing plant on the surface. But as the miners probed deeper a new plan was needed. It was decided to install cable hoists and lift kimberlite from the mine in large skips. The skips were not suitable for passengers, so the miners were provided with a zig-zag 'travelling way' sunk through the barren country rock that adjoined the pipe.

One of the very few with memories of early days at the West End is Hans van der Walt of Postmasburg, who started working there early in 1923. 'I was not yet 20 years old, but they put me in charge of a gang of labourers,' he recalls. 'A few months later I got my blasting certificate and I became a miner. The manager was Mr Erleigh and we were organised in a day shift and a night shift. Each shift worked 12 hours a day five days a week. Then on Saturdays the day shift worked from 7 am to 1 pm and the night shift from 2 pm to 8 pm. There was no work on Sundays.'[4]

The pipe was being mined in 'cuts' or horizontal slices, each one 15 metres deep though the width of the pipe gently narrowed on the way down. When a cut was nearly worked out it was time to prepare for the next one. The travelling way was sunk to the new level and a 'cross-cut' was driven through the country rock to connect with the pipe. Meanwhile a trench was cut in the centre of the pipe, seven metres long,

14. Taungs limestone quarry, a cliff worked with cocopans.

Northern Lime Company

15. Limestone kilns at Buxton quarry, predecessor of the operations at Lime Acres near Danielskuil.

Northern Lime Company

16. Raymond Dart examines a cast of the Taungs skull, *c* 1924.

Africana Museum

nearly two metres wide and 15 metres deep. At the bottom of the trench the miners cut niches in the sidewalls and installed long camelthorn logs that spanned the trench and served as anchors for the hoist cables.

There were two hoists at work in the West End, facing one another across the pipe. The drivers sat in high boxes that gave them a good view of operations far below. Each driver operated two skips that were raised and lowered on parallel cables that served as rails. At the bottom the cables were anchored to the camelthorn logs and at the top they were wound around drums so that they could be tightened or slackened as necessary. Loaded skips were pulled up the cables and at the top the kimberlite ore was tipped into bins.

Ore remained in these bins until required for processing, when it was fed into large cocopans. An endless rope haulage pulled the cocopans to crushers. The ore was tipped out and crushed, then fed into rotary washing pans. At intervals gravel from the pans was tapped into buckets and carried to long, narrow sorting-tables. There it was emptied and teams of black sorters scrutinised it for diamonds. At each table a white supervisor kept an eye on the sorters but even so it was not difficult for them to steal stones should they feel so inclined.

Down in the mine, after completing the trench and attaching the hoist cables to the logs the miners began drilling into the walls of the trench and then blasted them into the hole. Broken ore soon covered the logs and weighted them down, so it was safe to raise the loaded skips to the surface. The miners steadily widened the cavity between the walls and installed ore boxes each two metres deep. The hole grew yet bigger and the miners laid down cocopan rails on the floor of the cut. Cocopans were loaded by hand, then pushed to the ore boxes before being returned for a fresh load.

Hundreds of men were at work in the West End, but over at Postmas Mine operations were more modest. Much of the drilling was of the 'hit and turn' variety rather than mechanical and the tonnage removed from the mine was much smaller. Even so, visitors marvelled at a spectacular cocopan railway connecting the mine with crushers and a washing plant located on a hillside about a kilometre away. The railway climbed a gentle incline and trains of cocopans ascended it at the end of heavy cables winched by powerful engines at the top.

Each week the managers of the two mines motored to Kimberley to deposit the diamonds recovered. There were few fears that they would be ambushed along the way. A greater threat was IDB, illicit diamond buying that encouraged workers to steal stones from the mines or the washing plants and offer them for sale. A high wire fence surrounded the West End mine and the black contract workers living in its hostel were not allowed to leave the mine area until they had fulfilled their contracts. But white miners and other workers were free to come and go as they pleased.

One of the white workers was Willie Bam of Postmasburg, who joined West End in 1925 to work as a hoist driver. Each day he travelled to and from the mine by motorbike but was never stopped and searched. 'I could easily have smuggled out diamonds if I'd wanted to,' he recalls. 'One day one of the sorters came to me at the hoist, just as I was going off shift. He showed me a Springbok tobacco pouch that was half-full of beautiful stones. He asked me if I could get him a second-hand push-bike—that was all he wanted. I could have taken the pouch and put it in my pocket and gone home.

'But I was too scared—I didn't want to take the chance. So I said to this man: "No, don't give me the diamonds. Take them to the office and they'll pay you for them and then you can buy a new bicycle." It would have cost only £5 then—I didn't understand why he only wanted a second-hand bike. I heard later he went to the office and handed in the diamonds, but then they chased him off the mine. He didn't get his bike and I didn't get to be rich.'[5]

Australopithecus

With a large diamond mine near the centre of the village, Postmasburg was becoming used to the dull thud of explosions and the uneasy tremor of shock waves. To the north, the people of Kuruman were also learning about large bangs. General dealers stocked dynamite along with dress lengths and barrels of nails and a thousand-and-one other items. The dynamite was bought not only by local asbestos miners but also by farmers wanting to excavate wells.

Some of the Northern Cape's biggest bangs during the 1920s came from a limestone quarry on the farm Buxton, about 12 km from Taungs station on the Kimberley–Vryburg line. The quarry had come into being in 1907 as the Nolan Lime Works, owned by H G Nolan. Production levels were modest until 1917 when Nolan Lime merged with a Transvaal rival, the Northern Lime Company, which quarried limestone in the Waterberg range. Northern Lime was another company founded in 1907 and its fortunes were controlled by John Orr, a Scotsman who was one of Johannesburg's most energetic financiers.

For a year both Northern Lime and Nolan Lime representatives sat on the board of the enlarged company but it was plain Orr was in charge. The Nolan men became disenchanted and bowed out. Their shares were taken over by Central Mining and Investment Corporation which appointed three directors to the Northern Lime board. From this time Nolan Lime ceased to exist as a separate entity and Buxton stone was sold as a product of Northern Lime Company. Then Northern Lime's quarry in the Transvaal closed down and Buxton was the company's only source of limestone.

An official of the South African Geological Survey visited Taungs during 1918 and his report includes a brief survey of operations at Buxton. The limestone deposit was nearly a kilometre long, he wrote, fronting a dolomite plateau and broken by a ravine that cut into the plateau. 'The quarries begin about one hundred yards to the south of the opening and considerably above the level of the bottom,' he continued, 'presumably to facilitate the handling of the material by gravity.'[6]

After blasting, limestone was loaded into cocopans and trammed to a battery of tall vertical kilns which burned off carbon dioxide and turned the stone into calcium oxide or quicklime. Small quantities of the quicklime were 'slaked' with water to be sold to the construction industry as 'hydrated lime'. The products were bagged and loaded on to ox-wagons to be carted to Taungs station. Most of Buxton's quicklime went to the Witwatersrand for use in the cyanide process by which the gold mines refined their product, or otherwise to sugar refineries or soap and chemical manufacturers.

The limestone deposit at Buxton consisted of white 'secondary' limestone rather than the grey 'primary' limestone that looks like dolomite—*kalk* as opposed to *jonasklip*. The main difference between primary limestone and dolomite is that the latter contains much more magnesium, but both can provide the elements that make up secondary limestone. Acidic reactions in the ground water table leach calcium and magnesium from the primary host rock and streams and rivers precipitate them outside its limits. The calcium is heavier and is precipitated first and the magnesium is washed away.

Over millennia, streams can deposit beds of limestone that are up to 100 metres deep. That is what happened at Buxton. Sometimes the streams left caves in the limestone that might fill with stalactites and stalagmites as water dripped from the roof. Sometimes they ran over relics of past ages and buried them in calcium which eventually turned them into fossils. An unusually rich haul of fossils was found at Buxton in 1920 when a blast uncovered the floor of an ancient cave. Among the fossils were a number of small baboon skulls and several were sent to the South African Museum in Cape Town.

Dr S H Haughton of the South African Museum examined the baboon skulls and realised they came from an unknown species. Early in 1920 he read a paper on the skulls before the Royal Society of South Africa, but it was not published until 1925. By that time Professor Raymond Dart had arrived in Johannesburg to take up the chair of anatomy at the University of the Witwatersrand Medical School. Dart was principally interested in brain matter and nerve-cells and had little affection for bones, but during 1924 one of his students brought him an interesting specimen and asked for his opinion.

The student was Josephine Salmons and she had spotted the skull on a mantelpiece in the home of E G Izod, one of Northern Lime's directors. It was one of the fossil baboon skulls unearthed in 1920. Dart was immediately interested for 'as far as I knew then, this was the first monkey fossil to be found south of Egypt', he explained later. 'I asked Dr R B Young, who happened to be going to Taungs the following week, to send up any further pieces of likely rock containing bones he might see down there.'[7]

At Buxton Young called on A E Spiers, the quarry manager, and there on his desk was a box containing a number of fossil bones that had been discovered the week before. The bones had been collected by a miner named De Bruin, and they came from a brecciated formation that was apparently the floor of an ancient cave. Spiers agreed to send the fossils to Dart and they reached him in Johannesburg during November 1924. One fossil clamoured for attention—the cast of the inside of a skull much larger than a baboon's, bigger even than a chimpanzee's.

Dart found that the cast fitted on to the back of another piece of rock. With mounting excitement he took out a hammer and chisels and even a pointed knitting-needle. For six weeks he gently chipped at the rock until the skull stood revealed. The Australian-born anatomist realised he had stumbled upon the remains of an unknown species, part-ape and part-man. He was looking into the face of a six-year-old infant, the first complete face of an extinct species of ape ever discovered.

'This little face was not the face of a chimpanzee baby', he recalled years later. 'It was something far more refined. Instead of having big peg-like canine teeth, such as a baby chimpanzee has, they were as small as those of a human baby. Its eye-sockets were not coarse and square but delicate and rounded; there were no eyebrow ridges such as you find in a chimpanzee's skull; and, instead of the skull being flat on top, a real forehead rose up above the eye-sockets. The cast of the inside of the skull also showed that the brain of this baby had not only been somewhat bigger but considerably more intelligent than that of a fully-grown chimpanzee.

'Finally,' concluded Dart, 'the globular form of the skull showed me that it must have been carried on top of a vertebral column much more nearly erect than that of any living ape.'[7] Dart realised he had evidence of what others might call 'a missing link' between ape and man—but they had expected to find it in Asia, not Africa. Palaeontologists had forecast that the 'missing link' would prove to have a large brain with big teeth and a massive forehead like a gorilla's—yet Dart's discovery was the other way round.

'Apes ought to live in steaming tropical forests and eat fruit,' said Dart, 'but there were no forests or fruit groves down there at Taungs on the arid eastern fringe of the Kalahari. The skull, too, had been found in a place that had obviously been a cave. These Taungs apes were clearly cliff-dwellers on the bleak Campbell Rand plateau, which overlooks eastwards the broad forestless plain of the Harts River watershed, that dips southwards towards the Vaal. The Taungs apes were definitely something new; different from any known apes and really of a kind people overseas would think impossible: two-legged and fleet-footed apes.'[7]

Dart named his new species *Australopithecus africanus* or 'Southern Ape of Africa' but it was inevitably dubbed Taungs Man. Articles on his findings appeared during 1925, but for a decade the scientific world remained sceptical. Then in 1936 Dr Robert Broom of Cape Town discovered evidence of an adult *Australopithecus* in limestone formations in the Transvaal. Subsequently more specimens came to light in the Transvaal and East Africa too. It was accepted that *Australopithecus* had lived in South Africa between 2,3 million and 4 million years ago, a forerunner of *homo habilis*, *homo erectus*, *homo sapiens* and today's *homo sapiens sapiens*.

CHAPTER FOUR 1926–1935

Donkey Work

THERE WERE two great sights in Postmasburg during the 1920s. One was the lights of the West End diamond mine as it worked through the night. The other was the queues of donkey-wagons piled high with camelthorn wood that the mine needed as fuel. Most of the wood was burnt to power big gas-induction engines that drove generators, hoists and other plant on the mine. The engines had an insatiable appetite and the mine's need for fuel provided work for many scores of transport contractors. One of them was Hans van Staden, who today farms near Sishen.

Hans van Staden's father had been a diamond digger at Delportshoop, and young Hans had grown up there with three brothers and two sisters. The family moved to Postmasburg when the West End opened but Van Staden senior found transport riding more lucrative than working in the mine. 'We lived quite near Gatkoppies,' Hans van Staden recalls. 'At first I worked with my father and then afterwards I had my own wagon. We went to Kathu Forest to collect the wood, carried it to Postmasburg, then went back for more. The complete trip took a week.'[1]

The Van Stadens and indeed nearly all the independent transport contractors preferred donkey power to the traditional spans of oxen. First rinderpest, then a mysterious disease known as '*lamsiekte*' had killed Northern Cape oxen in hundreds of thousands, so donkeys had been introduced as an alternative. Transport riders soon found that donkeys ate less and had more stamina than oxen, and that their feet stood up to hot sand whereas oxen's feet quickly became sore. Even more important, they seemed immune to '*lamsiekte*' and other diseases that affected cattle or horses.

During 1914 government researchers working near Vryburg discovered the cause of '*lamsiekte*'—the bones of victims of rinderpest, abandoned in the veld. Cattle and sheep searching for phosphate were eating these bones and with them a deadly parasite. The government undertook a massive clean-up in a bid to rid the whole Northern Cape of infected animal remains, but it was years before British Bechuanaland and Griqualand West were restored to health. Oxen were safe again, but transport riders stayed loyal to their donkeys, and were convinced they were more efficient.

'Most of us had spans of 24 donkeys and a wagon up to six metres long,' says Hans van Staden. 'The wagons had big iron-rimmed wheels at the back and smaller ones in front. The donkeys were in pairs with collars around their necks that were attached to long traces running down the middle. A piccanin walked in front and led the first pair of donkeys. The driver might sit up on the wagon but usually he walked alongside. Each donkey had its own name—Blouberg, Vrystaat, Koffie, whatever—and we used to hiss to make them go and whistle to make them stop.'[1]

Kathu Forest was government land and transport riders had to obtain a permit to collect wood. 'A permit cost 10/-—a Rand—per load,' says Van Staden. 'We paid the money on the way in, then we could collect as much wood as we could carry. We didn't need to cut any wood—there were lots of dead trees lying there, bone dry. We stacked them on the wagon, three or four metres high, and tied them with rope. Then we began trekking towards the West End which was three days away. We travelled about 25 km a day and outspanned at about six o'clock each evening.'[1]

At their outspans, the transport drivers played draughts or cards or even boeresport like finger-pull or *skilpadtrek* (tortoise-pull). Sundays were rest days. Drawing close to the mine, most outspanned on a farm named Beeshoek. First thing next morning a long procession of wagons filed over the last hill and stopped at the mine gates. Each wagon was weighed as it entered the mine, then weighed again after discharging its load. The driver was paid by the weight he had delivered—about £8 or £9 for a full load.

With money in their pockets, the drivers might linger in Postmasburg. But soon they were on the road back to Kathu. Occasionally they broke their routine by delivering wood to the Postmas mine or perhaps to the small asbestos mines of the Kuruman district. Some drivers found it profitable to ignore wood and haul general cargo instead. Postmasburg was supplied from Douglas station on the Orange River and Kuruman from Taungs, arrangements that continued until South African Railways laid a line to Koopmansfontein and served outlying centres with a long-distance lorry service.

For years donkeys were the backbone of the Northern Cape's transport system, but policemen of the Cape Mounted Rifles introduced more exotic animals for patrols in the sandy Kalahari. The police were an important presence in the Northern Cape of the 1920s, stationed in all the main communities and also far out in the wilds. Normally they patrolled on horseback or perhaps on motorbikes, but in the Kalahari they preferred camels. So did a locust control officer named Chalon St Quentin whose job was to look for 'hoppers', baby locusts that gave notice of a coming swarm.

St Quentin worked for South Africa's Department of Agriculture and was based at Moroquin, today's Morokweng, about 150 km north of Vryburg. During 1924 he and a companion camped on a stretch of veld about 80 km from Moroquin. 'I'd just off-saddled my camel when I noticed a strange rock formation,' he says. 'There were ribbons of blue sandwiched between layers of red and brown. I took some samples and later showed them to my father who lived in Vryburg. He told me I'd found asbestos, and next thing I knew the Cape Asbestos Company was sending in a prospector.'[2]

The man recruited was not a regular prospector but Charles Stewart of Moroquin police. Stewart's son John says that his father had no experience of minerals but he did know the region and he knew the farmers. 'My father rode a horse,' says John Stewart, 'and he had his equipment in a little ox-cart pulled by four oxen. He found asbestos on the farm Cheddar and later on Botallack. The farmers agreed to let Cape Asbestos mine there. They asked my father to stay on as manager. In 1927 he opened a mine on another nearby farm that was named Pomfret.'[3]

Both oxen and donkeys played important roles in opening the three new mines. There was a shortage of water so each day a span of five oxen ferried water from a neighbouring farm. Local contractors used both ox-and donkey-wagons to haul fibre to Vryburg station. As Pomfret mine went underground, 25 donkeys were trained to haul cocopans up an incline. 'The donkeys had to pull quite a long way', John Stewart explains. 'There were two lanes—one up-bound and one going down. Each donkey pulled up a loaded cocopan, then it was unharnessed and led to the bottom while empty cocopans ran down under their own steam.'[3]

The Soutie Touch

Afrikaners know those who come from other lands as '*souties*' meaning 'salties' as they are from across the salt sea. *Souties* tend to be English-speakers, whether British, Irish, North American or Australasian. The people of Griquatown remember that *souties* worked in local galena mines during the 1920s but say they all left long ago. As a result very little is known about these workings and strange myths are developing. After examining the low, narrow adits at the Balloch mine one leading geologist concluded that they must have been developed by female Bushmen.

The Balloch workings are 60 km north of Prieska, closer to Niekerkshoop than Griquatown. A government report of 1940 stated that Balloch's galena consisted of 'a series of parallel veins carrying galena and subordinate amounts of zinc-blende in a gangue of quartz and amberite. It was prospected in 1919–20 when about 200 tons of galena were produced. During the period 1923–27 it was worked as the Balloch Lead Mine and altogether 684 tons of galena were produced. Local reports say that operations were discontinued largely due to the fact that the price of lead had practically collapsed.'[4]

The present farmer at Balloch, Kosie Jacobs, has been there since the 1960s. He believes the deposit was first outlined by the prospector Bleloch of Vogelstruisbult fame. A 'W E Bleloch' played a part in opening the West End diamond mine in 1919 and was almost certainly the 'William Bleloch' who had been well known in Transvaal gold-mining circles at the turn of the century. All that Griquatown people recall of operations at Balloch is that it was worked with cocopans. The abandoned mine is a maze of tunnels that extend 30 or 40 metres into the outcrops.

The low, narrow adits off the main drives are evidence of a long-vanished mining method. Miners had to crawl into such adits on their stomachs and work at the face with hammers. The ore body consisted largely of quartz so the galena could be recovered without using explosives. Broken ore fell on to a sack or blanket lying under the miner's nose, and when he had collected enough he eased himself back out of the adit while dragging the ore in his wake. In the main drift the ore was loaded into a cocopan, then trammed out to the sunlight.

Outside the workings the galena-bearing quartz was cleaned to dispose of waste rock, a process much like the hand-cobbing of asbestos. Then the ore was hand-sorted and stacked ready for despatch to a lead smelter. Similar procedures would have been used at the Bushy Park galena mine about 25 km north-east of Griquatown, where the long-forgotten miners are recalled by a deep pit filled with water. The mine began producing in 1927 but was soon abandoned when the lead price fell. Only 48 tons were mined, but much lead remains where that came from.

The mine at Bushy Park was opened by a small company launched in 1926. Behind it were men associated with the Postmas diamond mine, notably Thomas Shone and Reggie Saner. The two were joined by a Johannesburg financier named John Dale-Lace. Their venture was named 'Union Manganese Mines and Minerals', formed not to exploit galena but to tap one of the Northern Cape's great unexplored assets. Back in 1907 a government geologist named A W Rogers had noticed manganese far to the north at Black Rock, but now deposits had been found close to Postmasburg.

Local farmers and others had long been familiar with the great black outcrops of rock that could be found all over the Postmasburg district, but most had assumed they were formed of *yster* or iron. That was a mistake often made in the past. Not until 1774 had it been realised that manganese was an element all on its own, and even then it was many years before scientists realised it was useful as a metal. In the meantime manganese dioxide or 'pyrolusite' was used as an ingredient of glass and paint and ceramic glazes, as it had been since the days of Ancient Greece.

During the 1830s a French metallurgist showed that the addition of a small quantity of manganese improved malleability in pig-iron—in other words, its capacity for being rolled out or shaped by hammering. It was also shown that manganese strengthened the iron. Then the British inventor Henry Bessemer introduced manganese into steel-making, and in 1882 Robert Hadfield of Britain used an alloy of iron and manganese to produce super-rugged manganese steel that was used to make armour plating in battleships.

In South Africa, small amounts of manganese had been mined in the Western Cape since early in the nineteenth century for use in paint. Limited quantities were mined in the Transvaal and despatched to a steelworks in Newcastle, Natal. In the world outside, steel-makers in continental Europe traditionally drew their manganese from Russia while those in Britain and the United States imported from India. Now there were new large-scale producers on the Gold Coast of West Africa and in Brazil, but worldwide steel production was expanding and there was room for South African exports providing they were competitive.

According to long-time Postmasburg residents, the first to take a close look at local manganese deposits were W B Collins, who had been involved in the West End mine, and a Frans van der Merwe of Olifantshoek. These two sent samples of manganese ore to steel manufacturers in the United States and asked if they were interested. Response was lukewarm, apparently because the Americans felt the Postmasburg ore contained too much iron and because it was so inaccessible. The nearest railing point was Douglas on the Orange River, about 120 km away.

Collins apparently left the Postmasburg district in 1924. Meanwhile Thomas Shone of the Postmas diamond mine had become disenchanted with diamonds and was looking for new fields to conquer. He installed a manager at the mine and invested in an old Cape cart drawn by two horses, and in this he began travelling all over the region. 'He took a prospector's hammer and some sample bags and a couple of native assistants,' says his widow Molly, who still lives in Postmasburg. 'He really wasn't interested in diamonds any more—he was looking for base metals, especially manganese.'[5]

After each expedition Shone returned home with a range of specimens. 'He went fossicking all over the district,' says Molly Shone, 'and if he found something special he was as excited as a little boy.'[5] More practically, he took options over all the most promising farms. According to a letter Shone wrote in 1943, he had first become interested in manganese during 1922, and his interest must have increased following a visit to the region by A L Hall of the South African Geological Survey who had been sent to investigate possible sources of iron ore.

Hall's first inspection was made in 1925 and he returned again in the following year, this time accompanied by A W Rogers of Black Rock fame. Their brief was to identify sources of raw materials that might be used in a state-run steel industry, but Hall was more interested in the chances of establishing manganese mines geared to export markets. The deposits were traceable for 60 km along the Gamagara River, he wrote, in many areas up to seven metres thick. All the deposits were easily accessible from the surface so could be mined by open-cast methods.

There was no shortage of cheap labour around Postmasburg, wrote Hall—there were many native reserves in the area. Besides, 'the deposits round Postmasburg are very easy to mine, and in excellent physical condition. It would thus appear that a South African industry would have a good chance of competing successfully for its share in the world's markets provided transport difficulties can be overcome. . . . The Postmasburg area holds deposits of manganese ore in large quantities comparable to the scale on which well-established sources in other parts of the world are being exploited.'[6]

Hall's report appeared in 1926 and early in the same year Shone, Saner and Dale-Lace launched Union Manganese. The three men had investigated a number of farms west and north-west of Postmasburg and were ready to mine on Beeshoek, Doornfontein and Paling. In looking over Doornfontein Dale-Lace had spotted what he thought was a mountain goat trapped high on a kopje. The other two were not convinced but Dale-Lace insisted they should rescue it. A difficult climb led not to a goat but to a rock covered in dried dassie droppings. The hillock has been 'Lace's Goat' or 'Bokkoppie' ever since.

As yet Union Manganese had produced no ore beyond samples that had been sent to Johannesburg for analysis. But that did not prevent Shone from writing to all the world's steelmakers with offers of high-grade manganese. Ironically, his enthusiasm sprang from a serious over-estimate of the amount available. When Shone took visitors on a tour of Union Manganese's farms he said there was manganese all around them when much of it was actually iron ore or simply black rock with no ore content.

This mistake was easy to make, for all these substances looked much the same. Indeed, the mistake was duplicated by a Postmasburg attorney named A J Bester and a Johannesburg speculator named Nils Langkilde. Together these men took options on a line of farms to the north-*east* of Postmasburg, parallel to the line held by Union Manganese. From the look of the outcrops it seemed that these farms held as much manganese as the ones prospected by Shone, even though Hall had not commented on them.

Langkilde already served on the boards of several mining companies active in the Transvaal and he had valuable contacts on the Witwatersrand. He persuaded several of these contacts to help him form a new company, and 'South African Manganese Ltd' was registered during December 1926. Bester and Langkilde transferred the rights they had acquired and were rewarded with cash and shares. They also bought extra shares in the new company, together with a host of subscribers including 'master bakers from Kimberley, garage owners from Christiana, bank managers from Pietermaritzburg'[6] and many more.

At about this time Langkilde approached the United States trade commissioner in Johannesburg and asked him about the chances of selling ore in America. The trade commissioner suggested he should contact Robert T Erwin, who was then in Postmasburg examining Union Manganese's deposits on behalf of the Mississippi Valley Iron Company. Langkilde travelled to Postmasburg and met the American but made no progress. At the same time he met a Dr Graf, who was in touch with representatives of a big German combine that was looking for manganese.

According to Graf, the German combine was interested in putting up money to build the necessary railway provided it could acquire its own source of manganese. Meanwhile an inquiry arrived from the London office of the Philadelphia firm Lavino's, stating that they were 'always buyers of manganese ore'.[6] Lavino's wanted to know if S A Manganese could provide ore at short notice. With encouragement like that the company's directors decided to open up their deposits without delay. Two prospectors, S Griffiths and W J Marais, were engaged to test each farm in turn.

Both S A Manganese and Union Manganese continued to lobby the South African government over the need for a railway, and in mid-1927 it seemed there was a breakthrough. Tielman Roos, the minister of railways and harbours, confirmed that certain 'American interests'—no doubt Mississippi Valley Iron Company—were prepared to advance £25 000 to South African Railways to help construct a rail line linking Postmasburg with Koopmansfontein, about 120 km north-west of Kimberley. They were also prepared to sponsor ore-handling facilities in East London in the eastern part of the Cape Province.

All this sounded promising, but both the would-be manganese producers found their cash resources were running low. That was why both welcomed approaches by Fraser Jones, a British entrepreneur who was based in South Africa. Jones represented another group of Americans who wanted to buy one or other of the manganese companies lock, stock and barrel. The rival companies showed Jones over their holdings near Postmasburg, and it was disappointing when the negotiations came to nothing.

Various Dutch and German companies glanced towards Postmasburg during the year that followed but even yet there were no firm orders. The 'American interests' had evidently cooled on the idea of subsidising a railway. Nothing much happened until Fraser Jones became involved with new principals, the British Swiss International Corporation which had interests in various mines in France and Spain. The corporation sent a Dr Richter, professor of geology at the University of Bonn, to look over the Postmasburg deposits at first hand. His report was positive and British Swiss opened negotiations.

The chairman of British Swiss was Norman Pickett, who had made money from buying and selling scrap armaments left over from World War I. A series of cables from Pickett is preserved in Johannesburg at the head office of 'Samancor' as S A Manganese has been known since its merger with Amcor, the African Metals Corporation. The first of these cables shows that Pickett proposed first to take over S A Manganese, then to negotiate with South African Railways.

> 'AM AT PRESENT ENGAGED IN ARRANGING THE FINANCIAL DETAILS OF A COMPANY TO ACQUIRE YOUR INTERESTS STOP IF TERMS CABLED TO JONES YESTERDAY ARE ACCEPTABLE TO YOU I WILL SEND REPRESENTATIVES IMMEDIATELY TO NEGOTIATE WITH RAILWAY AUTHORITIES AND WILL FOLLOW MYSELF TO CONCLUDE THE BUSINESS.'[6]

S A Manganese's response must have been favourable, for Pickett promptly urged the directors to meet their counterparts at Union Manganese to arrange joint exploitation of the Postmasburg deposits. The two sets of directors did come together but neither had realised that Pickett was dealing with both. They could not agree and Pickett was less than happy as he made clear to S A Manganese:

> 'UNDERSTAND FROM FRASER JONES THAT YOU ARE UNABLE TO AGREE WITH UNION STOP STRONGLY URGE YOU MAKE AN ARRANGEMENT WITH UNION AS ALONE NEITHER CAN HAVE A COMPLETE SUCCESS STOP TOGETHER WITH THE WORLD MARKET AS IT IS I ANTICIPATE EXTRAORDINARY DEVELOPMENTS.'[6]

Even then no agreement could be reached. S A Manganese was prepared to settle for 10 per cent of a new company to be formed and to allow Union Manganese 20 per cent. But Shone and his partners felt they were worth a lot more. All this time Fraser Jones was playing one company against the other as he tried to organise favourable terms for himself, and that created further bad feeling. For S A Manganese, a third cable from Pickett was the last straw:

> 'HAVE RECEIVED LETTER FROM JOHANNESBURG INDICATING THAT GOVERNMENT GEOLOGICAL EXPERTS DO NOT AGREE THAT SOUTH AFRICAN MANGANESE PROPERTIES ARE VALUABLE AND STATING THAT A MEMORANDUM IS BEING PREPARED ON THE SUBJECT WHICH WILL WRECK ANY CHANCE OF AN ISSUE BEING SUCCESSFUL STOP WHOLE MATTER HAS BECOME SO INVOLVED DUE TO PERSONAL QUARRELS IN SOUTH AFRICA THAT I WILL NOT PROCEED UNTIL I HAVE PERSONALLY INVESTIGATED MATTERS ON THE SPOT.'[6]

Pickett did visit South Africa, but he negotiated only with Union Manganese and left S A Manganese alone. His dealings were to have far-reaching implications for the whole Northern Cape.

A Lucky Escape

By 1927 the Postmas diamond mine had run out of payable kimberlite and was closed down. A caretaker, Johnny Vertue of Campbell, was appointed to keep an eye on the silent machinery and long lines of parked cocopans. The caretaker and his family lived in the manager's house near the top of the long incline railway used to haul cocopans out of the mine. Vertue's son Pieter says that on Sunday afternoons his mother and father liked to doze. That gave Pieter and his friends a chance to get up to mischief, and a favourite exploit was taking rides in the cocopans.

'At the top of the incline there were barriers on the rails,' says Pieter Vertue, 'so we pulled them out of the way. Then we uncoupled one of the cocopans and rolled it to the top of the incline. We pushed off, three or four of us jumped in, and soon we got up quite a speed. The mine was filling up with water but that was half a kilometre away. When we got down there the cocopan hit the water with a splash, but the pan wasn't attached to the wheels so it floated free while the wheels went on down the rails. We pretended we were on a ship being launched from a slipway.'[7]

Postmas mine was out of action but as if to compensate an old mine had been reopened. The Frank Smith pipe near Windsorton had been closed since before World War I but in 1926 new owners had felt it was worth a fresh look. Soon a company was formed to mine not only the main pipe but nearby fissures as well, and a steep incline was sunk into the kimberlite. Winches hauled cocopans to new crushers and a washing plant erected on the surface. As yet profits were small but that was because diamonds were undervalued.

The West End mine in Postmasburg was still profitable, in spite of a huge mass of dolomite that interruped the pipe about 80 metres down.

Removing the dolomite proved costly, but there was blueground underneath and it seemed the mine's problems were over when a new menace appeared. The sidewalls of the pipe were drying out and crumbling and huge falls of ground threatened the workings below. Much of the fallen ground was removed and mining continued, but an ominous crack was opening to the north-west where the travelling-way was located.

'We were still working a day shift and a night shift,' remembers Hans van der Walt. 'David Brown, Erleigh's son-in-law, had taken over as manager. Norman Nicholson was mine captain. I was one of the shiftbosses. The day we noticed the crack by the travelling-way it was just a few millimetres wide and old Brown told the boys to fill it with cement. But the next day I got to the mine and the four miners on my shift refused to go down and told their men not to go down until I'd examined the crack. I found it had opened, it was now a centimetre wide.

'After that the miners refused to go down. Brown was standing nearby but I went to find Nicholson and told him what had happened and he told me to let the men go. He was firing them. I said that I was leaving too. I was a bit annoyed when he took that attitude when we'd all been working there many years. I felt he could have shown more consideration, we could have talked it out. So I left and went to my farm and that was the last time I worked for the West End. That must have been early in 1930.'[8]

The company hired new miners to take the places of those who had been fired, among them Alwyn Vorster. 'Nicholson took me down the travelling-way and said, look here, this is what drove the men away', says Vorster who has retired to Murraysburg, not far from Graaff-Reinet. 'The crack was so wide I could put my hand in it. They decided they had to blast away the dangerous rock and sent men down the sidewalls to drill holes with hand jumpers. We gave the men safety harness, belts around their middles with ropes leading up to the surface.

'The men were working about 10 or 15 metres down inside the hole. We had trouble making them wear the safety harness but it was as well they did. At five o'clock in the morning the wall gave way and the rock fell out from under them. There were 15 men there and they were left hanging at the end of the safety ropes. I looked down to see if they were all right and three were hurt—they were covered in blood. They'd been cut by flying rock. We pulled them up and the first to come was called Jantjie—he was too shocked to speak and just pointed up at heaven.'[9]

Fortunately there was nobody in the mine at the time of the fall. The washing plant was processing tailings. Willie Bam the hoist driver was still working at West End and he explains: 'The government inspectors had already visited the mine and said it was unsafe. Now they said the company would have to sink a shaft at a safe distance from the pipe, but the company said that wasn't worthwhile. Diamond prices were too low. They told us they were shutting down the mine and we could all go. They gave us a month's notice. That was in May 1930.'[10]

West End fell silent as the Postmas mine had done, and Postmasburg's village management board took over the tailings heaps to gravel local roads. The heaps contained many diamonds missed during sorting, some weighing as much as three carats. Especially after rain, numbers of small boys and adults too could be seen pacing the roads in search of tell-tale glints. But before long the CID diamond branch intervened and suggested that the council should draw its road gravel from another source.

Even at depression values the windfall diamonds were a boon to those who found them. The depression had been signalled by the New York Stock Exchange crash of October 1929, though many believed the world would soon recover. Most of those laid off by the West End soon found work in Postmasburg's manganese industry which during 1929 had undergone a radical change. Norman Pickett and his company had reached agreement with Union Manganese and leased its mining rights. To work them Pickett had formed a new company, Manganese Corporation, which was to underwrite a new rail line to Postmasburg.

One of Manganese Corporation's first employees was Syd Brownrigg, a metallurgist recruited from the Gold Coast. 'I'd been in West Africa since 1924,' recalled Brownrigg when interviewed in 1980. 'I was due to go on leave when I received a cable asking if I'd like to go to South Africa. I said yes—you can have just so much of the Gold Coast. In London I went to see the Manganese Corporation board and was quite impressed. They were prepared to put £1 million into South African base metals at a time when South Africans themselves were only interested in gold.'[11]

Brownrigg reached Postmasburg a few days before the Wall Street crash, but for the time being the district's problems were climatic rather than economic. 'Half a year's normal rainfall fell out of season in that first week,' he recorded, 'and the taxi journey from Kimberley took a good seven hours, sliding precariously along the edges of dongas and down the river bank on to the pont at Schmidt's Drift. That first evening in Postmasburg was cold and dreary, not much of a welcome for a young enthusiastic stranger, yet all the talk was of big things to come.

'Exploration of the village did not take long; three or four general stores, two optimistic garages, a bank, an indifferent hotel, raw brick dwellings and an attorney's office. The stoep of this was the only apparent scene of human activity, because it was here that the more prominent citizens gathered to discuss manganese options, new mining companies, cattle prices, or merely to gossip. The main point of interest, though, and especially for the manganese-minded, was a narrow office

17. A miner and his gang at the Gloucester manganese mine: labourers sort and load manganese while a mule waits to haul a cocopan.

Associated Manganese

18. Old cocopans form the roof of an unusual kaia at the Lohatlha manganese mine.

Humphry Clinker

19. Pioneers of Associated Manganese at Beeshoek, *c* 1934: behind the table stand Syd Brownrigg (*second from left*) and Jumbo Harris (*third from left*).

Associated Manganese

entrance with a brass plate alongside the door: "Capt T L H Shone—Mineral & Gem Explorer."'[12]

Brownrigg found Shone to be a man of enormous charm, 'ever ready to digress on any and every subject except the business in hand'. He was now over 60 years old but was still full of energy and enthusiasm. 'Implements of his trade littered his office,' continued Brownrigg: 'sample bags of minerals, hammers, lumps of rock and camping equipment. A glass-fronted case was crammed with specimens while various nooks and crannies were filled with books; few on minerals and prospecting but many on travel for he had wandered about quite a bit.'[12]

An intriguing glimpse of Shone the prospector is provided by Gene Stanton, manager of the recreation club at Lohatlha manganese mine. Stanton's father farmed at Bishop south of Sishen 'and Shone used to bring his wagon to our farm and prospect from there. He had a team of boys who'd been with him for years—he sent them off into the mountains to fetch samples. Meanwhile he sat under a big camelthorn tree and entered all the samples on cards. At the end of the week he sat under the same tree while he paid everyone—it seemed to us a great deal of money.'[13]

Shone later remembered many of his helpers in his will, but his favourite was a Griqua named Jan Frey. 'Shone never sent Jan Frey to fetch samples,' says Gene Stanton. 'But instead he sent him miles to fetch water from a special spring. It was very clear water and he'd never drink anything else.'[13] Another favourite of Shone's was an aged Bushman named Jacob who was supposed to have been born during the 1810s. Shone had promised Jacob that when he died his skull would be presented to a natural history museum. Each Saturday Jacob let Shone check his 'specimen' for bumps and was paid a shilling for his trouble.

At the time Syd Brownrigg arrived in Postmasburg South African Railways had not yet started building the rail link between Postmasburg and Koopmansfontein. New plant ordered by Manganese Corporation was being brought in by donkey-wagon—not least a complete power station that is retained at Gloucester manganese mine in case of emergencies. Manganese Corporation quickly won contracts to supply manganese to French customers but the first export consignment was destined for Japan. It was carried to Koopmansfontein aboard donkey-wagons and Hans van Staden was one of the drivers.

'The trip to Koopmansfontein used to take two or three days,' says Van Staden, 'with another two or three days to get back to Postmasburg. We had to load the wagons ourselves—the manganese was in big lumps, two or three tons to a load. At Koopmansfontein we first parked the wagons where they were to be unloaded, then outspanned the donkeys, then worked for hours to stack all the manganese.'[1] Before long Manganese Corporation switched to motor transport, but wagons had right of way on the atrocious roads and lorries stuck behind them had to move at the pace of the donkeys.

The power plant was assembled on the farm Beeshoek, now known as 'Mancorp Mine'. A tall loading chute of solid concrete was erected ready for the railway. Offices went up not far away and the corporation also built a square hostel block to house 500 black labourers. A small village was established next to the offices and the first to move in were Syd Brownrigg and his wife. The second house was occupied by the mine captain, Jumbo Harris, who was something of a celebrity. During his university days in Johannesburg he had been South Africa's champion sprinter.

On one occasion Harris had been matched against a greyhound in Johannesburg and large bets had been placed on the result. The greyhound won, but only just. During storybook rushes on the Lichtenburg diamond fields discovered in the Transvaal, Harris and other fleetfooted students had run ahead of a pack of diggers thousands strong and had pegged claims on behalf of others. Now Harris's great love was rugby and it was not long before he became active in the little rugby club organised in Postmasburg—though in these early days the district's leading sport was cricket.

The first mine manager at Mancorp Mine had been a Scotsman named Pringle-Smith, another graduate of the Gold Coast. Pringle-Smith had departed at the start of 1930 and was snapped up by S A Manganese, which continued to hope for a magic takeover like the one that had saved Union Manganese. Pringle-Smith was replaced by Jimmy Templeton from the Transvaal, but he too stayed only a short time and was replaced by David Brown from the West End. Mine managers came and went with such frequency, noted Syd Brownrigg, that 'to be an ex-manager of a manganese mine became an essential qualification for future success in other spheres'.[12]

The swift turnover reflected growing anxiety in Manganese Corporation, not about a shortage of customers but about the difficulty of supplying them with high-grade ore. According to a company report published in 1931 Manganese Corporation had won contracts with buyers in France, Britain, Germany, Belgium, Japan and the United States. 'Some of these contracts are in the nature of trial orders,' the report explained, 'but . . . we do not anticipate any difficulty in selling our whole production of ore, even during the present period of depression in the base metal market.'[14]

According to Syd Brownrigg, 'our main contracts at that time were with the French company Société de Manganese. But like our other customers they were only interested in high-grade ore, say 50 per cent manganese. We had deposits of high grade ore on Beeshoek and Doornfontein but they were very scattered. We had plenty of lower-grade ore too but at that time you couldn't give it away—nobody wanted it. We even opened up Paling and laid a narrow-gauge railway to link it with Beeshoek but that didn't work either—there was lots of ore but the grade was too patchy.'[11]

Searching for new supplies, Manganese Corporation began buying ore from a newly formed company, Hay Base Metals, which was mining on farms held by two other companies. One was Postmas Manganese Fields which owned Lylyveld, much later developed as an iron ore mine. The other was Gamagara Manganese which held mining rights on the farm Sishen. But even this new source of supply was not enough and in desperation Manganese Corporation turned to S A Manganese with offers to buy quantities of high-grade ore. Unfortunately S A Manganese was in no position to supply it.

During November 1930 the railway had at last reached Postmasburg, but for Manganese Corporation it was becoming more of a liability than an asset. In persuading South African Railways to build the line Pickett had promised that the corporation would rail at least 200 000 tons of ore during its first year and at least 350 000 tons every year for nine years after that. If it failed to meet its commitment, the corporation would be made to pay a penalty of £100 000. It would have been simple to rail large quantities of lower-grade ore—but there would be no customers for it.

By October 1931 Manganese Corporation was ready to give up the fight. Nearly all the staff had been laid off and only Syd Brownrigg and one or two others remained. 'The mine was practically dormant,' said Brownrigg, who was now acting manager. 'We filled orders from stockpiles. Things seemed very bleak but I stayed because in those days if you had a job you hung on to it.'[11] Not only miners had left Manganese Corporation for several directors had quit too. One was Thomas Shone. His son Terry believes he must have had 'a hell of a row'[15] with the rest of the board.

By a curious twist of fate, now that he was free Shone was soon invited to join the board of S A Manganese. He was taking the place of Nils Langkilde who had died during 1931. The rival company's position was not much stronger than Manganese Corporation's but it was free of debt and it had assets in the form of mining leases and a stack of ore mined by Pringle-Smith. The company had yet to sell a single ounce of ore but its duck was broken when a Natal steelworks ordered 1 400 tons—not of manganese but of haematite.

S A Manganese's financial position had always been precarious but Shone was prepared to inject new life into the company to prepare for the time when economic conditions improved. He suggested potential buyers for the stockpiled ore and lent the company £600 to cover option fees. His fellow directors were so impressed that when the reigning chairman resigned during December 1932 Shone was appointed in his place. As if in celebration, the Natal steelworks ordered more haematite. Better still, two weeks later South Africa went off the Gold Standard and the economy was released from a straitjacket.

The Depression

River diggings of the Northern Cape were strangely quiet during the later 1920s. Nearly all the diggers were at Lichtenburg in the Transvaal, where alluvial diamonds had been discovered in 1926. Half-a-dozen major rushes attracted diggers in tens of thousands—on one occasion 26 000 men lined up to try their luck. Daniel Ludick was there, and so were scores of others who later returned to the Northern Cape. The exciting years at Lichtenburg had been an apprenticeship that would serve them well for the rest of their working lives.

By the early 1930s the Lichtenburg fields were largely worked out and diggers were trickling back to their old haunts. Many returned no better off than when they had left. One diamond man who seemed dangerously close to the breadline was H S Richter, who during 1930 shared a farm kaia with a young shepherd fresh from school. The shepherd was Alwin Austin, who was later to build the village of Lime Acres and today farms near by. In 1930 he was only 14 years old. 'I took a job with a farmer named Moller,' he says. 'Richter came to the farm and asked if he could prospect it.

'As far as I could make out Richter was going from farm to farm all over the district. He didn't have any boys with him so he'd ask farmers to lend him one and give him his keep. The farmers thought he was a tramp but there was no harm in that, so they'd given him a boy and he'd go walking over the farm and digging holes—one hole here and another one 100 metres away and so on. With only one boy that took quite a long time. He must have stayed on the farm for nine months, but he didn't have much to say. People on other farms said they'd seen him riding in a cart with an old horse pulling him, but he didn't have it when he came to us.'[16]

Alwin Austin remembers the depression years as a nightmare period when the economic crisis was made all the worse by a crippling drought. 'To earn a little cash, many farmers had to cart firewood into Kimberley',[16] he says. Those living around Kuruman accepted pick-and-shovel relief work on the roads. Their efforts produced the first proper road between Kuruman and Vryburg. During 1932 a new missionary arrived at the Moffat mission in Kuruman and was appalled by the conditions—Humphrey Thompson, who still lives in the district. He has recorded some sobering impressions in his autobiography, *Distant Horizons*.

'I shall never forget the pitiable sights of our first two years in Kuruman,' writes Thompson, 'whole families trekking with their flocks and herds, their few belongings piled up on waggons drawn by teams of emaciated donkeys, sheep, goats and cattle, choking in the dust and falling out one by one to die miserably in the merciless heat. Our main roads in those days were crossed by many gates and at every farm boundary could be found a crudely lettered notice: "*Geen uitspanning sonder betaling nie*" ("No outspanning without payment"), and as there was no money with which to pay, the pitiful cavalcades just had to go on.

'The farmers who put up such notices could not be blamed as they themselves had little enough water and grazing for their own stock and could themselves be on the road within a couple of weeks. Along all the main roads the rotting corpses of horses, cattle, sheep, goats and even donkeys, the last the hardiest of all four-footed creatures, averaged at least one to the half-mile. Even in the normally prosperous city of Kimberley the diamond mines too had closed down and the shops were offering 25% discount off genuine prices for the very few who had any cash to spend.'[16]

The closure of Kimberley's diamond pipes meant that the only mines still operating in the Northern Cape were Buxton limestone quarry at Taungs and some of the asbestos producers. Among them were several mines owned by Cape Asbestos around Koegas and Pomfret. A new syndicate was working Warrendale near Danielskuil. Elandsfontein was still operating, and in 1927 the South African Saltpetre Company that owned it had been renamed Griqualand Exploration and Finance Company or Gefco for short. All these producers were dispensing with 'contractors' and were hiring their own miners instead.

Near Kuruman the main asbestos producer was now Dominion Blue Asbestos, an offshoot of the Turner and Newall conglomerate. Dominion Blue had taken over mines previously worked by the Gillanders and Campbell Syndicate, among them Hurley, Klipvlei, Maipeng and Mansfield. Most of the asbestos produced was carted to a sorting plant in Kuruman where it was bagged for export. Dominion Blue also erected a mill to deal with short fibres that would otherwise go to waste. On each mine the company appointed a manager who told miners where to work and ran the store from which they obtained provisions.

One of Dominion Blue's managers was Faan Riekert who still lives in Kuruman. Riekert's initials are S J P K, which stand for Stephanus Johannes Paulus Kruger. Like Daniel Ludick he was involved in the invasion of South West Africa during 1915, then took a variety of jobs around Kuruman and in 1926 became manager of Klipvlei asbestos mine. 'The miners were being paid by the day,' he remembers. 'There were 22 miners there and they all had blasting certificates. Many of them were former contractors. They drilled with hand jumpers, hit and turn.

'The miners usually drilled at an angle and each of them had a mug full of water. Every so often they poured a little water into the hole to keep the dust down. They wound an old cloth round the jumper to stop the water splashing. A blasting hole was drilled deep enough to take two or three sticks of dynamite. Once these were in the hole was capped with a detonator, then the miner attached a fuse that was at least a metre long. Normally ten or fifteen holes were charged and detonated together.'[18]

The workings at Klipvlei went up to 40 metres into the hillside and once they reached the asbestos the miners stoped out a chamber. Blasted rock was loaded into wheelbarrows and pushed out of the workings where it was tipped on to sorting floors. 'The rock containing fibre was cobbed by native girls', says Faan Riekert. 'They had to chip off unwanted rock with little hammers and they were paid by the weight of the fibre they cleaned. They used to collect it in paraffin tins, empty sugar pockets, baskets, anything that was handy.'[18]

Much of the waste rock was taken back into the workings and packed into pillars that held up the hanging wall. 'We couldn't use wood,' says Faan Riekert. 'That would have contaminated the asbestos.' Miners were normally paid by footage. 'Sometimes they were given good-fors instead of cash. They could exchange them at the mine store or otherwise they might wait for the company paymaster to turn up. I paid them by tally once a fortnight—I had to keep a daily tally of what they did.'[18]

Faan Riekert worked at Klipvlei until late in 1927 and was then transferred to Mansfield. Here mining methods were similar but the work was done by self-employed 'tributors' as contractors were known around Kuruman. 'We measured claims for them,' says Riekert. 'They took out asbestos, cobbed it and sold it to us. We gave them free dynamite but they had to buy their own rations. The tributors each had their own hand-cobbers, usually their womenfolk. We paid them by weight and I had to watch them carefully because some tried to cheat by putting waste rock in the sacks.'[18]

In quick succession Riekert was moved to Hurley, then to Maipeng (today within Bophuthatswana), then to Sardinia. 'They thought of me as a trouble-shooter,' he says. 'When there were problems they sent me. At Hurley we had cocopans to tram fibre to the sort floor and we had Blantyre labourers from Nyasaland, which is now Malawi. There was a shortage of labour locally so they brought in 50 of the Blantyres and it worked out quite well. Elsewhere about half of the miners were Herero from South West—and nine out of ten of the cobbing girls were Herero too. It was the only work they could get.'[18]

During 1931 Dominion Blue, Cape Asbestos, Gefco and several independent producers still mined asbestos but all were troubled by falling prices. Canadian, Russian and Rhodesian asbestos was on offer at bargain rates and demand from the United States had shrunk to almost nothing. As a result, during 1932 Dominion Blue stopped operating and Faan Riekert and others were left without work. Cape Asbestos cut back production at Koegas and closed down Pomfret. The decision marked the debut of Cape Asbestos's new manager, Bob Falck, who had been appointed in 1931 in succession to Rundle Olds.

There was another new manager at Elandsfontein, where Gefco had appointed a Cornishman named Harold Pascoe. 'Normally it was a very pretty farm,' recalled Pascoe's widow Nora in a letter to an old friend, 'with a pretty little running stream called Sand River, bordered by the grandest grove of Kameeldoorn that I've ever seen, and with grand kloofs and purple-shadowed kopjes on the horizon.'[19] But when Harold Pascoe arrived, there had been five years of drought and Elandsfontein was a stony desert. Cobbing women sat under the spreading camelthorns and their babies lay pillowed on asbestos dust.

A remarkable chart of Elandsfontein in this period survives at Gefco's offices in Kuruman. The mine was a maze of tunnels leading into the hillside that contained asbestos and each tunnel had a name drawn from Southern Africa's history or geography. 'Smuts' and 'Botha' paralleled 'Khama' and 'Shaka', 'Shangaan' and 'Basuto' were neighboured by 'De Beers' and 'Lobatsi'. All these tunnels were on 'Hertzog' horizon, connected with lower horizons named 'Griquatown' and 'Bushman' by winzes named 'Gamsa' and 'Kimble'.

The chart of Elandsfontein marks in tramlines used by cocopans and also air and water lines that served newfangled mechanical 'jackhammers' operated by compressed air. Survey stations were pinpointed and outside the workings were a blacksmith's shop (where jumper bits were heated up to be sharpened), toolsheds, watertanks, engine houses and a repair shed. Worked-out stopes were marked and spattered across the chart were symbols representing the length (and hence grade) of fibre in each locality—*A*, *B*, *C*, *S* and *SS*.

Old-timers recall that *S* and *SS* meant 'short' and 'supershort' respectively. *D* and *E* were extra long. *A*, *B* and *C* were the medium grades most acceptable to asbestos spinners in Britain and Italy. Traditionally they were measured against an old-fashioned matchbox that would have been bigger than those used today. *A* fibre was as long as a matchbox was deep. *B* fibre was supposed to be as long as the box was wide. *C* fibre, the most valuable grade, matched the box from end to end.

CHAPTER FIVE 1935–1945

White Leghorns

THOMAS SHONE's career as chairman of S A Manganese lasted only 18 months. His friend Reggie Saner had joined the board during 1933, and early in 1934 it was decided that Saner should take over as chairman while Shone became managing director. All were convinced the depression was ending. Shone aimed to open S A Manganese's properties in hopes of a spate of orders from the steelworks of the world. Most of Postmasburg's professional miners had gone off to the goldfields, so Shone recruited a number of local farmers and equipped them with gangs of black labourers.

Shone's farmers did not have blasting certificates so their gangs worked with picks and shovels rather than drills and dynamite. Professional miners referred to the farmers as 'white leghorns' because they only scratched at the manganese. Shone directed them to pockets of high-grade ore on the farms Kapstewel, Doornput and Klipfontein. An old photograph shows one of the gangs at work beside a high kopje. The leghorn watches while some of his labourers smash rocks with heavy hammers and others hand-sort the manganese according to grade. One member of the gang pushes a wheelbarrow.

Shone lived in Postmasburg and made himself responsible for every phase of S A Manganese's activities. He supervised both leghorns and labourers, chose the areas to be mined, checked on the grades of ore produced and made arrangements to despatch it. Unfortunately the work was taking toll of his health. He was now nearly 70 years old and the mine secretary, a Mr Macdonald, informed the board in confidence that Shone was suffering from dizzy spells. The directors recruited a young man to help him but there were quarrels and a few weeks later the directors had to think again.

Manganese Corporation was back in production as well and Syd Brownrigg brought in 'white leghorns' just as Shone had done. Some worked on Doornfontein and some on Paling. Orders for manganese were coming in but morale in the company was not high. The directors still lived under the shadow of the penalty due to South African Railways. Len Aldridge of British Swiss had succeeded Pickett as chairman and told shareholders that the board was 'neglecting no opportunity or circumstance which will enable them to arrive at a favourable settlement with the (SAR) Administration'.[1]

S A Manganese was trying to persuade South African Railways to extend the Postmasburg railway into the heart of the manganese fields, certainly to Kapstewel and if possible to the farm Lohatlha. There was no suggestion that the company would guarantee tonnage. On the contrary, S A Manganese suggested that the Department of Mines should underwrite the line to promote South African base metals. The government agreed and the line to Lohatlha was approved, meaning that ore trains would be able to reach a point halfway up the manganese belt outlined by A L Hall.

The farm neighbouring Lohatlha among hills to the south was named Gloucester and it too held manganese. It was owned by Guido Sacco of Johannesburg and his three partners, who had bought it in the 1920s and had floated a company, Gloucester Manganese. As yet they had produced no ore and in 1920 they had unsuccessfully tried to sell the farm to Manganese Corporation. Now Gloucester was on the rail route, so Sacco approached a new Johannesburg mining house with a proposition.

The mining house was Anglo-Transvaal Consolidated Investment Company, or Anglovaal for short. It had been founded by Slip Menell and Bob Hersov in 1933 at a time when gold values were rocketing. Besides launching a new gold mine the two men quickly became interested in outside ventures, and Sacco was introduced to them through Louis Moshal who was married to Hersov's sister. Moshal had recently founded the Ore and Metal Company to deal in minerals of all kinds and that was how he had come across Gloucester Manganese. Sacco wanted Anglovaal to back a large-scale manganese operation that would include not Gloucester alone but other farms too.

Anglovaal was keen, and during 1935 its representatives met the board of Manganese Corporation and offered to take over its mines and pay a royalty on the manganese produced. The offer was accepted, and during 1936 Anglovaal launched a new company named the Associated Manganese Mines of South Africa Limited with both Sacco and Moshal on the board. Today the company is better known as Ammosal (on the manganese fields and in rugby circles) or Assmang (in the financial world generally but especially on the Johannesburg Stock Exchange).

Guido Sacco was the Godfather of Associated Manganese and asserted his authority from the beginning. He wanted to open the Gloucester deposits without delay and appointed Jumbo Harris as Ammosal's mine manager. Syd Brownrigg stayed on as assistant manager and chemist, and the two men began a close association that lasted until Brownrigg's retirement in the late 1960s. In their private lives they were worlds apart, but in the context of the mines Brownrigg's good-humoured conservatism was a neat foil for Harris's no-nonsense efficiency.

As soon as was practical much of the machine plant at Beeshoek was dismantled and carted to Gloucester, partly by way of the dry bed of the Gamagara River. So was machinery brought from the defunct Postmas diamond mine. A skilled stonemason used local dolomite to build offices, a repair shop and a powerhouse that still exist. A hostel was built to house black labourers but white miners and other workers lived in Postmasburg and were transported to Gloucester aboard an open lorry.

Further north, Associated Manganese decided to open workings on the farm Bishop which was close to the new railhead at Lohatlha. Two former diamond diggers, Colonel Vorster and Tok Erasmus, were put in charge and recruited some 80 'white leghorns' who were to be paid on results. Each leghorn was given a few labourers with picks and shovels and had to heap ore in neat rectangular piles like stacks of bricks. The leghorns slept in tents or zinc kaias where they worked, and in many cases their labourers slept in the open.

The leghorns were supposed to sort their manganese into three grades and Syd Brownrigg checked their accuracy and measured their stacks. Most of the ore was bound for Germany or the United States. Luckily for the manganese companies, an economic recovery in the middle 1930s was giving them all the orders they could have hoped for. Tragically, they were beset by a mystery fever that ran rampant through their labourers' quarters. Hundreds of men fell sick, and every day six or seven men died.

'We had no idea what had hit us,' said Syd Brownrigg. 'Local doctors could not identify the disease, and no remedy worked. We called in the Institute for Medical Research in Johannesburg. Fortunately they sent a man who had experience of the disease and he immediately spotted it was relapsing fever caused by insects like ticks that had been brought in years earlier by labourers from Malawi. The ticks were in the brick lining of the hostels and had lain dormant until the buildings were occupied again.'[2]

The sick were treated with injections, but for many help came too late. 'We must have lost about six hundred men,' said Brownrigg. 'They were buried in manganese rubble in an area adjoining Lohatlha, and their graves are still there. Hundreds more needed to convalesce after their illness. Many went home, but others wanted to keep working to earn money so we got them to build us a golf course on Beeshoek. About 300 men were involved, and the course was completed in 1937.'[2]

The mystery disease hit S A Manganese as well as Associated, and morale was at rock bottom. Shone had retired and soon Saner dropped out too. The company needed a shot in the arm and called in Bill Douglass, a former Lichtenburg digger who had been playing the Johannesburg Stock Exchange but who had been hard hit by the exchange's 'Black Friday' of September 1937. Douglass agreed to motor to Postmasburg to look into the situation and reached Kapstewel mine in time to be there when miners were supposed to start work.

The mine manager was away that day, but eventually the mine secretary arrived and admitted there were problems. No white labour was available and black contract workers were deserting because of the sickness. Several had been caught and were to appear in Postmasburg magistrate's court that morning. Douglass attended, and heard one of the labourers tell the magistrate: 'Shoot me dead, cut my throat, but don't send me back to the mine.'[3] Douglass returned to Johannesburg and put in a report, and S A Manganese's directors asked him to take over as mine manager.

Douglass's first task was to put paid to the tick problem, so he laid concrete floors in the compound. Next he needed labour, so he went to the Vaal River to look up some of his old digger friends from Lichtenburg. He wanted them to bring their teams of labourers to Postmasburg and dig for manganese instead of diamonds. The diggers responded and soon spread themselves over S A Manganese's four farms. Their gangs worked with picks, shovels, wheelbarrows, cocopans from the river diggings and in some cases cranes with a swinging boom which had proved their worth in deep-level claims.

Even as the diggers started work, the upswing in the manganese market abruptly reversed itself. A year earlier the United States' steel industry had been working at capacity. Since then it had slumped to a quarter of its strength. S A Manganese's agents declined further shipments and Associated Manganese was hit too. Germany's economy was in better shape but the Nazi government limited the amount of cash that might be spent on imports. S A Manganese's agents in Germany had reached the limit and now they could only offer goods like glass eyes, mouth-organs and trucks.

In these unpromising circumstances Bill Douglass was told to reduce production and concentrate on Lohatlha. At the same time Associated Manganese closed Bishop. Both leghorns and diggers were leaving the manganese fields, and in October 1938 Douglass was told to close Lohatlha. He and his wife were living at the old Kapstewel farmhouse where he had built several kaias to extend office space—the nucleus of the village of Manganore. The S A Manganese board put him on half-pay but he was so bored he felt he deserved double. Soon he resigned and went to live in Vereeniging.

The Ghaap Plateau

The early 1930s had seen a boom in South Africa's gold-mining industry. General Jan Smuts's decision to take South Africa off the Gold Standard had allowed the value of gold to float upwards, at least in relation to the devalued South African pound. That made it worthwhile to start new gold mines, expand existing ones and revive several that had closed. The increased gold production meant increased orders for lime used in the refining process. South Africa's leading supplier was the Northern Lime Company of Johannesburg which drew its lime from Buxton quarry near Taungs.

Northern Lime also received substantial orders from the fledgling South African Iron and Steel Industrial Corporation, the state-owned iron and steel industry known as Iscor for short. Iscor needed raw limestone as a flux for smelting operations at works in Natal and the Transvaal. Northern Lime was gaining on swings what it was losing on roundabouts, for the whole South African mining industry was abandoning old-style carbide miners' lamps in favour of battery models. The carbide manufacturers had been one of Northern Lime's best customers, but that was all over.

Overall, Northern Lime had to step up production so commissioned new lime-burning kilns at Buxton and opened a new quarry on the farm Thoming, about 10 km away. Like Buxton, Thoming held rich deposits of secondary limestone. Northern Lime was by far the largest producer of lime in the country, but several tiny companies had at least a finger in the pie. One of the small operations was White Limes Ltd which had been quarrying at Makapansgat in the Transvaal. Makapansgat was to be proclaimed a national monument so the company asked a prospector to scout out a new deposit.

The prospector was named Leopold Kramer and his search took him to the edge of the Ghaap Plateau, close to Delportshoop. That was where George Stow had spotted 'stalactitic limestone of very great thickness'[4] when he had explored Griqualand West in 1872. Kramer was not alone on the Ghaap Plateau. One Henry Adler was there too, representing 'Glencairn Lime' which apparently belonged to him. It seems the two prospectors obtained options over various farms that abutted the plateau, and as soon as they were secured both men headed for Johannesburg.

According to an article written by A B Robertson, 'endeavours were made to bring the prospectors together, but these failed and Leopold Kramer took his option to Lewis and Marks (*a leading Johannesburg finance house*). Mr Henry Adler in turn went to the Johannesburg Consolidated Investment Company Ltd. Both houses took up their options, and JCI turned theirs over to Anglovaal.'[5] Bob Hersov and Slip

Menell were already looking towards the Northern Cape for they were in the process of launching Associated Manganese. Besides, they already controlled a cement company.

The prospectors had gone separate ways, but the mining houses they approached thought it better to work together. The boards of Lewis and Marks and Anglovaal agreed to float a new company in which both would have shares—the Union Lime Company. It was agreed that Lewis and Marks would become Union Lime's managers, consulting engineers and buyers. Anglovaal would become sales managers. Union Lime came into being during 1936 and bought limestone rights on the farm Die Puts close to Delportshoop from one George Ricketts, whose father and mother had been among the first arrivals on the Vaal river diggings.

George Ricketts retired to another farm in the district, but his son Eddie persuaded Union Lime to sell him trading rights on the coming quarry. As yet the site had no roads and no buildings, nothing but a high cliff of white limestone that fronted the Ghaap Plateau and commanded wonderful views of the flat plain stretching to the south. Union Lime's first directors recruited a former Postmasburg miner named James de Kock to begin cutting trees and clearing access roads. De Kock was the first employee, but soon others were taken on to build zinc kaias that doubled as offices and homes.

One of the directors travelled to Britain and asked an engineering firm to design the necessary lime-burning kilns and erect them on the new site. He also advertised for an experienced works manager. One of the applicants was Eric Lowther who had been working at a limeworks in England's Lake District. Lowther was asked to take the job but at the same time had to consider an offer from a sugar firm based in Trinidad. He and his wife Elsie looked through books in their local public library to decide which country had more to offer. South Africa won, and soon they were on their way.

Elsie Lowther today lives in Cape Town and remembers her first impressions of Die Puts. 'After the Lake District, it was a bit of a shock,' she says. 'There was nothing but a few iron huts and some low wattle trees. The farmhouse was empty. Eric used one of the huts as an office and slept there during the week, but I stayed in Kimberley for the first six months and he joined me there at weekends. Even so, things went fast. The lime plant was being built, they were beginning work on the quarry, and they were building houses.'

When the manager's house was ready the Lowthers moved straight in. Eric Lowther decided it was time the little community had a name so chose 'Ulco' in honour of 'Union Lime Company'. As new families arrived he and his wife set out to make Ulco a pleasant place to live. Beside their house they developed a sunken garden and a bowling green and planted many different species of trees to see which grew best.

'It was obvious summers were going to be hot and dusty,' says Elsie Lowther. 'I wanted someone to recommend a tree that would spread all over Ulco, so I went to see Miss Wilman who was curator of the museum in Kimberley. She suggested the mesquite which originally came from Mexico. We planted some seeds and in a few years we had trees. Now they've spread all through the district.'[6] Charles Langeveld, long an Ulco resident and now living in Barkly West, points out wryly that the trees have helped local traffic police who hide among them to trap speeding motorists.

To start with, Union Lime's output was to be much more modest than Northern Lime's efforts at Buxton. The original plant consisted of two vertical kilns and a hydrator to 'slake' the burnt lime. A conveyor belt on a wooden gantry carried limestone from a storage pit at the quarry to three storage silos beside the kilns. The company also built a 12-kilometre rail spur to link the plant with the Kimberley–Postmasburg railway and brought in its own locomotive to shunt trucks. The first shipment of lime produced in Ulco's kilns was railed in August 1937.

In those early days Ulco quarry occupied only a few miners and a few score labourers who lived in an adjoining hostel. Elsie Lowther has a number of photographs that show how things were done. Blasting holes were drilled by jackhammer or in later years by high 'jumper drills' like the ones farmers used to bore for water. The jumper operators pulverised rock by dropping a heavy weight on it, mixed the waste rock with water and removed the resulting slush in a hollow tube. The holes were charged with dynamite and when all was clear a section of cliff was blasted into the air.

Labourers used their hands or long-pronged forks to load broken limestone into cocopans, which were then pushed through the quarry to a special storage pit. On the evidence of Elsie Lowther's photographs the pit was about 30 m long and 10 m wide. Cocopan tramlines were laid on both sides, and cocopans were parked on them and tipped over to discharge their load. Topping the pit was a strong 'grizzly' of tapered steel beams that served as a sorting screen. One row of beams was laid over the sorting pit from end to end, a second row lay across them.

The grizzly became an institution at Ulco, and one who remembers it in action is Daniel Ludick's son Piet who worked at Ulco during school holidays and is working there today. 'They needed that grizzly because there was no crusher,' he says. 'The limestone was tipped on to the grid and if a stone was small enough it fell through into the storage pit. If it wasn't it stayed up on top. A gang of boys worked on the grizzly and their job was to chop up the big rocks with 16-pound hammers until they were small enough to fall through.'[7]

Piet Ludick and in later years his father were among many men and boys from Delportshoop who went to work at Ulco. Like other diggings, Delportshoop was severely depressed during the later 1930s. For years diggers needing work had had to leave their wives and families and go elsewhere for months at a stretch. More than a few had joined Bill Douglass at Postmasburg, but now there was a source of work almost on the doorstep. Houses were becoming available at Ulco but many preferred to live in Delportshoop and commute by bicycle in spite of the state of the roads.

'Everything was sand and soil,' says Elsie Lowther of the roads around Ulco. 'That wasn't so bad if you didn't get stuck, but the real problem was punctures. Tyres weren't all that strong anyway but they didn't stand a chance if they picked up a nail. The roads were full of nails left over from the old wagons that used to carry wood to Kimberley.'[6] Motorists starting a trip from Kuruman or Postmasburg thought nothing of carrying two spare wheels and a number of spare inner tubes that could be fitted as required. Of course, they needed to take a pump as well.

For Charles Langeveld, the worst feature of Northern Cape roads was ruts—not side-ruts with a *middel-mannetjie* down the centre but 15 cm corrugations between close-packed ridges that spanned the road. 'There were no graders,' he says. 'Each vehicle that passed kicked up more dust and the ridges grew higher and the corrugations grew deeper. Your car shook and rattled as it ran over the ridges and you had to grit your teeth and go like hell. Of course if it rained you got bogged down in mud and then you'd need donkeys or oxen to pull you out.'[8]

During the 1930s Charles Langeveld was living in Barkly West and remembers it as the diggers' capital. 'During the week Barkly was quiet like any other country town,' he says. 'But on Saturdays—well, that was when the diggers came in. They had diamonds to sell, they had provisions to buy and Saturdays was when they did their socialising. The diamond buyers did business in a little row of huts near the mining commissioner's office. The diggers went from one to the next until they were offered the price they thought their diamonds were worth.'[8]

Sadly for the diggers, diamond prices were well down. That was why Delportshoop diggers saw Union Lime as a fairy godmother, and many took jobs at Ulco. Then came news of a new kimberlite fissure close to the old Frank Smith mine. As diggers tell the story, the finder spotted a diamond while relieving himself against a bush. The fissure was named 'Sover', the mining commissioner proclaimed a new public diggings and there was a rush for claims. But few diggers could afford the heavy equipment needed to work kimberlite and before long most claims were sold to a handful of companies.

Koekie Daniels is a veteran digger who acquired his certificate during the 1930s and recalls how claims were worked at that time. Daniels grew up on Longlands diggings between Delportshoop and Barkly West and he works claims there today, though in the meantime he has probed for diamonds at half-a-dozen other locations. On a tour of his claims at Longlands he first pointed out a narrow circular shaft about eight metres deep. 'The first job was to see if there was payable ground,' he explained. 'Once you hit bottom you tried a couple of washes to see what came up.'[9]

If the ground proved payable, Daniels continued, many diggers rigged a windlass over the top and sent down labourers to tunnel a drive. If the ground was not too deep, they might prefer to bring in a swinging crane and work the claims as an open pit. Once the ground was on the surface they probably put it through a 'dummy', a handy sifting device that combined the best features of babies and rockers. Daniels was still using a dummy himself. His consisted of a shallow tray with a mesh bottom, about 1,3 m long and 60 cm wide, suspended on four sturdy poles about 1,6 m high.

One of Daniels's labourers shovelled ground into the tray of the dummy. Daniels grasped a handle at one end of the tray and began pushing and pulling it with sharp jerks. As he did so the tray swung wildly on straps attached to the poles. Gravel filtered through the holes in the tray bottom until only bantams were left on the mesh. Daniels scanned the bantams for diamonds but none were there. Now the remaining gravel was ready for his rotary washing pan. In the 1930s a rotary pan would have been operated by two labourers but today it is driven by an engine.

Daniels's pan was about two metres in diameter. A central shaft rotated four arms carrying long teeth that stirred a 'puddle' of mud and gravel. The teeth swept heavier materials to the edge of the pan and at intervals they were tapped through a hole at the side. Next a labourer tapped gravel into a bucket and carried it to a washing trough. There he poured the gravel into a metal funnel which channelled it into a bank of sieves. Like drawers in the old rockers, each sieve had a different mesh and the widest was on top so that finer materials filtered to the bottom.

Next came the most skilled part of the operation—the 'gravitation' of the gravel under water. The labourer picked up the top sieve and with deft hand movements spun the gravel horizontally while at the same time shaking the sieve up and down. If he was doing the job properly, centrifugal force was drawing the material with the heaviest specific gravity to the middle of the sieve. Diggers long ago discovered that diamonds have unusually high specific gravity, so when a sieveful is upturned any diamonds it contains should be sitting on top and in the middle like a cherry on a cake. On this occasion Koekie Daniels had to go without.

Folds and Patches

Dawie Voges grew up on a farm in the Langeberg and starting in 1927 worked for firms of attorneys in Kuruman, Danielskuil and Postmasburg. By 1932 he was in Griquatown and was on hand when out of the

20. Frik Scholtz, a miner who helped to pioneer both the Sishen iron-ore mine and the Lime Acres limestone quarry, stands next to a giant excavator bucket of the sort used in both operations.

Iscor

21. Northern Lime's quarry at Lime Acres in the early 1950s.
Northern Lime Company

22. A township in the veld: Lime Acres's first four streets meander through open country.
Northern Lime Company

blue his firm received a letter from a gem cutter in Germany. The cutter was George Riem of Idar-Oberstein and he wanted to know if there was still tiger's eye around Griquatown. None had been produced since 1911, but if any was available he wanted to buy it. Voges's boss gave him the letter and soon he located old tiger's eye workings on Griquatown commonage. He sent samples to Idar-Oberstein and received an order by return.

'That was the start of the modern tiger's eye industry,' says Voges, who today lives in Kuruman. 'The Germans first ordered half a ton, then a ton, and gradually quantities increased. My wife and I bought a farm near Niekerkshoop and began farming cattle and mining tiger's eye as a sideline. The seams lay close to the surface and I employed tributors to dig through layers of sand and banded ironstone to expose them. Then they used crowbars to chip out slabs of tiger's eye. They cobbed off the banded ironstone and then I bought the clean tiger's eye by the pound.'[10]

Voges's customers wanted both golden and blue tiger's eye. The blue was soon dubbed 'hawk's eye' and sometimes Voges came upon green material that was sold as 'cat's eye.' He also stumbled on a way of producing a quite different coloour. When golden tiger's eye was heated in a fire it turned bright red. Voges named his new variety 'bull's eye' and sent samples to Germany where they were well received. 'Bull's eye' has been a staple of the industry ever since.

Dawie Voges believed the best tiger's eye came from around Niekerkshoop but there was also substantial deposits close to Koegas and Prieska. Andries Estebeth today farms near Prieska and in 1937 he went to work at Koegas where the asbestos miners took a keen interest in tiger's eye. 'They knew it was related to asbestos but couldn't decide how,' he recalls. 'Some said the two had come into being by separate routes, some said tiger's eye was originally asbestos that had hardened, some said asbestos was tiger's eye that had gone soft. You could take your pick.'[11]

To make the debate even more poignant, miners sometimes came on seams that contained both substances. 'You'd find blue tiger's eye on the surface, but as you followed it in you found beautiful asbestos fibre,'[11] Estebeth says. The phenomenon was a great puzzle to Bob Falck and Ollie Harrison, who were manager and assistant manager at Koegas. At about the time Estebeth joined them Harrison was about to leave Koegas to start a new Cape Asbestos division at Kuruman. Demand for asbestos was increasing rapidly, and the company was reopening several mines that had belonged to Dominion Blue.

'I went to Koegas straight from school and they gave me a job as a lorry driver,' says Estebeth. 'At the time there were very few white people there—just the manager, assistant manager, mine secretary, a couple of miners and a couple of drivers. We lived in Koegas but most of the mining was across the river at Westerberg. We crossed on a pont—weighted down with a loaded lorry the pont often stuck on sandbanks. Some of the mining was still being done by tributors but gradually Bob Falck was bringing in day workers who were paid by footage or volume.

'A good many of the tributors and day workers had blasting certificates, and to earn them they had to answer questions about explosives—how to charge up, how to handle dynamite. Each one had two red boxes, one for dynamite and one for detonators. They drew dynamite once a week. Most of them drilled holes with long steel jumpers hit with a hammer. The drills were sharpened in a blacksmith's shop. It was amazing how deep they could go. But then Bob Falck introduced compressors and jackhammers and gradually Koegas and Westerberg were mechanised.'[11]

Another innovation of Bob Falck's was mills at both Koegas and Westerberg. Most fibre was despatched in the form of stamped cobs as before. But there was always a good deal of waste and this was processed as 'milled grade' asbestos. That made new openings for freelance *tsollas*, widows or other women without men to support them who scavenged for dropped cobs and waste fibre. Most women at Koegas–Westerberg hand-cobbed for tributors or were paid by the mine, but the *tsollas* worked by themselves and sold their production to the mine at the end of each month.

Bob Falck's innovations were matched at Gefco's Elandsfontein, where Harold Pascoe was learning much from Herero tributors. It was apparently tributors who helped Pascoe to understand the 'main marker' of asbestos formations, a distinctive stripe in the strata that could be traced for hundreds of kilometres. 'Locate the main marker,' says Louw Markram, a Gefco surveyor who lives in Kuruman, 'and you know there is a good chance that you will find asbestos below.'[12] Pascoe spotted it on the farm Bretby between Kuruman and Danielskuil and prepared to investigate.

'Up to this time,' wrote Pascoe in a delightful article entitled *Asbestos Fever*, 'nobody had really wondered about the why and the wherefore of blue asbestos. There were those who asserted fondly that it was a purely surface manifestation. Water had percolated through the cracks and asbestos had crystallised out of the solution. Others were looking for "rolls", saying that asbestos deposits were always associated with folding. Again, all the known deposits were in the hillsides so of course it could not be found in the flats while search must be confined to the vicinity of the outcrops.

'Could it be, one thought, that asbestos alone of all the minerals, obeyed no natural laws? Must its occurrence always be entirely haphazard? Surely not, and gradually dim theories were formed and hesitatingly applied in practice.'[13] On Pascoe's recommendation Gefco's directors bought Bretby and Pascoe prepared to sink inclines and test his theories. Neighbouring farmers thought he was mad, for all Bretby's visible asbestos had been removed by two old partners named Whitelock and Gericke who had earned themselves a reputation for great eccentricity.

'The working methods on Bretby had been very primitive,' says Louw Markram, who grew up in the area and knows it well. 'The old men collected a couple of tons of hand-cobbed fibre and then brought it to Kuruman on an old donkey-wagon. They gave it to a contractor who carried it to Taungs, and from there it went to Britain. Whitelock and Gericke weren't paid until the asbestos reached their customers so they waited months for their money. But each time they came into Kuruman they picked up money received for an earlier shipment.

'With the money in their pockets the old men went round the pubs and they might spend days at it. Then one of them would decide he was tired and wanted to go home. Often there was a quarrel and one took the wagon and returned to Bretby while the other was left in Kuruman and had to find his own way back. Often that meant a walk of 50 kilometres.'[13] With Whitelock and Gericke off the farm, Pascoe's shafts went down 30 metres and proved there was asbestos. To haul it to the surface, Pascoe erected two ingenious donkey whims that were soon the talk of the district.

Each whim consisted of two big drums on a vertical pole. The donkeys were underneath and they walked in circles to make the drums rotate. There were two sets of rails in each incline, and one drum hauled cocopans coming up the left-hand rails while the other pulled cocopans on the right. But one cable was wound up clockwise and the other anti-clockwise. This meant that as the donkeys walked clockwise, a loaded cocopan was being hauled up one side of the incline while an empty one went down the other. When the donkeys went anti-clockwise it was the other way around.

It was said that Bretby donkeys became so used to the action of the whims that they knew when a cocopan had reached the top of the incline. They gave the labourers time to tip out its contents, then automatically reversed direction to haul up a loaded cocopan on the other track. 'We had great larks on Bretby,' Pascoe's wife Nora wrote to a friend. 'Our temperatures soared and fell daily between hopes of great riches and fears of dire poverty.'[14] She found the 'asbestos wife' played a key role in all that happened and wrote a poem about it—*Folds, Seams and Patches*:

I sing, if any care to hear, the Life
And Duty Whole of an Asbestos Wife.
Post-honeymoon, the gaily-trousseau'd bride,
Undaunted, though the unpeopled veld was wide,
Housed (with a bug or two) in tin-roofed shack,
(Having of all mod. cons. a candid lack)
Woke on the first Blue Monday working morn
To hear her Man speak, as by passion torn,
Of Faults reversed; of Patch; of Seam; of Fold.
Her Housewife's conscience pricked, she cried, 'don't scold!
My Faults Reversed I'll Patch!' But as a wall
Is blind and deaf, he heard her not at all,
Nor shared her Being. She was Not. 'The Strike
Must like athwart the Dip,' he cried. 'The dyke
Runs close beside the fault. Now here come through
Three seams of fibre—rich, but never blue . . .'
Appalled, yet dutiful, thus roughly hurled
From her Vocabulary, Being, World;
Meek, speechless, clad in khaki shorts and shirt,
She took her place in the asbestos dirt.

★ ★ ★ ★ ★ ★

Time is for slaves, not miners. Meals, Life, wait
On the Asbestos Lust. Now is their Fate
Of non-inflammable blue fibre spun.
They think in Shafts and Tunnels. Their veins run
Crocidolite. Their temperature will rise
To heights of wealth whose limit is the skies
And fall to chasmed penury, by the hour.
Asbestos Fever has them in its power,
While the Wan Wife, conditioned, eats her crusts
And cuts her cloth of blue asbestos dust.

★ ★ ★ ★ ★ ★

Years passed. Now more Asbestos Wives appear,
Marvelling to see this rocklike pioneer.
Pillared in poise now; passionless; serene;
While they still quaver, hope and fear between,
Until they see that, like Lot's wife of old,
She's turned a statue in a woman's mould;
Not made of salt, but fibrous through and through;
Immune to heat, cold, time. Asbestos—(Blue)![15]

At the time World War II broke out there were 15 separate asbestos mines in the Northern Cape. Twelve of them belonged to Cape Asbestos, though Koegas–Westerberg was counted as one and produced more than the remaining eleven put together. Westerberg, indeed, was the world's biggest asbestos mine. Gefco had Bretby and Elandsfontein. The fifteenth mine was Warrendale near Danielskuil, which for some years past had been mined by one Barry Burrow of Kimberley. During 1939 Warrendale was taken over by Burrow's sons Binks and Sonny and a partner of theirs named Harry Bailey.

Sonny Burrow supervised the mine while Binks Burrow managed sales. They and Bailey launched a new company, Consolidated Blue Asbestos, which continued working Warrendale until 1958 when it was sold to Cape Asbestos. At the time the new company was launched there was activity on a farm next door to Warrendale, by name Brits. There was no water on Brits so its agricultural value was small, but it did hold asbestos and an even greater prize. As early as 1930 H S Richter had discovered that Brits held a large pipe of kimberlite.

Brits was set in asbestos hills that overlooked the farm Bowden, where Thomas Shone had unearthed several kimberlite fissures. Bowden was privately owned and there it would have been legal to prospect for precious stones. But Brits was owned by the government, and during 1928 the government had brought in legislation making it illegal to prospect for precious stones on state land. At the time so many new sources of diamonds were coming to light that some people feared their value would be destroyed. Besides, the government was ready to mine its own stones for itself.

Richter stumbled on Brits in the course of one of his prospecting ventures. From the lie of the land and the evidence of vegetation he outlined the top of a kimberlite pipe, though he could not be sure it contained diamonds. He sank two prospecting pits into the kimberlite, one of them 14 m deep. But then his activities came to the attention of the mining commissioner in Barkly West, who pointed out he was prospecting illegally and warned him off. For years Richter kept clear, but in 1939 he came up with a plan that involved two financial partners.

Richter's partners were Stephanus van Niekerk, a store-owner at Longlands river diggings, and Joe Cawood, a farmer who had several times gone prospecting. These two and Richter applied for a prospecting permit covering Brits—not for precious stones, but for asbestos. That was legal, for the 1928 legislation had no effect on prospecting for base minerals. But we may draw our own conclusions about the partners' intentions from a letter written by Richter to Van Niekerk. It was addressed 'Bowden, Silverstreams' and was dated 'October 16 1939'.

'I am now getting on well with my work at Brits,' runs Richter's letter. 'Before the end of this week I hope to have six shafts in yellow kimberlite mine ground, and ready for the rotary. I was quite right in my estimation, she is one of the largest mines in South Africa and it is absurd to think that a mine of at least 2 000 claims is not going to be payable. We want no experts, no opinions and no cheap talk. The rotary must speak, the eating of the pudding is the proving thereof; and the diamonds found on the surface are also of good quality so that my expectations of the potentialities are great.'[16]

Richter had indeed found a large mine. Today it is famous as the Finsch diamond pipe. Richter was so excited that he could not keep the news to himself and told a Barkly West diamond buyer named Bernard Goldberg. Shortly afterwards he met Van Niekerk and Cawood in a hotel in Danielskuil. When Cawood learnt that Richter had let out their secret he was furious. He reported Richter for illegal prospecting and the unfortunate man appeared in Griquatown magistrate's court and was fined 'about R40'.[16] Van Niekerk asked Cawood why he had done what he did. Cawood replied: 'I'll have the lot, or I'll have nothing.'[16]

The Brits venture had ended badly. Van Niekerk went back to his store-keeping and Cawood to his farming. Richter prospected for a local farmer to earn his keep but shortly afterwards he left the district. And that was the last that anyone heard of him.

Looking North

War clouds were gathering over Europe and nations like South Africa were becoming conscious of strategic materials, not least manganese. During 1937 the South African Geological Survey sent a team of geologists to re-examine the Postmasburg district. F C Truter was to cover the Postmasburg townlands; D J L Visser was sent to the Langeberg and their northern extension the Korannaberg. His job appeared especially arduous because he would have to do a lot of climbing. The central area that contained the manganese beds was assigned to Leslie Boardman who had a suspect heart condition.

Leslie Boardman had grown up on a Transvaal farm with minerals all around him. The Premier diamond pipe was close by, and on the farm where he lived an old miner worked small pockets of copper. In spite of these influences, at the University of Pretoria Boardman chose to read forestry because he longed for the open air. But the first year of his forestry degree included a course in geology and Boardman switched horses. On graduating he joined the Geological Survey and found himself teamed with several who had had close associations with the Northern Cape, among them A L Hall.

Boardman died in 1976, but accounts of his experiences were recorded in S A Manganese's official history. He set off for the manganese fields in a new Ford car complete with a radio set. Once near Postmasburg, the only station he could pick up was Grahamstown and even then only after dark. Each evening in camp he followed news of the Spanish Civil War. Besides his surveying and geological equipment, he was carrying a little cottage tent with a groundsheet, a stretcher, a canvas bath and wash-stand, cooking gear, cases for papers and specimens and two sets of crockery and cutlery.

The manganese fields had last been surveyed in 1928, again by men of the Geological Survey. Boardman wondered what chances there were of finding anything to add, but he soon found that the earlier survey had been very general. He made it his task to plot every pocket of manganese and iron ore. The project lasted two years and at intervals he returned to Pretoria to work on the data he had collected. He was astonished by the huge haematite reserves of Sishen and neighbouring farms and wrote a special report on them, but British officials who saw it said he must be exaggerating.

Boardman's survey took him over the farms being mined by Associated Manganese and S A Manganese and he also visited two new operations. One was the farm Aucampsrust, about 10 km west of Beeshoek. There, Thomas Shone and Reggie Saner were back in business with 'New Union Manganese Mines and Minerals', a shadow of their first company. Shone and Saner had promising contracts with German buyers, and all went well until war broke out and one of their shipments was sunk. That knocked the heart out of them and soon 'New Union Manganese' was placed under judicial management.

The other new operation was at Demaneng, a farm close to Sishen. A new company, African Metals Corporation or Amcor for short, planned to produce semi-processed alloys for specialised steelmakers. Amcor was the brainchild of H J van der Bijl, a pioneer of South African science and industry who had done much to create Iscor and also Escom, South Africa's Electricity and Supply Commission. Amcor's geologist, Wilhelm Kupferburger, believed that Demaneng was a promising source of high-grade manganese and advised his company to buy it. Unfortunately the ore was patchy and Amcor had to think again.

Late in 1938 Amcor approached S A Manganese with a confidential inquiry. Could S A Manganese provide a monthly supply of specially-selected, high-grade ore for the production of ferro-manganese? The inquiry arrived at the time when German buyers ran out of funds. S A Manganese was only too delighted to accept the new customer and before long the companies became intertwined through an exchange of shares. Amcor became S A Manganese's secretaries and technical consultants, and two Amcor nominees were appointed to S A Manganese's board.

For South Africa, World War II began in September 1939. Freighters carrying South African minerals had to run the gauntlet of German warships with South African asbestos around their boilers and South African manganese in their armour plating. The allies were building warships too and indeed armaments of all kinds so placed large orders for manganese. S A Manganese was concentrating on South Africa's domestic market but to meet the demand Associated Manganese had to find new sources. The company looked to Black Rock, even though it lay 100 km north-west of the existing mines.

Black Rock was an anomaly: a long, low kopje of medium-grade manganese poking through the flat sands of the Kalahari. A survey beacon perched on top of the kopje pinpointed the boundary of three farms—Nchwaning, Belgravia and Santoy. A colony of baboons lived there but prudently made way when local children climbed up for picnics. A W Rogers had noticed Black Rock's manganese as early as 1907, but nobody had supposed it had economic significance until a prospector named A T Fincham inspected it in the mid-1930s and took options on the three farms.

In earlier years A T Fincham had lived on a farm south of Kimberley and had produced salt on a local saltpan. Then sudden floods had destroyed the best part of a year's production and had wiped him out of business. He had sold the farm and gone to Postmasburg, where his son Thorny had opened a café. Fincham senior had gone fossicking all over the Northern Cape and in South West Africa too. One day Fincham met Amcor's Kupferburger in the Postmasburg hotel and mentioned that the Black Rock options were for sale.

Kupferburger told S A Manganese about Black Rock and the directors were interested but felt Fincham wanted too much money for his options. At about this time, and quite by coincidence, the Geological Survey sent Leslie Boardman to inspect Black Rock. Boardman had now bought himself a caravan and was living more comfortably than on his earlier excursions. He compiled a report on the outcrop and concluded that there might be a considerable body of high-grade manganese all around it. Black Rock had the makings of a great mine and the only problem was its distance from a railhead.

By this time Fincham had sold his options to a speculator who now approached Associated Manganese, where he found a receptive ear. 'Before that we'd never suspected there could be manganese so far north of Beeshoek,'[2] said Syd Brownrigg. The company called in the noted geophysicist Oscar Weiss to examine Black Rock and he sent a team equipped with a gravimeter. On the results Associated Manganese bought 100 morgen—86 hectares—from each of the three farms at Black Rock. The combined 258 hectares covered the whole of the kopje and also a margin around the base.

By road Black Rock was 170 km from Beeshoek and according to Brownrigg there were 88 farm gates on the way. 'You had to open and shut every one of them,' he said. 'If a farmer caught you leaving one open he had the right to fine you 10/-—in today's money, a Rand.'[2] Jumbo Harris was still at Beeshoek early in 1940 when Associated Manganese began developing Black Rock, but soon he joined the South African Army and went off to war. Brownrigg took over his job and drove to Black Rock and back at least once every week. A small contingent of labourers was stationed there with a handful of miners to supervise them.

One of the miners was Piet Coetzee of Postmasburg, who in the mid-1930s had worked with Thomas Shone at S A Manganese. He and another miner travelled up with a portable compressor and a couple of jackhammers. 'As yet there was no dynamite at Black Rock,' he says. 'That was brought from Gloucester on a donkey-wagon. We first drilled holes for three weeks, and then when the dynamite arrived I spent a whole day charging up. It was twilight when I started blasting, and next morning the farmers of the district came to find out what all the noise was about.'[17]

At first the miners worked on manganese outcrops, but soon it was decided to begin tunnelling into the kopje. All went well until they hit banded ironstone which was too strong for their drill bits. 'That was in the days before tungsten carbide steel came in,' said Syd Brownrigg. 'We were using the old star-bits—steel jumpers with a cross at the end that could be sharpened when it became blunt. But in that banded ironstone we were getting through 18 bits to the inch—that's nearly seven to a centimetre. We couldn't go on like that, so we tried something different.

'I'd heard about a method the old-timers used—heating rock and then splashing it with cold water to crack it. We brought in an oil-burning flame-thrower and aimed it at the rockface. When it seemed hot enough we sprayed on water—but it made hardly any impression. The banded ironstone was there for keeps.'[2] At a later stage the miners had more success with mud blasts, packing sticks of dynamite against the rock and covering them with mud. Progress was still slow, but the early miners of Black Rock did sink six incline shafts along the line of the ore body.

A strange feature of Black Rock was that the ore body was folded over upon itself. A shaft sunk vertically would have intersected it three times. The inclines entered the rock from a basin that had been opened in the middle and donkeys hauled cocopans up the inclines and into the fresh air. Beside the kopje there were three sort-floors where the manganese was stacked according to grade. It was carted not to Lohatlha but to Gloucester along a road running down the dry bed of the Gamagara River. But lorries trying to approach Black Rock itself ran into difficulties.

'The problem was deep sand on the farm track,' remembers Kiewiet Reinecke, who arrived at Black Rock in 1941 and later married Betta

Pretorius, a daughter of the farmer at Nchwaning. Indeed, today he farms there himself. 'The lorries had to stop about eight kilometres away so a contractor called Jan Nel brought in donkey wagons. Later we improved the road and laid down manganese chips and the lorries came all the way.'[18] Donkeys were also needed to pull a cart that brought water from the neighbouring farm Santoy.

The early miners of Black Rock lived in zinc kaias consisting of bedrooms and kitchens, except for Piet Coetzee who lived in the Nchwaning homestead. Mining was dirty work so he soon built himself a bathroom. 'I cut one oil drum in half to heat the water and another one lengthways to make the tub,' he says. 'Then I surrounded the tub with a lot of oildrums standing up on end.'[17] Late in 1940 Coetzee married a Postmasburg girl and invested in a tin bath, but otherwise the couple set up house with a table and chairs made of old dynamite boxes.

Black Rock worked to capacity until 1943, when Syd Brownrigg ordered a rapid cutback. Very little shipping was available to carry manganese, not least because the United States was processing low-grade manganese of its own regardless of the high production cost. Only two miners and a handful of labourers remained at the mine and they too were withdrawn in 1945. The manganese required was drawn from Gloucester, where Brownrigg's miners each ruled a section of the mine as if it was a kingdom. Fuel was scarce, so donkeys towed cocopans and wagons and the mine captain and shift bosses made their inspection rounds on horseback.

Beeshoek and the other mines of the south had closed down yet Associated Manganese's mine offices were still there and so was Syd Brownrigg. Periodically he visited Kimberley, and if there was time he dropped in at Ulco to see Eric Lowther. To his great surprise, he had discovered Lowther was an old school friend. 'I grew up at Keswick in Britain's Lake District,' he explained. 'We lived beside Lake Derwentwater and walking to school there were no houses until you came to the Lowthers'. Eric and I were even in the same class.'[2]

Like Brownrigg, Lowther had not been able to volunteer for the armed services because his services to his mine were too important. Lime and limestone were strategic minerals just as manganese and asbestos were, and to step up production Union Lime had built five more kilns. Each time a new one was completed there was a small party for the workers and Elsie Lowther pressed a button to start the kiln's career. Meanwhile the Lewis and Marks group had been absorbed by another concern and Anglovaal had become Union Lime's managers and consulting engineers.

Not everyone at Ulco believed South Africa should be at war, but Elsie Lowther organised a women's club to raise funds for service charities. 'We prepared food and sold it and we embroidered cushions and sold them, and every month we sent away money,' she says. 'What impressed me was that even if the women didn't agree with the war, they were still ready to help the boys who were fighting.'[6] Ulco children followed suit when they organised concerts to raise money for children hurt in London's blitz. Several families entertained British sailors sent inland for a break.

Elsewhere in the Northern Cape, there was considerable anti-British feeling as there had been in World War I. On one occasion saboteurs cut the telephone line between Kuruman and Vryburg and fired on the repairmen sent to mend it. Families kept in touch with war news through crystal radio sets and the letters of those at the front. At home, the clearest evidence of the war was petrol rationing, bans on white bread and cake flour, and shortages of a thousand items ranging from butter and soap to crockery, motor spares and building materials.

CHAPTER SIX 1945–1954

Men of Iron

World War II petered out in 1945 and the Northern Cape returned to normal. The limestone quarries of Taungs and Ulco were still hard at work, and so were the asbestos mines of Bretby and Koegas–Westerberg. Several small diamond mines probed the Sover kimberlite fissure near Boetsap and diggers still worked claims on the Vaal, Harts and Orange rivers. On the manganese fields Associated Manganese concentrated on Gloucester but S A Manganese had operations on ten farms. On three of these farms S A Manganese was producing iron ore.

All the farms of the manganese belt contained haematite in greater or lesser quantities and S A Manganese had mined small amounts early in the 1930s. Now S A Manganese partnered Amcor in launching 'Manganore Iron Mining Ltd' to work haematite deposits on Kapstewel, Doornput and Klipfontein. The ore was found in pockets surrounded by dolomite and these pockets were assigned to individual miners supervising large gangs. Most of the miners lived in Manganore village but some worked so far away that they found it easier to sleep in kaias erected in the veld.

To test ore reserves, the new company used a steam-driven jumper drill. An arm on the drill raised a heavy weight, then dropped it on to the rock down the hole. The operators poured water into the hole to turn the pulverised stone to slush. At intervals they lowered a hollow tube with a loose plug at the bottom. Slush pushed up the plug and coursed into the tube. When the operators hauled up the tube the plug returned to its hole, and on surface the operators tipped out the slush and examined it for minerals.

The Klipfontein workings were on a hill overlooking Manganore village. There, broken ore was loaded into cocopans and pushed to the top of a fascinating mechanism that survives today—an endless rope haulage about 500 metres long. The 'endless rope' was really a series of cables connecting pairs of cocopans that went up and down an oval track. Cocopans were loaded at the top and unloaded at the bottom, so the weight of full cocopans running down the righthand incline pulled empty ones up on the left.

Manganore village was a little less spartan than in Bill Douglass's time but it was not yet comfortable. A smart manager's house had replaced the old homestead and there were new offices and a guest house, but the miners and their families lived in iron houses that were not much more than kaias. Many had no floors, not even concrete. There was no power and no water supply beyond old oildrum 'canteens' left outside to catch rainwater and replenished from a donkey-drawn watercart. Like Piet Coetzee at Black Rock, several miners cut oildrums in half from top to bottom to make bathtubs.

Most of Manganore's iron ore was going to steel and alloy works run by Amcor, which was expanding. Europe's iron and steel industries were in the doldrums in the post-war period and there was a call for increased production in South Africa. That was why Iscor was pressing ahead with a fully integrated steelworks at Vanderbijlpark south of Johannesburg, which was to complement the existing Iscor works in Pretoria. The Pretoria plant drew iron ore from Thabazimbi mine in the northern Transvaal, but Vanderbijlpark needed a supply of its own.

Iscor was studying several possibilities, among them the farms in the Northern Cape that had been the subject of Leslie Boardman's report of 1938. They included Sishen and its neighbours, and in 1945 Iscor had taken options on them. The next step was to send in a young geologist to examine them more closely. The geologist was named Lynn and he was helped by a miner named Lombard and a gang of labourers who dug shallow prospecting pits. All slept in tents pitched on the sandy bed of the Gamagara.

Lynn's results were promising enough to persuade Iscor that it was worth prospecting Sishen in detail. A miner named D S Theron was put in charge and with him was a geologist named Greyling. Theron recruited two more miners, Hendrik Noeth and Frik Scholtz who today farms near Postmasburg. Their first job was to look for water. 'We knew there was water at Kathu but Iscor wanted to know if there was enough for the mine,' says Frik Scholtz. 'There were several springs used by local farmers and we went to the most powerful and dug pits through the mud until we came to the solid rock.'[1]

In digging the pits Scholtz and his gang unearthed ancient animal remains and artefacts like those found by the Viljoens during the 1970s.

Prehistorians from Bloemfontein Museum were called in to inspect them. Meanwhile Iscor was less than satisfied with results at the wells and sent in a drill to probe the rock—not a jumper drill, but a water-cooled diamond bit rotary drill capable of drilling to great depths. Two diamond drills had been brought to Sishen to launch a full scale prospecting programme and Frik Scholtz was to be put in charge.

A diamond drill is designed to retrieve rock samples in the form of a 'core', a long rod of rock some 10 cm in diameter. Its drill bit is studded with industrial-grade diamonds and contains a hollow chamber connected with a tube-like 'core barrel' that rotates with the bit. 'We went down 60 metres,' says Frik Scholtz. 'All of a sudden we hit water. It welled up like a fountain, a metre above the surface. That was when we realized there were tremendous reserves of water under the rock. We capped the hole and later Iscor tapped the water and pumped it to the mine.'[1]

There was no secret about the prospecting venture and Frik Scholtz discussed it with a local farmer—Hans van Staden, who was adding a third career to a repertoire that already included transport riding and 'manganese digging'. After years of collecting wood from Kathu Forest Van Staden knew the area better than most. Scholtz introduced him to D S Theron and the two men discussed the lie of the haematite. 'Theron said the ore body ran east to west,' says Van Staden. 'I said it ran south-east to north-west. I said I knew of iron stones where he said they had no right to be.

'I took Theron riding and showed him the iron stones. He said they must have come from the sky—he meant they were parts of a meteorite. But later I found more stones in other places and eventually he was convinced. He gave me a job looking for stones—it was the first real job I'd ever had. He also contracted me to haul in a big wagon drill with my team of donkeys. That was the last time I used them—it was 1948. From then on everyone used petrol lorries and to protect the veld the government brought in laws limiting the number of donkeys you could own.'[2]

Theron, Scholtz, Van Staden and the others working at Sishen lived in tents as Lynn and Lombard had done. Scholtz, Noeth and their gangs worked with the diamond drills. During 1949 Albert Hartman of Thabazimbi arrived as drill foreman and took over D S Theron's job too. Iscor wanted some deep prospecting trenches so a gang equipped with hand jumpers drilled holes for explosives. A young Iscor miner named Mike Pauer was being transferred from Thabazimbi to a mine in South West Africa and was instructed to call in at Sishen to charge the holes and blast them.

'That was in January 1950,' says Mike Pauer. 'I was supposed to stay for a week or two and I've never left.' That may be because of what happened to his car on the way down. 'The tar road ended at Klerksdorp,' he recalls. 'Then there was a dirt road to Vryburg and that wasn't too bad. But from Vryburg to Sishen the roads shook the car to pieces and once it reached Sishen it never worked again. A tree fell on it.'[3] When an Iscor geologist failed to reach Sishen as expected, Pauer and others went to look for him and found him driving at a snail's pace with both rear wheels flat.

During 1950 Pauer and the rest of the prospecting party continued to live in tents in the Gamagara, but in the next year they moved into zinc kaias. Iscor was now ready to open a mine and L F Vorster arrived as the first manager. He and his family moved into the old Sishen homestead which until then had been occupied by two sisters from the island of St Helena. Vorster had a new job for Hans van Staden—erecting modest houses to form the nucleus of a mine village. Van Staden's brother Jaap was called in to make bricks and concrete slabs used to build interior walls.

The Van Stadens eventually completed 28 houses in two rows back to back. More elaborate homes were built for the mine manager, secretary, engineer and doctor. Mine offices and stores were added to the complex and outside contractors began erecting an ore-handling plant. The community grew still bigger when a party from South African Railways arrived to lay a rail link between Sishen and Lohatlha. The line was to be opened in 1953. As yet Sishen had no store of its own, but there was a general dealer's at the hamlet of Dingle close by and further west lay Olifantshoek.

This was the first time Olifantshoek had seen anything of the mining industry, but with Postmasburg and Kuruman the village served the heartland of the Northern Cape. 'Olifantshoek nestles in a cluster of hills which might remind one of a herd of grazing elephants,' noted a Sishen correspondent in Iscor's house magazine. 'On Tuesdays and Fridays, Mr J F Basson and his native assistants sally forth to Olifantshoek in a lorry to do the shopping for the village. Each housewife gives him a shopping list and he returns with his lorry laden with packages which he delivers to each home.

'Groceries, vegetables and fruit and delicious mutton can be obtained there and there is also a dry-cleaning depot. Occasionally the residents make private trips to Olifantshoek to do some personal shopping. There is an establishment called the Kalahari Hotel which has a magnetic attraction for thirsty men, while the women may satisfy their craving for pretty things by paying a visit to "Olga's". Here one may buy all the things dear to a woman's heart—bless Olga!'[4] Several Sishen children went to school in Olifantshoek which was about 35 km from the mine.

As yet there was no power at Sishen and families made do with paraffin lamps. Housewives baked their own bread and Hans van Staden's little dairy herd provided Sishen's milk. Many of the women already knew each other from years spent at Thabazimbi and soon formed a lively book club. Their menfolk had plans to build a recreation hall but first created a shooting range. All these activities took place under a pall of red dust that drove many Iscor women to despair, especially on washing days. Close to the village an Iscor shift-boss named Jan Kotze had opened the first quarry.

Jan Kotze was from Thabazimbi where Iscor mined underground. Sishen was to be an open pit. 'I arrived in mid-1952,' he says, 'and the first task was to prepare our equipment. Five big dumper trucks arrived by road. At the time they were the biggest in the country but by today's standards they wouldn't seem exciting. Each truck carried components of two big excavators that were put together at the mine. We also had a couple of wagon drills. We picked a spot in the veld where the ore came close to the surface and we put the wagon drills to work.'[5]

To help him, Jan Kotze had two miners. One was Mike Pauer. 'Our job was to built up a stockpile for the ore-handling plant,' says Jan Kotze. 'We were drilling and blasting the hard rock and the excavators cleaned the face. But we also used the excavators on beds of detrital ore that was easy to handle. The original ore-handling plant had crushers and screens but no washing process. There was no way of blending ore so we had to know which grade we were supplying. In the early days the ore-handling plant was filling 40 rail trucks a day.'[5]

L F Vorster remained mine manager in Sishen's early years and Mike Pauer remembers him as a hard taskmaster. 'He wanted us to keep the ore stockpile full at all times, no matter what,' he says. 'We began work at six in the morning and usually we didn't finish till nine at night. On Saturday it was even longer. Vorster wanted us to make sure there'd be a full stockpile for first thing Monday morning. Sometimes we worked till midnight. That didn't leave much time for fun and games but we were quite satisfied. We thought we were well paid.'[3]

The Sishen operation was controlled from Iscor headquarters in Pretoria rather than from a traditional mining financial centre like Johannesburg or Kimberley. In a way, the capital's influence was a symbol of the times. During 1948 Jan Smuts's United Party had been defeated at the polls. Its conqueror was the Nationalist Party led by D F Malan, which was pledged to enforce segregation of South Africa's whites and non-whites. Blacks were declared to be residents of tribal homelands, and mining companies wanting their labour had to recruit them on contract or not at all.

Shuttle Service

By 1948, Associated Manganese was ready to reopen Black Rock, the only underground manganese mine in the southern hemisphere. Jumbo Harris was back and Syd Brownrigg was still his assistant manager. To

23. Thomas Shone, pioneer of the Postmasburg manganese fields.

Samancor

24. Leslie Boardman, discoverer of the northern manganese belt.

Samancor

25. Mining manganese ore at Beeshoek with pneumatic drills, sledgehammers, forks and cocopans.

Associated Manganese

26. At the Adams mine, a Sterling lorry is loaded with manganese ore for despatch to the railhead.

Associated Manganese

27. At the Gloucester manganese mine, labourers use forks to load special rail wagons.

Associated Manganese

help them travel the 'milk run' between Beeshoek and Black Rock the company bought an aged De Havilland Dragon Rapide, a 'Bamboo Bomber' biplane with canvas wings. The aircraft came from Tommy Mitchell, a veteran test pilot who took a close interest in the 'Bamboo Bomber's' progress. Beeshoek's airstrip remains 'Tommy's Field' to this day.

The aircraft's pilot was the mine doctor and there was room for five passengers. To service it the company engaged a young aircraft mechanic trained in the South African Air Force—Pieter Vertue, who had arrived in Postmasburg when his father took a job at Postmas diamond mine. 'Not everyone wanted to fly,' he says. 'The aircraft didn't look very safe. But two or three times a week she flew up to Black Rock and back, stopping at Gloucester on the way.'[6] There were soon airstrips at Sishen and Manganore too and Northern Cape farmers became used to having aircraft overhead.

At Black Rock compressors, jackhammers, cocopans and other equipment had been kept in storage while the mine was closed. New miners moved into the zinc kaias and the Nchwaning homestead and new labourers filled the nearby hostel. One of the first arrivals was Percy van der Walt who still works at Black Rock. 'I was in charge of grading,' he says. 'I began with the stacks of ore left from the earlier operations. Mr Brownrigg helped me establish what was what and it was ready for despatch.'[7]

Before, Black Rock's ore had been carried to Gloucester by independent contractors. Now Associated Manganese bought trucks of its own—huge Sterling semi-trailers that travelled at an average speed of 90 km/h. But on steep uphill stretches they slowed down to 6 km/h and at all times they sent up clouds of dust that played havoc with the nerves of motorists stuck behind them. At first the company introduced two Sterlings only, but as they proved themselves the fleet was increased until eventually there were 12 of them operating a shuttle service that continued 24 hours a day.

'Every truck had two drivers, each with an assistant,' says Pieter Vertue who was put in charge of servicing the Sterlings. 'One driver loaded the truck at Black Rock and drove as far as Deben. Then he handed over to the other driver who took the truck to Gloucester, unloaded it and brought it back to Deben. Then the first driver took over once more and drove to Black Rock. The whole cycle took 24 hours. The drivers rested at Deben and the company put up single quarters for them. The service shop was at Gloucester and each truck was overhauled on every trip.'[6]

If there were breakdowns, Pieter Vertue sent out a van. A lorry patrolled the road to pick up flat wheels. After a puncture the drivers could remove the flat wheel and fit a spare and were instructed to leave the flat beside the road. Drivers' assistants had to work hard, for in addition to helping with repairs they had to open farm gates. In some cases drivers saved them the trouble by removing the gateposts on the way through. Gradually the company replaced the gates with cattle grids made of reinforced concrete that was strong enough to take the weight of loaded lorries.

Henry Maritz arrived at Black Rock in 1949, fresh from the copper mine at Tsumeb in South West Africa and before that several years in the South African Army. 'At that time there were only four white men on the mine,' says Maritz, who like Percy van der Walt still works at Black Rock. 'They were the mine captain, two miners and the grader. I was a miner too. We were working underground with stopes that followed the ore body. We left pillars as we went, and in places the ore was so thick that our pillars were 30 metres high.

'In siting the pillars we had to play it by ear—it depended on the state of the hanging wall. In places we could dispense with the pillars, but we had to be careful because once a pillar had gone you couldn't put it back. We laid cocopan rails right up to the face and pushed the cocopans to the winching station. The boys spun the cocopans on a turntable and hitched up the cable and they were winched up the incline and on to the sort floors. There the cocopans were tipped out and the sortboys graded the ore and threw it into different wheelbarrows ready for the stacks.'[8]

Even with the Sterlings, Black Rock was isolated. Fortunately for the young miners, the farmer at Nchwaning had five daughters and other local farmers had daughters too. Henry Maritz married one of them. 'Sunday was the only day we didn't work,' he says, 'but we were free in the evenings. I used to go visiting on horseback. We built a tennis court at Black Rock and a little swimming pool too. Often we were invited to eat with the Pretorius family at Nchwaning—they were very good to us, and so were all the local farmers. Once a month Mr Pretorius lent us his car for a drive into Kuruman.'[8]

Nearly all the leading hands and labourers at Black Rock were Tswana and they soon gave nicknames to the white men. Percy van der Walt was '*Madol*' or '*Knees*' because he was tall and skinny and his kneecaps stood out. Henry Maritz was '*Matachise*' or 'Hurry Up' because he was always chasing labourers to work. The other two miners were dubbed '*Klakatan*' or 'Lion's Head' and '*Rhadigotsane*' or 'Big Pockets'. Whites and blacks got on well together, and when the soccer-mad blacks organised a kickaround in the evenings the whites often joined in and had a game with them.

Black Rock's living standards remained spartan, and in comparison Beeshoek's seemed palatial. Not the least of Beeshoek's comforts was electricity—a generator in the village provided electric light every night until 10 pm, and one afternoon a week there was power for ironing. As yet Lohatlha lacked such luxuries and housewives relied on candles and oil lamps. Meals were cooked on wood-burning stoves which also heated water for the weekly wash. Officially Manganore remained the senior community, but Lohatlha was slowly overtaking it.

Most of the workings of Lohatlha were close to the village, which meant miners could return home for lunch. The midday break was signalled by a gong hanging from a camelthorn tree. Having the workings so close meant that Lohatlha had a dust problem, especially when the wind blew. A quartet of donkeys dragged a heavy iron girder over the roads to sweep the dust to one side. The same donkeys pulled a cart that made a weekly tour of the village to deliver wood and coal. Water came from a huge barrel strapped on to an old lorry chassis and was delivered to oildrum 'canteens'.

Lohatlha neighboured Gloucester though a hill separated the rival operations. As yet there was no village at Gloucester and miners still commuted from Postmasburg, though the open lorry had been replaced by a bus. Associated Manganese and S A Manganese were keen competitors so guarded their secrets closely and there was minimal contact between them. Even so, their mines were worked on very similar lines. Groups of miners were supervised by shift-bosses and each miner was allocated a section of ground and a large gang to help him work it.

Daan Koorzen arrived at Lohatlha in 1950 to work for South African Railways. He joined S A Manganese three years later and is today the mine captain at Lohatlha. 'During the 1950s the S A Manganese properties were worked in two sections,' he says. 'Manganore and the surrounding farms made up the eastern section. Lohatlha was the chief element of the western section but it also included Demaneng, the old Amcor mine, and Aucampsrust which had belonged to New Union Manganese. Lohatlha was divided into sub-sections each run by a shift-boss with three or four white miners and their gangs.

'The typical gang was divided into three teams with a leading hand in charge of each. One team did the drilling, one trammed the cocopans and the third was on the sortfloors. The drilling was up at the rockface and several of the hands worked with jackhammers to drill holes about 50 cm deep. The miner charged them with dynamite and prepared them for blasting. The cocopan tramlines went close to the face so we protected them with sand. Everybody took shelter while the ore was blasted—the miner in his kaia, the leading hands in a second and all the labourers in a big one.

'Once the ore was blasted, some of it had to be broken up with heavy hammers or pom-pom drills that worked like pavement breakers—up and down rather than round and round. With really big rocks the miner might try a mudblast, packing dynamite against the rock and covering it with mud. That had the effect of a really big hammer and it saved on drilling. When the rock was ready hands began sorting the ore from the waste. Ore went to one side of the cocopan tramlines and waste to the other. The loading hands lashed the rock into cocopans and trammers pushed it away from the face.

'We loaded waste in the morning and manganese in the afternoon. The waste went to a dump and the manganese to the sortfloors where the sorting hands took over. The ore was tipped on to a long heap stretching along the sortfloor and the sorting hands looked at each rock and classified it. They sorted it by eye and sometimes they needed to use a little hammer and chip a piece off the rock to see what was inside. They had to distinguish between nine different grades. They tossed the rocks into wheelbarrows behind them, a separate barrow for each different grade.

'The sorting hands were picked by the sortfloor leading hand and it took six weeks to train them. One chief leading hand knew the ore so well that you could give him any rock and he could tell you where it came from, anywhere on the mine. When the wheelbarrows were full, hands wheeled them to the different stacks and added the rocks like bricks. Now they were ready for shipment but first we had to test them. That was my job. Our system was to take six forkfuls from various parts of the stack. Five forkfuls were thrown away and we kept the sixth and that was sent to the assay office.'[9]

Much the same methods were used at Gloucester, except that in several cases donkeys were used to haul cocopans up inclines. Willie Bam remembers that they were obedient but not always patient. 'Once they'd hauled up a cocopan the hands unhitched them and they walked down for another load without needing an escort,' he says. 'But when they heard the lunch siren they stopped work and brayed loudly and went to where their food was kept. At the end of the day they trotted back to their kraal and if the hands weren't quick they'd take their harness with them.'[10]

Jumbo Harris and Syd Brownrigg were firmly in charge at the Associated Manganese properties. At S A Manganese there was a new manager, a Natalian named Mike Wilson, who had experience of gold mines and also of Natal's sugar industry. Wilson and his family arrived at Manganore during 1950, and at about the same time S A Manganese acquired a new field geologist—Leslie Boardman, persuaded by Wilhelm Kupferburger to throw in his lot with the manganese industry. To be on the safe side Boardman insisted that he should be employed by Amcor rather than S A Manganese.

Not the least of the factors that persuaded Boardman to return to the Northern Cape was his marriage to a girl from Griquatown, Joey Wandrag. At Griquatown he came to know a young man named Flippie Badenhorst and suggested he should contact Mike Wilson and ask for a job at S A Manganese. Badenhorst was accepted, and some of his earliest assignments were to accompany Boardman on his field trips. Boardman had already checked S A Manganese's existing properties and on his recommendation Amcor had bought the farm Lylyveld that neighboured Sishen. Now he was moving northwards.

'The first time I went with him he was visiting farmers,' says Flippie Badenhorst, today mine secretary at Lohatlha. 'He wanted to persuade the farmers to give him options on the farms and allow him to prospect on them.'[11] Not all the farmers were pleased to see him. Some had seen prospectors before and had found the money they were paid barely covered the damage that was done. But others were more positive and invited Boardman and Badenhorst to stay at their farmhouses. 'Boardman preferred to sleep out under the stars,' says Badenhorst. 'We lit a camp fire and wrapped up in blankets.'[11]

Badenhorst's next trip with Boardman was a prospecting venture. Boardman had persuaded Kupferburger to buy a magnetometer like the one used by Oscar Weiss's team at Black Rock. He had never worked with one before so asked the mine captain at Black Rock for permission to try it out. The mine captain—Piet Coetzee, returned from Gloucester—told him he was welcome and Boardman made a full traverse of the outcrop from east to west. He started and finished in the sand outside the ore body and the readings he collected showed his magnetometer was a powerful tool.

'My job was to carry the magnetometer along the prospecting lines that Boardman chose,' says Flippie Badenhorst. 'At the beginning of the day it seemed quite light but it became heavier as we went along. There was a tripod and a platform for the instrument and I had to set them up every 100 metres. Then Boardman balanced the platform and took his reading and noted it down in a logbook. Each reading took about five minutes. We kept on with that for days on end and covered a good many farms. It was all supposed to be secret because Boardman didn't want Associated Manganese to know.'[11]

Boardman was specially impressed by high readings on the farm Wessels which lay north of Black Rock. He persuaded Wilhelm Kupferburger to send in a diamond drill but initial results were disappointing. The drill was moved to the farm Diaboghomo next door and went down 150 metres without detecting any sign of manganese. Kupferburger said there was no point in continuing but Boardman insisted and at 280 metres the drill entered manganese that assayed at 55 per cent—phenomenally high by any standards.

With results like those, S A Manganese took steps to buy the freehold of Wessels, Diaboghomo and their neighbours. Meanwhile Boardman was investigating a farm in a quite different area—Smartt, which lay 30 km north of Deben. Magnetometer readings showed there was ore close to the surface and an old wagon drill was carried north from Manganore. The drill went down 15 metres and there was manganese as Boardman had predicted. Again S A Manganese bought the farm and others that lay close to it, and the company was in a strong position to start a new mine.

Giant Cocopans

Ulco quarry and limeworks had been a family affair from the start, nowhere more than among the Bredenkamps. 'Old man Bredenkamp was working at Ulco and his kids grew up here,' says Lydia Swartz, herself an Ulco baby today married to Ulco's hostel manager. 'Freddie was the eldest and he started here as an apprentice while his sister began as a typist. Next there were twins—Myra came as a typist and her brother as an apprentice. Enid was a typist, so was Jeanette, and Dudley the youngest became an apprentice. That meant eight of them worked here together.'[12]

In 1948 Ulco's cozy atmosphere abruptly changed when outside contractors arrived to erect a major cement factory next to the limeworks. For several years Eric Lowther had urged Anglovaal to consider building such a works and supplying it with limestone from the Ulco quarry. Anglovaal liked the idea, and during 1947 Anglo-Alpha Cement had bought an interest in Union Lime and had made preparations for the new venture. The factory was to be a multi-million investment and specialist workers were brought to Ulco from a score of countries.

'Everyone at Ulco was 100 per cent in favour of the new factory,' says Charles Langeveld. 'It meant more people, more work, more opportunities. The factory was a huge venture in itself, and in addition a lot more houses were built to accommodate the people who would be working in it. Even then there weren't enough houses so the company helped people to build their own homes in Delportshoop. At the same time the recreation hall was expanded to provide a mess for the construction men, and that's been a lasting benefit too.'[13]

The rising cement factory soon dwarfed the original limeworks. Meanwhile Lowther and his men were mechanising the quarry and opening new faces of lower-grade limestone that were adequate for cement production but not for lime. The old grizzly was replaced by a large jaw crusher and the old hand-loaded cocopan fleet was supplemented by new giant cocopans that were filled by an excavator. 'The big cocopans had axles two metres long and they stood three metres off the rails,' says Charles Langeveld. 'They were far too heavy to be pushed so we installed a system of winches.'[13]

Unfortunately the new system was not a success. 'With the old hand-pushed cocopans, we laid light tramlines that could be moved from one place to another,' says Langeveld. 'Even if they were damaged by falling rock they were quickly straightened. But the new rails were like locomotive tracks. Once they were in place you couldn't move them, and they were constantly being damaged by falling rock. After a few months Mr Lowther decided to scrap the big cocopans and bring in a fleet of trucks—International horses and reinforced semi-trailers.'[13]

A glimpse of Ulco quarry's new look comes from an article in the *Northern Cape Bulletin* of September 1949. It seems that Eric Lowther favoured a single large explosion every two or three weeks, at the time 'the biggest well-hole blast in the Union. . . . The operation is tricky. At the foot of the 150 ft (*c 50 m*) cliffs there are excavators, shovels, lorries and men. Beyond them are the lime kilns, conveyor belts, power station, huge silos, the lime and cement works and the township. A mistake may cost lives, machinery—destroy an industry which has taken 12 years to build up.

'But nothing is left to chance. Eleven holes 15 feet (*c 5 m*) apart are bored by a modern machine. Natives unload the 16 lb (*c 7,3 kg*) dynamite cartridges from the lorries, which climb up the cliff on winding roads. Supervised by blasting experts, over 950 lb (*c 440 kg*) of dynamite is gently lowered into the well holes. Mirrors guide the men. The explosive must be evenly distributed. Smoking is forbidden. The preliminary arrangements take hours. Then comes the hushed moment for the blast. Everybody runs for cover. The earth shakes and thunders. The cliff crumbles, boulders hurtle down the slopes, and a huge white cloud envelops the site.'[14]

Charles Langeveld remembers that the dynamite cartridges were bundles tied with string. Five or six cartridges were lowered into each well hole on lengths of twine that ended in a hook. 'The hook was brass so that it couldn't make a spark,' he says. 'The moment the cartridge touched bottom the hook came loose and you pulled up the twine and lowered another one. When all the cartridges were in the miner inserted the electric detonator and filled up the hole with sand. Then the boys tamped down the sand with a long wooden stick.'[13]

Today's quarries trigger sequences of explosions that may last many seconds, but in 1950 all the cartridges went up at once. 'It looked as if the whole cliff was coming at you,' says Charles Langeveld. 'Then the rock dropped and you saw the smoke and heard the bang.'[13] Ulco's blasts were among the great sights of the Northern Cape and they were an event even for Ulco-ites. There was even greater interest when news spread that a blast had opened an enormous hidden cavern halfway up the rockface that was filled with stalactites and stalagmites.

'The cavern was a wonderful crystal palace,' says Charles Langeveld. 'I've never seen anything so beautiful. The cave was big enough to hold 30 motorcars but the floor was very uneven so it wouldn't have been much of a garage. You could see water dripping and that was what had formed the stalactites and stalagmites. Some had joined and you couldn't detect the break. Everything was crystal and there were lots of different colours but mainly everything was white or brown. And to set off the effect there was a light dusting of limestone powder left over from the blast.'[13]

Union Lime had many times discovered fossils in the limestone—grass, twigs, leaves and on one occasion a complete honeycomb. But the limestone grotto was something new. Someone rigged up a rope ladder strung from one of the stalactites and many clambered up to the cave for a first-hand inspection. Everyone knew that before long the cave would be destroyed, so many chipped off souvenir stalagmites and lowered them to the quarry floor in sacks. When blasting resumed, many Ulco-ites gathered on the fallen rock and scoured it for more crystal to add to their collections.

Limestone was the main constituent of Anglo-Alpha's cement but the new factory also needed substantial amounts of shale and gypsum. Fortunately there were supplies close at hand. Gypsum was being quarried at Melkvlei near Barkly West, and Eric Lowther arranged for adequate supplies to be railed to Ulco at regular intervals. The shale was even closer—beneath the deposits of limestone. 'We quarry the shale in exactly the same way as the limestone,' says Eric Cockcroft, Ulco's general works manager until 1982. 'Not nearly so much is needed so every couple of weeks we divert excavators and trucks from the limestone and load shale instead.'[15]

Eric Lowther remained at Ulco to see the cement factory on its way and resigned in 1950. His place was taken by a German-Swiss engineer, Lu Matter, who was to remain at Ulco for a quarter of a century. Lowther took a job with an engineering firm in Kimberley and he was visited there by Alwin Austin who had worked with him at Ulco. 'Mr Lowther was sitting in his office and he showed me some stones,' says Austin. 'He asked me: "Alwin, what do you make of these?" Now the stones looked to me like ordinary dolomite, so I said: "We farmers call that *jonas*."

'Mr Lowther then said: "Would you believe it was limestone?" I said: "What, like *kalk*?" That's our name for limestone, but he explained *kalk* was only *secondary* limestone. His stones were *primary* limestone and they were just like dolomite except they contained much less magnesium. He told me the stones came from near Danielskuil. Everyone had assumed they were dolomite but then someone lit a fire on them and threw some water over them and they began to evaporate—just like the hydrated lime produced at Ulco. The fire had burnt the lime and the water slaked it.'[16]

The man responsible for the discovery was Digby Roberts, a geologist working for the Corner House financial group which had a major say in the Northern Lime Company and in many gold mines too. The Corner

House wanted Roberts to locate new sources of limestone for use in a secret industry: the processing of vast quantities of low-grade uranium recovered from waste residues in gold mines' slimes dams, a technique developed during World War II in preparation for atomic warfare.

Northern Lime already held options on a group of farms containing limestone that were located west of Douglas. But they were considered too far from the railhead to be worth exploiting. In Kimberley Digby Roberts heard stories of 'stones that evaporated' and tracked down three businessmen who were manufacturing gravestones. The businessmen had been disappointed to find the rock they were quarrying developed brown stains when it was exposed to the air. They thought it was poor-quality dolomite, but Roberts recognised it for what it was—primary limestone.

The businessmen were quarrying their 'dolomite' near Danielskuil and Roberts went there to visit farms and ask for permission to prospect. One farm he visited was Silver Streams where he met the Hoelson brothers, Stan and Norman. 'Digby told us he was doing some sort of survey for Corner House but he didn't tell us what he was looking for,' says Stan Hoelson who still farms in the district. 'It was all very secretive. Some of us thought he was after diamonds, others thought gold, but nobody guessed limestone.'[17]

One major difference between primary limestone and dolomite is that the limestone reacts to dilute hydrochloric acid. 'Quite simply, it fizzes,' says John Wotherspoon, who for years served as Northern Lime's geologist in the Northern Cape. 'The dolomite doesn't fizz. Digby Roberts went prospecting with a little bottle of acid and tested rock where it lay.'[18] Roberts's results uncovered a large block of limestone lying between Danielskuil and Papkuil and Northern Lime took out options on a number of farms close to the railway between Koopmansfontein and Postmasburg.

Eric Lowther had now left his engineering firm and had gone to Johannesburg as Northern Lime's general manager. He was seen as South Africa's leading authority on limestone, and now he sent a drilling rig to Danielskuil to make an in-depth appraisal of Roberts's deposits. The drill proved that high-grade limestone existed in depth so Northern Lime bought the farms and put Jack Goldswain of Taungs in charge as a quarry was opened and contractors erected kilns. Goldswain and his party pitched tents in the veld and signed on a miner—Frik Scholtz.

We last met Frik Scholtz at Sishen where he was part of D A Theron's prospecting party. His first job at Sishen was to open a well and it was the same on the limestone fields. 'They'd sent down a borehole but the water supply was too weak,' says Scholtz. 'I was told to sink a well two metres across. We took the well down 38 metres and entered the solid rock and that was where we found water. The rock formation was broken so we bricked the sidewalls from the bottom to the top. As far as I know that well's still there.'[1]

Next Scholtz opened the quarry. 'I'd never worked on an open mine before,' he says, 'but they wanted me to develop an incline following the lie of the rock. The limestone beds were set at an angle. We drilled holes with jackhammers, blasted the ore and then broke it up by hand using heavy hammers. Then we loaded it into wheelbarrows and pushed it to stacks. Ordinary road lorries came down the incline to load up the rock and they took it to Silver Streams station. From there it went off to the Rand Water Board in Johannesburg which had kilns of its own.'[1]

By the standards of what was to come, the limestone shipments to Johannesburg represented little more than pocket money for Northern Lime. But they did make it possible to open the quarry and prepare for the time when the new kilns came into operation. For some time Goldswain, Scholtz and others on the Northern Lime farms had lived in prefabricated kaias erected by Alwin Austin, who was also contracted to dig foundations for the kilns. 'Each kaia had a bedroom and a bathroom,' says Austin. 'There was also a long hut we used as a mess and we installed a dartboard and a table tennis table and a big radio set.'[16]

Now Austin was commissioned to build permanent houses for Northern Lime employees. An early photograph shows that the houses were erected along two parallel roads winding through the veld. The roads were crossed by a third 'Burma Road' that led on to the quarry and the lime kilns which first came into operation during 1954. The Burma Road cut the other two in half, and each of the four halves was named after one of the farms bought by Northern Lime—Bowden, Smuts, Shone and Adams. Together they made a village that Eric Lowther named Lime Acres.

Pascoe's Indaba

During the war years, Gefco's Bretby had worked to capacity producing asbestos for the British government. With the help of a skilled Herero prospector named Piet Thomas, Gefco's Harold Pascoe scoured the region for new deposits and located his 'main marker' on the farm Riries north-west of Kuruman. There were no fresh asbestos outcrops on Riries, so Pascoe brought in a bright red jumper drill to test the strata and located a rich asbestos horizon 100 metres under the surface. He wrote to the directors suggesting a new mine and they approved.

Now Pascoe had to persuade some of his workers to make a move. Most of them were Herero like Thomas and liked to reach decisions by means of an indaba or forum. The men sat in a circle and took turns to speak until consensus was reached. In discussing Riries, their main concern was grazing for their donkeys and goats. Pascoe and Piet

Thomas assured them that Riries was good farming country, and Thomas said the asbestos was so rich that they would certainly make their fortunes. The indaba set its stamp on Riries and a number of the Herero made plans to travel there with their families.

Riries was more than 65 km from Bretby, so the Pascoes moved to Kuruman to be close to both. The house bought for them became Gefco's administrative headquarters and Gefco general managers have lived there ever since. At Bretby, Pascoe sank a new deep incline shaft and to save money devised a home-made winch at the top. The winch was an old lorry differential with the propshaft shortened, the whole apparatus mounted on four stout poles. Soon it became an even greater talking point than Pascoe's donkey whims.

A film made in about 1950 shows the Pascoe winch at work. The lorry's cab is still in place but the bonnet has been removed, and in place of the radiator there is an attachment leading to an oildrum full of water. The front wheels have gone and the back wheeldrums serve as cable winders. The winch is located about 30 metres in front of the top of the incline which is blocked from view by a high ramp. Cables from the winch pass over pulleys above the ramp and are attached to cocopans hauled up the incline and tipped out at the top.

Gefco was a much smaller concern than Cape Asbestos, and after the war years most of its products had been used to make battery boxes. Cape Asbestos continued to supply spinning mills and also sold asbestos for ship insulation. Most of its fibre came from Koegas–Westerberg but the company still possessed a score of much smaller operations around Prieska, Kuruman and Pomfret. That was the situation in 1947 when a new shift-boss arrived at Koegas. His name was Doug Todd, and during the war he had flown anti-submarine Venturas for the South African Air Force.

Todd was a gold-mining man and was fascinated by the primitive mining methods still used on many of Cape Asbestos's mines. 'The company was still using tributors,' he said in the course of a lengthy interview before his death in 1980. 'The "mines" were often just holes. Some sections were being worked with jackhammers, some with hand jumpers. But in most cases the tributors and day workers were going deeper than in the old days. They were sinking vertical winzes to reach the bottom of the asbestos horizon. Once at the bottom they tunnelled outwards to begin stoping.

'In places the horizon was two or three metres high, containing many strata of asbestos. The miner aimed to bring down the hanging wall, sort out the fibre and send it to the surface. Often he drilled a single hole, put in a stick of dynamite and blasted as he went along. The miner's helpers sorted the fibre from the waste and put it into buckets which were hauled up the winze by hand or windlass. The waste was usually left where it had fallen and the miner stood on it to drill new holes. When he was finished he abandoned the winze and started on a new one elsewhere.'[19]

At about the time of Todd's arrival, Cape Asbestos began introducing tungsten carbide drills that were far tougher than the ordinary steel drills used previously. 'The old star-bits were no match for unoxidised banded asbestos or riebeckite—*blou bliksem*, as it was known,' recalled Todd. 'But tungsten carbide was a different matter.'[19] The new technology persuaded Cape Asbestos to reopen the deep winze sunk at Koegas in Rundle Olds's time, and before long the company decided to close its smaller mines and concentrate on Koegas–Westerberg and Pomfret.

The rationalisation might have left Doug Todd without a job, but just then he was approached by Gefco which invited him to take over as general manager. The directors wanted to free Harold Pascoe from the grind of administration so that he could track down new sources of sub-surface asbestos. Todd established himself in Kuruman and persuaded Gefco to buy him a Cessna 182 so that he could fly himself to the company's two mines, Bretby and Riries, and further afield. Riries was now in full production and was more than fulfilling Pascoe's high hopes.

'The fibre was phenomenally rich,' says Mollie Franke, a German-born mining engineer who joined Gefco in 1950 and now lives in Natal. 'So rich that the miners had trouble drilling holes in it. Their jumpers became tangled in the asbestos and their jackhammers overheated.'[20] Miners directed their drills into banded ironstone instead. Both top-quality and lesser fibres were lashed into cocopans and winched to the surface where they were tipped on to a heap for the hand-cobbers, who often raced one another to pick out the best cobs.

Hand-cobbing was still an important part of the asbestos industry, and at Riries the man in charge of the operation was Faan Riekert. 'We laid a special stone floor and about 100 cobbers worked there,' he says. 'It was a big operation and there was a lot of singing and chatting, quite a commotion. The girls used little square hammers and many brought in metal hammering blocks. The girls were paid according to the weight of what they stamped. The lesser fibre was taken to a stamping mill and bagged ready for customers, but the hand-cobs were graded and bagged separately.'[21]

Mollie Franke was at Riries to help erect a new mill, but before very long he was lured away to join a new asbestos company that had mushroomed into being—Kuruman Cape Blue Asbestos Ltd, or KCB for short. Behind the new venture were three brothers, Douglas, Charles and Percy Armstrong. Percy Armstrong was a former diamond digger and prospector who had a farm near Vryburg, and in 1949 he had gone on a hunting trip in the Kalahari. With him had been a man in his eighties who showed him asbestos formations in the Heuningvlei area, about 100 km south-west of Pomfret.

Heuningvlei was a long way from the nearest railhead, but there were tenuous road connections with Kuruman. Percy Armstrong arranged a mining lease over three farms that belonged to the state. Then he and his brothers prepared to build a mill on one of these farms and to allocate mining sections to independent tributors. Following a Transvaal precedent, their tributors would be white miners and diggers responsible for providing their own equipment and hiring their own gangs of labourers. They relied on friends of theirs to spread the word.

Early in 1950, the Armstrongs set up camp at Heuningvlei and began putting up their mill. At first they slept in their cars, soon they erected zinc kaias, and ultimately they built a small village of 12 concrete bungalows. One by one their tributors arrived, most of them former diggers or gold miners. An exception was the former sawmill proprietor from Pretoria who had recently come to grief in a dairy farming venture. His name was Sarel de Witt, and in spite of having no mining experience he invested in equipment and a truck and joined the Armstrongs at Heuningvlei.

'We tributors delivered asbestos to the Armstrongs' mill and they paid for it by weight and grade,' says De Witt, who now lives in Kuruman. 'Each of us had our own section to work and our own labourers and hand-cobbers. For 18 months I lived in a tent, but I learnt about asbestos and began buying out my neighbours.'[22] To work the new sections De Witt hired a number of Irishmen. 'They were all on the run,' he says, 'some from women, some from debt, some from prison. They were glad to be hidden in the bush. I gave each one a kaia and a pick and shovel and told him to mine.'[22]

Heuningvlei was prospering, and the asbestos company Turner and Newall made a takeover bid—the first time the corporation had involved itself in the Northern Cape since the folding of Dominion Blue Asbestos in 1932. The Armstrongs accepted the offer, but within a short time Percy Armstrong was prospecting again. Sarel de Witt left Heuningvlei too, and with him went a one-armed former gold miner named Sam van Rensburg who had become his lieutenant. De Witt learnt that a water borehole drilled on the farm Carrington had intersected asbestos, so obtained a mining lease.

'I had to learn the hard way,' he says. 'Sam van Rensburg was with me and also a small gang of labourers. I decided to sink a shaft beside the borehole and we worked on it around the clock for seven weeks. We went down 170 metres. I had great hopes of establishing a rich mine and began developing drives into the asbestos reef. But then the asbestos pinched out. It took us only two weeks to take out the fibre and that was all there was. It was the last time I tried to start a mine without prospecting first.'[22]

Carrington was a dead loss, but then De Witt teamed up with Piet Thomas, the old Herero prospector who had worked with Harold Pascoe. Thomas took him over the farm Langley which neighboured Carrington and showed him an old prospecting winze sunk by Gefco but abandoned when it produced no asbestos. 'Thomas said they'd stopped too soon,' says De Witt. 'He said there'd be asbestos just below the bottom of the winze. We went down another five metres and there it was. That man was a born prospector, and he was the master of the markers in the asbestos formations.'[22]

De Witt wanted to start mining but his cash position was less than strong. He decided to join forces with the Armstrongs, who were starting a new mine on the farm Whitebank south of Kuruman and had registered KCB to work it. Percy Armstrong was chairman and De Witt became managing director. All the men involved in the new mine put in long hours, but their wives were not so enthusiastic. One day several of the men were to dine together in Kuruman but at the last moment told their wives they would be late. They asked the women to keep something for them, so when they arrived the wives served up hot plates piled high with asbestos.

CHAPTER SEVEN 1954–1961

More Manganese

MANIE PYPER grew up on the farm Middelplaats, about 30 km north of the hamlet Deben. He was on hand in 1953 when S A Manganese prepared to open a new mine on Smartt, the farm next door. 'I was the first man they signed on,' says Pyper, now the chief storekeeper at Pomfret asbestos mine. 'Koos van der Merwe was up from Lohatlha to take charge, and a man named Stoltz arrived to look after earth-moving equipment. Our job was to clear vegetation and remove the overburden to expose the ore body. That meant digging through 12 metres of sand.'[1]

The earth-moving equipment consisted of a mechanical horse pulling a scraper and a bulldozer pushing from behind. The scraper cut into the sand like a plough and collected it in a deep bin. When the bin was full the bulldozer drew back and the mechanical horse towed the scraper to a dump well clear of the workings. In those early days the only sign of explosives was a small quantity used to sink a prospect winze. 'The winze went down 20 metres and it was 1,3 m square,' says Pyper. 'We lined it with timber lagging but even so there were many problems with drifting sand.'[1]

Smartt's ore contained a high proportion of manganese and was destined for Amcor's ferro-manganese smelter at Meyerton in the Transvaal. Production began early in 1954 when Hendrik Schoeman arrived to start mining. 'The plan was to cut into the ore body at a gentle angle and lay tramlines for cocopans,' says Pyper. 'We installed a winch to haul them to the surface and when there was room we sent in a mechanical shovel. With the ore face exposed we drilled well-holes about ten metres deep and inserted long cartridges of dynamite but we only blasted once a week.'[1]

Copying Associated Manganese's arrangements at Black Rock, S A Manganese planned to transport manganese ore by truck. South African Railways had begun operating at Sishen and both manganese companies developed ore stockpiles at the new railhead. S A Manganese bought five International trucks which were loaded at Smartt each evening, then collected by their drivers at about midnight. The trucks left Smartt at 90-minute intervals to allow adequate unloading time at Sishen. On arriving back at Smartt they were refuelled and serviced and if necessary loaded for another trip.

While S A Manganese opened Smartt, Associated Manganese developed a new mine at Devon which lay two farms to the north. Here too ore was being produced for a ferro-manganese smelter, in this case a new works being built by Anglovaal at Cato Ridge in Natal. Devon was seen as a 'colony' of Black Rock while Smartt's links were with Lohatlha, but both mines drew supplies from Kuruman. Meanwhile, Associated Manganese decided to build a village at Gloucester. Two large hostels for contract labourers had existed there since the 1930s but white staff had commuted from Beeshoek or Postmasburg.

Some years earlier Associated Manganese had asked the South African Post Office to register a postal agency at Gloucester. Unfortunately there was already an agency of that name elsewhere and the Post Office refused to duplicate it. Associated Manganese had to submit another choice of name and decided on 'Glosam', short for 'Gloucester Associated Manganese'. To avoid confusion over the postal name the new village was called Glosam too. Houses were erected around a central square that was soon equipped with tennis courts, a playground and a swimming pool.

Glosam was a near neighbour of Lohatlha, where S A Manganese was replacing the old iron houses with new homes built of brick. The village was also given a brand new recreational hall. Lohatlha and Manganore joined forces to field a Samangan rugby team which practised on a grassless pitch and played occasional matches against the clubs in Postmasburg, Kuruman, Olifantshoek and Griquatown. Players travelled to away fixtures aboard two open bakkies. But the fixtures which Samangan men most enjoyed were against a new club formed at Associated Manganese.

In earlier years Associated Manganese men had played for Postmasburg, but Jumbo Harris had long hoped for a club based at Beeshoek. One of 'Ammosal's' first players was Pieter Vertue, who remembers that the club started in 1953. 'Colonel Harris coached us,' he says, 'and because Ammosal was an open club our teams included local farmers and teachers too. We started with two teams and soon we were beating

28. Early prospecting on Brits farm, the site of Finsch diamond mine.

De Beers Consolidated Mines

29. At the opening of Finsch mine, Thorny Fincham (*right*) and Harry Oppenheimer, chairman of De Beers, flank Dr T E Dönges, then South Africa's state president elect.

De Beers Consolidated Mines

30. Sishen township, where trees have grown to shade homes from the Kalahari sunshine.

Iscor

31. Night and day, Sishen's excavators load relays of heavy trucks that carry ore to the crushers and waste to the disposal tips.

Iscor

everyone we played against. The secret lay in regular practices, several times a week. Colonel Harris expected us to put rugby ahead of everything else.'[2]

Jumbo Harris had built a fine rugby stadium which was the pride of Beeshoek. Not to be outdone, Syd Brownrigg extended the golf course to 18 holes and lured many of the rugby players from practices. During summer Brownrigg helped organise occasional cricket fixtures against players from Lohatlha, where the leading enthusiast was Mike Wilson. At least once a season Ammosal and Samangan players teamed up to challenge a team from Kuruman that was captained by Doug Todd of Gefco. Todd, Brownrigg and Wilson became close friends.

All through the middle 1950s Leslie Boardman continued to explore the northern manganese fields. Often he had to pit his wits against geologists working for Associated Manganese who were equipped with substantial funds to persuade farmers to sign away options on their property. Already the map of the manganese fields looked like a chess-board, for what one company had spurned the other had snapped up. Boardman was confident he had traced the eastern limits of the manganese, though he was less sure of patterns to the west as the ore body dipped to deep levels.

It was a surprise, then, when manganese was found on the farm Langdon Annex, north of Devon and well to the east of Boardman's deposits. The owner, Atta van der Westhuizen, had called in a *siener* or diviner to look for water on his property. The *siener* was an elderly gravedigger named Van Rensburg who came from Lichtenburg. Van Rensburg walked over the farm and failed to find water, but he did report 'seeing' masses of black rock. Van der Westhuizen sank a pit on the spot and three metres down hit high-grade manganese.

Water diviners are to be found all over the world, but in South Africa there have been many reports of diviners 'seeing' metal. Indeed, a few of the most gifted can distinguish between minerals. An academic at the University of Stellenbosch has researched the subject and suggests that *sieners* have high tension within themselves, and that by holding a steel wire tightly they can detect changes in magnetism as they walk from one geophysical feature to another. Boardman was sceptical of *sieners*' powers, but Langdon Annex was positive proof.

Rather than approach the established manganese producers, Van der Westhuizen contacted an independent Johannesburg financier named Benny Struck. It was decided to open a mine at Langdon Annex and Struck and a partner floated a new company that was registered as National Manganese. Langdon ore was drilled, blasted, loaded into cocopans and hand-sorted ready for shipment. As required it was loaded on to contractors' lorries and carried to Sishen to be railed to the coast. Many shipments were routed to Lourenço Marques in Mozambique, today's Maputo.

National Manganese is still operating today, and must not be confused with the National Mining and Exploration Company that began mining manganese at about the same time. National Mining had rights to the farms Aasvoëlskop and Rooinekke which lay north and south of Postmasburg respectively. Within a short time the properties were taken over by Consolidated African Mines or CAM, an offshoot of a shipping agency that specialised in ore shipments to Japan. The shipping agency had contracts with National Mining, and when the company failed to meet its commitments the agency stepped in and took over.

Meanwhile, Van Rensburg the *siener* had been called back to the Northern Cape to look for water on the farm Hotazel. Again he reported seeing masses of black rock. Hotazel was owned by a farmer named 'Kaiser Bill' Boshoff who had fought with Smuts during World War I, but the former owners of Devon wanted to buy the property and they called in Leslie Boardman. Remembering what had happened at Langdon, Boardman and a geophysicist colleague travelled to Hotazel without delay and set up a magnetometer. Boardman was training the geophysicist to take over his fieldwork.

The magnetometer's early readings were unpromising, but suddenly the needle jumped off the scale. The geophysicist thought the instrument was broken. Boardman tested it and realised it was registering a phenomenally high value of manganese. He and his colleague traversed the farm and outlined a circular block of ore that geologists would call a Graben structure, a section of rock that had sunk below its original surface level and had therefore escaped the processes of erosion. Boardman concluded that the ore must once have been connected with manganese to the west.

The discovery at Hotazel came as a godsend for S A Manganese. Smartt had fallen short of expectations because its high-grade ore was patchy and inconsistent, and the company had to battle to meet Amcor's needs. The initial drilling programme had been carried out over too wide a grid and had failed to reveal Smartt's shortcomings. Hotazel's ore seemed a perfect substitute, but before buying mineral rights the S A Manganese directors wanted to make sure a new mine would reward their investment. A drilling crew was sent to make a full exploration.

The drilling programme showed Hotazel held enough ore to support a mine for decades to come, though it was later discovered that in places it was flawed by intrusions of banded ironstone. The directors agreed to exercise their options and launch a mine in grand style. Initial plans called for a fully mechanised operation backed by a modern mining village of 30 houses with offices and stores. Outside contractors were put in charge of construction and South African Railways were persuaded to extend their line north of Sishen. To start the mine, Koos van der Merwe was sent from Smartt.

'Van der Merwe and his miners made good progress,' reports S A Manganese's official history. 'The sand cover was stripped off by three scrapers and the bulldozer from Smartt, but from that point methods differed. At the new mine engineers had planned an access road, evenly graded at eight degrees, to run down into the workings through sand, limestone and manganese or whatever lay in its path. The ore body would be tackled from the road, with the ore blasted and then loaded into rear dump trucks by mechanical shovels.'[3]

Much of the waste limestone removed from the mine was used to make concrete for Hotazel village. As construction proceeded Mike Wilson was a regular visitor, and it was a red-letter day when the first Hotazel families moved into their homes. Most of the families were from Smartt, and the old iron houses they had been living in were dismantled and sent to Manganore. Mike Wilson spent much of his time consoling 'Kaiser Bill' Boshoff, who still lived in Hotazel homestead and took a keen interest in everything that happened. He often cautioned Wilson against unnecessary waste.

In planning the new village, it had been realised that not all South Africans would welcome the name 'Hotazel'. Alternatives were suggested, but then it was found that South Africa's Place Names Commission had already approved 'Hotazel' and the Post Office had registered it too. The company let it stand but planned an opening ceremony with some trepidation. During November 1959 several planeloads of visitors were flown from Johannesburg, among them the minister of mines, Jan de Klerk.

The minister was a religious man and it was known that he considered Hotazel's name both ugly and blasphemous. At the lunch held to welcome the visitors there were several speeches, one of them delivered by 'Kaiser Bill' Boshoff. But in deference to Jan de Klerk, not one of the speakers allowed the offensive word to pass his lips.

Rush on Bellsbank

Early in the 1950s a former Lichtenburg digger named Danie de Bruin was prospecting for diamonds near Boetsap, not far from the Sover fissure. One day he met the manager of Bellsbank Estates, named Tommy Mitchell like the famous aviator. Mitchell told him of old prospect pits on Bellsbank that had been dug by H S Richter, and De Bruin went to investigate. He obtained permission to prospect there and in deepening one of Richter's pits he found several diamonds. The pit probed a kimberlite fissure that ran straight and narrow for at least three kilometres.

For most of its length Bellsbank's fissure was between a metre and 1,4 metres wide, but in places it widened into 'blows' that had the shape of miniature diamond pipes. Richter had sunk his pits in one of these blows and De Bruin followed suit, digging out oxidised 'yellow ground' and putting it through a rotary washing pan. 'I was very unlucky in the beginning and found only a couple of diamonds each week,' he says. 'But then things improved and there were stones in every wash. Some parts of the fissure were rich, some had nothing, and I had to find out by trial and error.'[4]

De Bruin's diamonds came from Bellsbank's 'main fissure' but he was to find about 20 lesser fissures. He was convinced that Bellsbank should be developed as a full-scale diamond mine but the mining commissioner in Barkly West could not agree. The mining commissioner wanted to proclaim a public diggings on Bellsbank and allow other diggers a foothold. That meant De Bruin would be entitled to no more than 30 discoverer's claims while Bellsbank's owners would be allowed 50. The proprietors were in Britain and De Bruin was told they were willing to sell their rights, so he bought them.

The mining commissioner fixed a date for the proclamation. De Bruin had to stop prospecting but he was allowed to peg his 80 claims, each one nearly 15 metres square. He arranged them in such a way that he covered the three blows and the sections of the fissure that adjoined them. Meanwhile, news of the coming proclamation spread all over the Northern Cape's surviving diggings. On the day selected nearly 400 certified diggers gathered on Bellsbank for the privilege of pegging a claim apiece. Among them was the discoverer, who was a veteran of half-a-dozen huge rushes at Lichtenburg.

All the diggers wanting to take part had notified the mining commissioner in advance and had been issued a ticket corresponding to a claim licence. The mining commissioner stood on a lorry and with him were his assistant and other dignitaries. The commissioner read the proclamation in both official languages, then began drawing envelopes from a ballot box and called out each number in turn. A report in the *Diamond News* of December 1954 noted that 'there was a good deal of the old-time atmosphere . . . some 374 claimants stepped forward to select their allotments.

'Many anxious and sun-burned faces surrounded the lorry, the focal point in the proceedings,' the report continued; 'and as each digger received his certificate he proceeded to select his own digging spot. Some of them ran to peg off their 45 feet square (*c 15 m square*) claims; while others merely ambled across the veld to make their choice at leisure. About 15 women were among the diggers, 200 of whom had spent the night before camped in the open.'[5] De Bruin found himself well down the field but still managed to peg an acceptable claim near 'middle blow'.

Many of the diggers involved in the Bellsbank rush admitted they were speculating. 'They intend afterwards to sell the ground pegged,' said the

Diamond News, 'as they regard it as impossible for a small digger to work.'[5] The mining commissioner had expected all the diggers to opt for claims straddling the fissure at right-angles, but not a few saw the advantage of 'diamond-shaped' claims with opposite corners pegged within the fissure. 'Such claims gave us an extra five metres,' says Pietman Selzer, who today lives at Delportshoop. 'The mining commissioner wasn't very pleased but it was all perfectly legal.'[6]

Like Danie de Bruin, Selzer grew up on river diggings and he too is a veteran of the Lichtenburg fields. A week after the Bellsbank proclamation Selzer, De Bruin and other certified diggers were allowed to peg five more claims in their own names. They were also allowed to have 12 more claims transferred to them by other diggers. Some bought, some sold, some exchanged, some went into partnership. Pietman Selzer joined forces with another experienced digger named Rodney Parker. Between them they held 12 claims and controlled nearly 300 metres of the main fissure.

Elsewhere on the diggings, men were pegging claims on the fissures that De Bruin had not explored. All proved barren except the 'Bobbejaan' or 'Baboon' fissure, so named because it was close to a ridge that was home to a baboon colony. Among those who pegged the Bobbejaan was Roelof Versluis, and Danie de Bruin was not far behind. Versluis secured a foothold on the main fissure when he bought the 13 claims that had been developed by Selzer and Parker and he later acquired 13 neighbouring claims that had been worked by Koekie Daniels.

Faan Deetlefs began working on Versluis's claims in 1958 and still manages them today. 'When I started he had five claims on the Bobbejaan and we were working them from the surface,' he recalls. 'We had a crane and we hauled ground in old oildrums fitted with handles and with the tops cut off. On the surface we had a small rotary washing plant and that was all our equipment. For weeks we found no diamonds at all, then suddenly we found a big one and we were ready to buy all Bellsbank. We worked hard because there was nothing else to do, and anyway we were on a percentage.'[7]

At Bellsbank, Danie de Bruin had followed in the footsteps of H S Richter. During 1956 he became interested in another of Richter's old haunts, the diamond pipe on Brits near Danielskuil which was closed to prospecting for precious stones. Like Richter and his partners in 1939, De Bruin obtained a licence to prospect Brits for base minerals. De Bruin says he had not previously heard of Richter's activities but he did know that Thomas Shone had found kimberlite close by, near the site of Lime Acres. He sent a veteran digger named Jan Krieg to prospect on his behalf.

Today Jan Krieg works for De Bruin on Sover fissure, and he says he spent nearly four months on Brits. 'I lived in a kaia at the edge of the pipe,' he says. 'We dug several holes there, one outside the kimberlite but the others inside. Each hole went down five metres or deeper. I also examined the old prospect pits left by Richter. But we didn't find any diamonds—I wasn't supposed to be looking for them, and anyway we didn't have a rotary pan so we couldn't try a wash. Officially we were prospecting for asbestos and the law was quite clear.'[8]

One afternoon De Bruin was in Kuruman for a meeting and met a young geologist from De Beers. 'He said: "Let's have a beer together,"' says De Bruin. 'Then he said: "What are you doing at Brits?" I said: "I'm looking for cotton (*asbestos*). I want to darn my clothes." He said: "Looking for cotton in kimberlite?" Now I was really shocked that he knew it was kimberlite. I decided I'd better stop prospecting. I belonged to the wrong political party and I thought if I continued at Brits the authorities might penalise me at Bellsbank. I realise now I was being foolish.'[4]

Jan Krieg was disgusted to hear that the Brits venture was over. 'He said he'd never prospect for me again,'[4] says De Bruin, who allowed his base minerals rights to lapse. They were quickly snapped up by Thorny Fincham of Postmasburg, who had several times joined his father in prospecting ventures. According to Syd Brownrigg, during 1950 the Finchams had for a time reopened the old Postmas diamond mine. 'But I rather suspect they already had the diamonds they supposedly pulled out of it,' said Brownrigg. 'They must have got hold of them in Namaqualand, a fairly common practice.'[9]

Fincham and his wife still ran a café in Postmasburg. At Brits, Fincham pegged three large base minerals claims but did no work on them. Instead, in 1959 he granted a twelve-month option on the claims to Willie Schwabel, a former digger and manganese assayer whose son Ernst was already prospecting for diamonds near Lime Acres. Schwabel had heard rumours of Brits's diamonds, but officially he would be looking for asbestos. Schwabel, his wife and son all moved to Brits and for several months lived in a tent.

Both Willie and Ernst Schwabel held diggers' certificates, yet they could not hope for official permission to look for diamonds on Brits until the existing Precious Stones Act was amended. Friends in the Orange Free State gave them contacts at the Department of Mines in Pretoria, but before anything was achieved Willie Schwabel's option lapsed and he and Fincham agreed to form a company and work together. Their company was registered as 'Finsch Base Minerals' to stress their joint participation, with Fincham holding 55 per cent of the shares.

Negotiations with the Department of Mines ground to a halt, so Willie Schwabel turned to an old digger acquaintance named Brahm Papendorf who lived in Johannesburg but had claims at Delportshoop.

'Willie knew I had valuable contacts,' says Papendorf. 'He said that if I could get the law changed he'd give me ten per cent of Finsch, taken out of his own shares. I went to see the secretary of mines in Pretoria and put Finsch's case, and soon the Department of Mines agreed that the law ought to be changed and it happened during the parliamentary session of 1960.'[10]

It was now possible to prospect for precious stones on state land. 'Finsch Base Minerals' gave way to 'Finsch Diamonds,' but as yet the partners had no idea whether their kimberlite pipe was payable. The Schwabels had not dared to attempt a wash and in any case they had no rotary washing pan. Papendorf borrowed a pan from a friend living near Postmasburg, and the mining commissioner was invited to travel out from Barkly West to watch the first wash. The assistant mining commissioner accompanied him and the chief of the CID diamond branch in Kimberley was there too.

'You've got to understand that at the time we were all stony broke,' says Brahm Papendorf. 'The Schwabels didn't have a cent. They were living in a scruffy kaia with a little fence around it to keep out grazing cattle. Fincham had his cafe but not much else. I was so short of cash that I'd had to ask a hotel manager in Danielskuil to let my family stay there on credit. I said I'd pay him back if we found diamonds. So we all had a great deal at stake when we began washing and there was a lot of anxiety. We had no idea what was going to happen next.'[10]

The Schwabels and Papendorfs nervously waited in the Schwabels' kaia as labourers cranked up the rotary washing pan. Fincham was watching, and so were his adopted son Bobby Campbell and the three diamond dignitaries. Campbell took charge as the first wash was sieved and turned upside down on the sorting table. That first sieveful produced two diamonds and there were three more in the second. 'Bobby brought them in to show us,' says Brahm Papendorf. 'From then on, not a sieve was blank. Within two hours of starting we'd found 26 diamonds.'[10]

Under their prospecting agreement, the three partners in Finsch Diamonds were entitled to sell the diamonds they found provided a small royalty was paid to the government. New diamonds were found daily and each man took a cut. Some of the money was invested in new equipment, some was used to hire more labourers. 'We built a hostel for the labourers and my wife and I built a log cabin for ourselves,' says Papendorf. 'We lived simply and at first my wife cooked in three-legged pots. But we weren't lonely—Lime Acres was close by and so were Danielskuil and Postmasburg.'[10]

Under instructions from the mining commissioner, the partners dug nine prospect pits to test different sections of the diamond pipe and tried sample washes from each. The commissioner wanted to proclaim a public diggings on Brits just as he had proclaimed Bellsbank. The partners had other ideas and invited Jan Haak, the deputy minister of mines, to inspect their pipe at first hand. On Haak's intervention the mining commissioner was restrained from making his proclamation and the way was opened for a full-scale diamond mine like those operated by De Beers.

Such a mine needed an investment of many millions which the partners did not possess. As they wondered what to do, they continued to prospect and recovered diamonds by hundreds of carats. 'At the end of each month we sorted what we'd found,' remembers Papendorf, the only survivor of the three partners. 'We had a sorting table the size of a bed and arranged the diamonds in rows according to category. There was one row for gemstones, another for chips, another for industrials, and so on. We took account of shape and colour and quality and we could pick them up in handfuls.'[10]

Among the partners' investments was a bulldozer that helped to heap ground for a mechanical shovel. One afternoon bystanders shouted in excitement as they saw a big diamond glint in the bulldozer's pan, only to disappear in a heap of kimberlite. A painstaking search was in vain, but next day the stone turned up in a wash. It was a diamond of prime quality and weighed 44½ carats. As Kimberley's *Diamond Field Advertiser* pointed out, Finsch Diamonds' pipedream was taking substance as a dream pipe.

Wheelbarrow Power

Escom, South Africa's Electricity Supply Commission, was erecting powerlines like tentacles reaching for communities and industries in all four provinces. Ulco had been an early customer, and by 1960 there were plans to extend Ulco's line to Postmasburg by way of Lime Acres. Gefco's Doug Todd believed that Escom should go further and route its line to Kuruman and indeed to Hotazel and Black Rock. He contacted Mike Wilson at S A Manganese and Syd Brownrigg at Associated Manganese and persuaded them to back his application. Then he wrote to Escom head office in Johannesburg asking for an appointment.

'They wouldn't even talk to me,' he said. 'Escom had recently burnt its fingers in supplying power to chrysotile asbestos mines in the Transvaal. No sooner were the lines in place than the mines closed down. Escom didn't want another fiasco. But then I persuaded Kuruman municipality to approach Escom and this time they had to agree to a meeting. A delegation of four of us went to Johannesburg and the Escom men hauled out maps and showed us the distances involved. The man in charge said Escom couldn't possibly justify the expense of erecting a line and that was that.

'Then I said: "What would it cost to put a line up there?" He said: "What do you mean?" I said: "Well, we might consider erecting a line at our own expense. But first tell me what it would cost. We can't commit ourselves until we know." The chap was completely stuck. He said: "You can't afford it." I said: "Of course we can afford it. I've got 40 engines at the Gefco mines alone." The atmosphere was quite different after that. Escom told their man in Kimberley to make calculations, and he and I worked on the project and came up with a proposition.'[11]

Doug Todd knew that the mines would be Escom's major customers while Kuruman and other communities would need only small amounts of power. It was decided to route the new powerline from mine to mine as far as Black Rock and serve Kuruman with a modest branch line. Gefco had to put up a guarantee covering 14 years' use. Before long wooden pylons were erected to carry electricity north of Postmasburg to the manganese mines, then to Bretby and the north by way of two new Gefco mines named Asbes and Mount Vera. Asbes was to be the terminus of the branch line serving Kuruman.

Asbes and Mount Vera had been prospected by Harold Pascoe and were evidence of Gefco's rapid expansion. The company was also opening new areas of Bretby and Riries and was overtaking Cape Asbestos as the leading producer of crocidolite. Tungsten carbide drills and new milling techniques were increasing productivity but Doug Todd was also introducing fresh mining methods. Rather than rely on incline shafts his mines were reaching for the asbestos horizons with twin vertical winzes that could be extended to deep levels. Such winzes were connected by horizontal crosscuts that helped ventilation and provided an escape route in case something went wrong.

In spite of the new arrangements, fibre was still hoisted to the surface in cocopans. Asbestos from the face was dropped into cocopans from a boxhole ore pass, and loaded cocopans were pushed to the bottom of the winze. Each pan was then attached to hoist chains and lifted clear of its wheels. Once on surface, it was dropped on to another set of wheels and pushed to a ramp where it was tipped over and emptied. Then the cocopan was pushed back to the winze, the pan was detached and lowered to the bottom, and it was restored to a set of wheels ready to fetch another load.

A Doug Todd innovation at Riries seemed like a step backwards but was designed to increase efficiency. 'To begin with we had used scraper winches, chevron-shaped scoops that dragged broken ore over the footwall and dumped it down an ore pass,' Todd explained. 'Unfortunately the scrapers chewed up the fibre and destroyed half our product. I decided to introduce wheelbarrows and underground sorting. One lasher loaded two wheelbarrows and while he worked the barrow handlers checked each forkful and removed the obvious waste. When the barrows were full they were pushed to the ore pass.'[11]

In many cases waste left down the mine was built into walls used to channel fresh air from the main shaft. Fans over the secondary shaft helped to suck out stale air. Todd saw no reason to leave pillars in the stopes if the horizon being worked was less than five metres high. 'It was better to remove everything,' he said. 'You could see the effect from the surface—the ground settled like a wave. But if we were working a horizon any higher than five metres then we usually left in pillars. We didn't want to cause sinkholes.'[11]

Vertical winzes and cocopan hoists were coming into use at asbestos mines run by other companies. At KCB, for instance, Sarel de Witt was extending operations on Whitebank and opening new mines on other farms. KCB did not have Gefco's capital resources and the new ventures were bold attempts to escape from debt. Mollie Franke says that KCB's underground workings broke all the rules in the book. 'We might have been excavating a cathedral, but we didn't bother with the pillars,' he says. 'Fortunately the hanging wall held and there were no disasters.'[12]

On surface, KCB's aged lorries were held together by chicken wire. Many of them had already seemed ancient when acquired from the South African Army. Now they 'rattled over corrugated roads,' says Franke, 'churning up huge clouds of white dust, and often they stood broken down along the route.'[12] A common sight on Whitebank was a black driver underneath his truck, armed with pliers and determined to nurse his load of asbestos cobs to the central mill. Franke and his staff were kept busy by outdated winches and milling machinery that had long since seen better days.

In spite of its difficulties, KCB was pioneering concepts of its own. One had been suggested by a sales associate, Frits Baunach. 'It was because of difficulties in selling very fine fibre produced at Langley,' says Franke. 'Nobody seemed to want it, but there was no problem in selling harsh fibre from Whitebank and another farm named Sardinia. Frits Baunach said that considering how tobacco and coffee companies blended their products, there was nothing to stop us blending asbestos fibre. We mixed fibres from the different mines in a rotating trommel and it worked very well.'[12]

Some time since, Langley had been sold to Turner and Newall but KCB continued to work its asbestos and paid modest royalties to the owners. These operations ceased during 1958 and KCB instead began mining on the farms Bestwell and Newstead. All fibre produced was sold to a Swiss-owned company, South African Asbestos or Asbesco for short, which had a stake in KCB and controlled its fibre shipments. In 1960 Asbesco's chairman, Ernst Schmidheiny, offered to buy KCB. The Armstrong brothers and Sarel de Witt accepted, and Percy Armstrong, De Witt and Frits Baunach were invited to sit on KCB's new board.

Sarel de Witt was still looking for asbestos on his own account, this time around Danielskuil. Helping him was Marthinus Uys, once a chrysotile asbestos prospector in the Transvaal and now owner of a Danielskuil hotel. With De Witt's backing, Uys took options on the farms Oudeplaas and Owendale where old-time tributors had worked oxidised surface deposits. De Witt was after unoxidised asbestos below. Drilling was positive, so De Witt formed a new company: Danielskuil Cape Blue Asbestos Ltd, or DCBA for short.

Several other prospectors were at work in the asbestos hills. 'We had an old chap at Danielskuil who was named Simmons,' remembers Marthinus Uys. 'He was the only man I've ever seen who was strong enough to lift another man on the back of a shovel. He lived in a little kaia called Angel's Rest and each evening he came to the hotel. One night he was walking home when he fell into a dry well. It was too deep for him to climb out so he struck a match and saw a snake lying there. He spent an uneasy night but next morning some workers found him and they pulled him to safety.

'That wasn't enough for old Simmons. He made the workers fetch a bucket and he went down into the well again and rescued the snake. He let it escape into the veld. Later we asked him why he'd done it and he said he'd made a bargain. He'd told the snake that if it didn't bite him he'd help save its life and he was honour bound to keep his promise.'[13] For a time Uys teamed up with Simmons and they located asbestos on the Groenwater native reserve. 'We tried to register claims but we were warned off,' says Uys. 'I wasn't impressed when one of the government men registered claims instead.'[13]

Mollie Franke remembers there were several prospectors active around Kuruman. 'Or rather, they weren't so much prospectors as speculators,' he says. 'They visited farmers and obtained options and then sold them. It was all very hush-hush.'[12] One of the most successful of these speculators obtained options over the farm Depression which lay close to Riries. He sold them to another former Transvaal prospector named Dave Wandrag who decided to launch a mine. Wandrag formed a company, Wandrag Asbestos, and arranged to sell his fibre to Gefco.

The asbestos mines of Kuruman and Danielskuil no longer seemed isolated, for Escom power was available and road and rail links were improving all the time. Cape Asbestos's Pomfret was another matter. Its road connections with Vryburg were little better than in Charles Stewart's time and few of Pomfret's miners were keen to brave trips into the world outside. Manie Pyper arrived at Pomfret during 1955 and found that the manager, Arthur Ackermann, ruled it as a private kingdom. Ackermann was the only *soutie* among the Northern Cape's mine managers, half-English and half-American, and he had spent many years looking for gold in Rhodesia.

'Major Ackermann was a bit eccentric,' says Pyper. 'He dressed in an old khaki helmet and a scruffy bush jacket and shorts, even when he went underground. He had a dog called Punch that never left his side. One day I was with the labourers loading cocopans at the bottom of the incline shaft and Ackermann told them to bring him an empty one. I couldn't guess what he had in mind but the shift-boss told the labourers to do as Ackermann said. They brought the cocopan and Ackermann jumped into it and so did Punch. He wanted to be winched up to the surface—the old devil was too lazy to walk.'[1]

The Matter-Horn

Telephone lines connected Northern Cape mines and farms with the rest of South Africa, but service was not always reliable. Northern Lime's Eric Lowther decided to invest in a two-way radio system to link Lime Acres quarry with Johannesburg. 'At first they kept the receiver at head office,' remembers Elsie Lowther. 'But it didn't work very well because of traffic interference. Eric brought it to our home in the suburbs and I became the operator. If something was to be done, the office telephoned me and I called up the mine and passed on instructions or asked for information.'[14]

The arrangement continued until Northern Lime applied for a telex link. Meanwhile, increasing demand for lime meant that the Lime Acres plant was producing at capacity. By 1958 three large rotary kilns were in service, and together they produced half as much again as the 22 old vertical kilns at Taungs. The works' best customers were uranium extraction plants. Original plans had called for four such plants but by 1960 there were 17 of them, processing slimes from 26 separate gold mines. The boom was a response to sudden demand for uranium stockpiles in Britain and the United States.

In charge at Lime Acres was J K E Douglas, a former Taungs works manager who had helped design the new plant. During the early 1950s he and Eric Lowther had travelled in the United States to study lime-burning techniques and decide on strategy. The Lime Acres township had not expanded beyond its original four streets but it now included a primary school and a recreation club. Anyone seeking diversion had only to visit Finsch Diamonds on the hillside overlooking the quarry. The kimberlite pipe was two kilometres from the limeworks and the washing plant was clearly visible.

Union Lime's Ulco had close connections with the diamond world too, and several Ulco employees worked Delportshoop river claims as a sideline. Ulco had settled down after the frenzied construction period and the new cement factory was in full stride. The limeworks was expanding too and two new lime kilns had been commissioned. Meanwhile, Ulco engineers found their kilns could be fed with larger stones than they were designed to burn and that improved their output. At the same time the hydrator plant was altered to produce new grades of hydrated lime.

Ulco's manager, Lu Matter, and his wife were keen naturalists and were determined to beautify Ulco's unpromising surroundings. 'We needed yet more trees,' wrote Matter before his death in 1982: 'hundreds of trees that would stand up to the drought years. We already had a good many indigenous species like swarthaak, withaak, wag-'n-bietjie and soetdoring and those we left where they were. We trimmed them and protected them and it was an unforgivable offence to cut one down or even to damage one without justification.'[15] The Matters took special interest in the 'location' where black families lived.

During the 1950s, Ulco's cement factory was absorbing about 60 per cent of the stone blasted in the quarry but it was of lower grade than the stone required for the lime kilns. Surplus limestone ready for the cement factory was heaped in a dump that Ulco wags called the Matter-horn, after Switzerland's famous mountain. To save on dynamite, quarrymen experimented with new methods of blasting. In one period they tried tunnelling ten or 12 metres into the base of the cliffs and drilling from the bottom up. Results were not impressive and they reverted to drilling from the top.

About 150 km away, the iron ore miners of Sishen now had six large drills at work, and four powerful excavators shovelled broken ore into ten heavy trucks. During 1957 L F Vorster had left Sishen and had been succeeded as manager by Justus van der Hoven, trained as a gold miner but fresh from Thabazimbi. Iscor now wanted Sishen to produce ore for its Pretoria works as well as for Vanderbijlpark, which meant filling more than 100 rail trucks every day. Van der Hoven decided to split his workforce into two shifts. In the mine, Jan Kotze ran one shift and Mike Pauer ran the other.

'With Van der Hoven in charge, our mine really began to go,' says Mike Pauer. 'Before, we'd been working detrital ore and outcrops. Now we were ready to mine the main ore body lower down. To reach it we had to remove a big tonnage of waste including gravel and shale and sand. The main ore body was thick and once we'd made a hole in it our blasts sliced it like a cake.'[16] Sishen's mechanisation meant that relatively few men worked in the mine and that made the four Van Staden brothers even more noticeable. Jaap was a miner, Piet drove an excavator and Hans and Joost drove trucks.

Meanwhile, Sishen's original 'dry' ore handling plant had been converted into a 'wet' plant that washed ore and allowed blenders to produce consistent grades as required by Iscor's mills. There were changes in Sishen township as well. By 1960 it contained 130 houses with a general store, clinic, primary school and church. The mine's recreation club had a swimming-pool, rugby field, tennis courts, bowling greens and a jukskei pitch. There were electric streetlights and well-watered gardens beside the houses, and housewives drew eggs, milk and meat from an Iscor farm.

Sishen's iron ore was railed south to Postmasburg, south-east to Kimberley, then north-east to Vanderbijlpark and Pretoria. Manganore's iron ore was bound for Amcor's plants in the Transvaal and Natal and Amcor itself was preparing to begin mining at Lylyveld, two farms away from Sishen. Associated Manganese held rights on the farm Bruce which separated Lylyveld from Sishen but as yet had no plans to mine there. Instead, during 1958 Associated Manganese had begun mining haematite on Beeshoek—the first time Beeshoek had been worked since the demise of Manganese Corporation.

'We started with three miners and about 60 labourers,' says Dirk Bleeker who was mine captain at Beeshoek and still lives there today. 'We began by digging out detrital ore and then blasted solid deposits in the kopjes. The ore was loaded into cocopans and pushed to stacks. Each cocopan was manned by two labourers who were paid by the number of loads they handled. Each team laid its own tramlines and worked where it felt it could make the most money. The ore was treated at a plant near the Associated Manganese offices and as required it was railed to Port Elizabeth.'[17]

Beeshoek was coming into its stride at a time of far-reaching political change. At the heart of it was the prime minister, Hendrik Verwoerd, who wanted to sever South Africa's constitutional ties with Britain or rather with the British sovereign as head of state. Fifty years after Union, South Africans voted in a referendum to decide their future. Natal was against Verwoerd's proposals but the other three provinces were behind him. During March 1961 Verwoerd terminated South Africa's membership of the British Commonwealth, and a few weeks later the nation became a republic.

CHAPTER EIGHT 1961–1968

Shafts and Winzes

SAREL DE WITT was ready to begin mining asbestos near Danielskuil but needed financial backing. During 1961 he contacted Ernst Schmidheiny of Asbesco, the Swiss company that had bought KCB a year earlier. 'Asbesco wanted to see me in Switzerland,' says De Witt, 'so I flew to Europe and attended a big meeting with 24 people around the table. I was a little apprehensive because I knew how the Swiss do business. One man is watching your left eye, another your right, and two more watch your lips and your nose. I sat beside Schmidheiny and tried not to show what I was thinking.

'I listened carefully while everyone talked, but as we proceeded I made notes on the back of a cardboard cigarette box. At that time I smoked Peter Stuyvesant. When my notes were ready I handed the box to Schmidheiny. He read the notes, then took a pen and signed at the bottom. He asked: "Can this be our contract?" Now we were negotiating in millions. He asked me to sign, then he made a photostat of the back of the Peter Stuyvesant box and gave it back to me. That's how I raised the money to launch DCBA and I still have the box today.'[1]

DCBA's drilling programme had outlined several blocks of asbestos under the farms Owendale and Oudeplaas. Each block contained several asbestos horizons superimposed on one another but they were treated as a single ore body and coded 01, 02, 03 and so on depending on when the block had been discovered. To see what they might be like, the DCBA men asked for permission to visit Warrendale mine which lay only a few kilometres away. Consolidated Blue Asbestos had sold Warrendale to Cape Asbestos, and the new owners were developing sections of the mine not previously explored.

Among the first miners recruited by DCBA was Corrie Pieterse, who had gone to school in Postmasburg and was later trained as a gold miner in the Orange Free State. During 1960 he spent a few months with Associated Manganese, but he arrived at Owendale in time to help sink DCBA's first shafts. 'That's what we asbestos miners call them, but in mining law they're too narrow to be shafts so they're known as vertical winzes,' says Pieterse, who later became mine captain at Owendale. 'Typically a winze measures two or three metres one way by a metre or two the other.

'At Owendale we decided to begin with the 02 ore body and our strategy was to sink twin winzes about 100 metres apart, then connect them with a footwall crosscut. That's a standard arrangement—if you're to have more than 50 people working underground, you must have a two-shaft system to provide an adequate ventilation circuit and an emergency escape route. We sank the winzes ourselves and sited them just outside the ore body. We bypassed four horizons and developed our footwall crosscut just underneath the bottom one, so that we could use it as a haulage for our cocopans.'[2]

The next step was to blast a series of boxholes sloping upwards to make contact with the various horizons. Some of the boxholes would serve as ore passes, some as travelling ways. Now 02's miners were ready to tunnel horizontal drives across the paths of the horizons, linking the twin shafts like the rungs of a ladder. Later they would blast chambers or stopes in the ore body but the drive would be left intact as a travelling way. Broken rock would be dropped down the ore passes to be loaded into cocopans in the footwall crosscut, then trammed to the bottom of the hoist.

That was the pattern in all the Northern Cape's asbestos mines during the 1960s, as can be seen from Harold Pascoe's article *Asbestos Fever.* 'Progress has been considerable,' wrote the man who had opened Bretby and Riries. 'Some of the deposits now being worked are upwards of seven metres in thickness on a low dip and it is now regular practice to lay out a complete system of footwall drives and boxhole ore passes before stoping begins.'[3] According to Pascoe, stoping often took the form of removing horizontal slices from the ore body, a method known as 'longwall cut and fill'.

After a blast, three-man teams of a lasher and two sorters loaded fibre and waste rock attached to it into wheelbarrows. Remaining waste rock was supposed to be left underground, but inevitably much escaped. Even so, the underground sorting greatly reduced the amount of rock that had to be hoisted to the surface and put through the mill. Yet more

32. A miniature locomotive hauls a 'train' of cocopans on rails laid at the Gloucester manganese mine.

Associated Manganese

33. Jackhammer drills introduced in place of hand-held jumpers led to dramatic improvements in productivity.

Associated Manganese

34. Black rock goes trackless: a front-end loader is lowered down the main shaft of the northernmost manganese mine.

Associated Manganese

35. A triple-boom hydraulic drill penetrates the working face at the fully mobilised Mamatwan manganese mine.

Tony Cox

36. At Lohatlha, cocopans have given way to trucks and mechanised conveyor systems.

Humphry Clinker

waste was intercepted by a team of hand-sorters attached to the mills. In several cases these surface teams consisted of women, many of them former hand-cobbers or their daughters who were heirs to a deep-rooted tradition.

Following a blast, a certain amount of broken rock was retained in the stope. This served as a platform for men drilling holes ready to bring down the next slice of the ore body. Meanwhile, waste rock was stacked high to make packs strong enough to carry the hanging wall. All asbestos-carrying fibre was tipped down ore passes. 'In this manner virtually no asbestos is lost,' wrote Pascoe, 'though continual checking is necessary to ensure that no recoverable long fibre is discarded into the waste packs.'[3] By the time Pascoe wrote, there was growing demand for short fibre too.

Crocidolite made up only a small proportion of the world's supply of asbestos, but as the hardest and toughest variety its popularity was out of proportion. In earlier years most of it had been spun as asbestos cloth or sprayed as an insulant. 'Asbestos is now used for multitudinous purposes,' reported Pascoe, 'for reinforcing concrete in roofing sheets and pressure pipes, for reinforcing plastics in battery boxes, for sound and heat insulation and fire protection. . . . New uses will be discovered as long as the peculiar properties of the mineral enable it to remain economically superior to similar artificial products.'[3]

There had been changes in processing asbestos. 'Hand cobbing followed by crude tromelling has been superseded by complete mechanical milling,' wrote Pascoe. 'The ore is partially sorted underground, where waste is vitally important for packing and providing roof support, is trammed to the surface, allowed to dry in the open air, and then taken to the mill. The ore is then crushed and resorted, put through secondary crushers, either cone or disc or hammermill type; the asbestos is sucked off by fans at all stages and goes through special cleaning processes before final bagging.

'The fines are put through fast running disintegrators and the asbestos is then further cleaned by aspiration and tromelling until almost the last vestiges of grit and dust have been removed. Frequent tests are made to ensure regular quality, in particular for wood contamination from underground props and packs.'[3] Gefco's Simon Spies explains that aspiration worked like a vacuum cleaner. 'After going through the crushers the fibre was light and fluffy,' he says. 'The aspirator was gentle enough to suck up the fibre while leaving heavier particles of grit and rock that were then treated as waste.'[4]

As yet none of the asbestos mining companies understood the dangers of asbestosis, a disease caused by inflammation of the lungs after inhaling asbestos fibres no matter how small. Underground asbestos dust was dampened by water used to cool jackhammers, but on surface dry dust flew freely. 'Some machines had so much dust coming out that you couldn't see the operator,' says Simon Spies. 'We didn't know any better. One especially bad area was the bagging table. The table had a number of big round holes drilled into it and the bags hung underneath. The fibre to be bagged was dropped into the middle of the table.

'Six or seven baggers worked at the table. They pulled fibre from the pile and stuffed it down the holes. To pack the fibre into the bags they pushed at it with stampers, heavy iron tubes with blunt ends. When the bag was full it was stitched by hand—all very primitive, but we thought it was clever. Then in 1962 someone invented the screw bagger, not for asbestos but for other products. We thought we could adapt it so we experimented and eventually came up with something like a sausage machine with the screw going round and round and disgorging asbestos into a bag at the end.'[4]

By 1962 Gefco had been in existence for 35 years, or 67 years if one counts its earlier career as the South African Saltpetre Company. All this time it had been controlled by a board of directors based in London. Nora Pascoe describes Gefco's old headquarters as 'dark, dismal, low-ceilinged, squalid, electric light necessary all day, and fabulously expensive and sought after, being in the City'.[5] There was a change when the directors accepted a takeover bid from a new South African mining house, Federale Mynbou, that was later to merge with the old gold-mining house of General Mining.

Gefco was now the leading producer of crocidolite. Besides its own asbestos it was milling fibre produced by Wandrag Asbestos on the farms Depression and England. KCB still concentrated on Whitebank and was operating on two other farms as well. DCBA was sinking shafts on Oudeplaas and the small Groenwater mine was in production near Postmasburg. Warrendale still belonged to Cape Asbestos though there were plans to sell it to DCBA. Cape Asbestos was still mining at Koegas–Westerberg and Pomfret and in several Transvaal locations as well.

Many of the asbestos miners and their families lived in asbestos villages like Pomfret, Koegas, Riries and Bretby. KCB's men lived in Kuruman, and Wandrag and Warrendale had a few houses apiece. In its earliest days DCBA transported its miners from Danielskuil on the back of a lorry. Then Sarel de Witt decided to build a few houses on Owendale for DCBA's mine manager, secretary and engineer. The houses were a great success, so De Witt erected a whole village. To design it he called on his sister Lena Marshall who had experience of landscaping in Kuruman.

Owendale's village was sited on rising ground opposite the mine, with its back to the asbestos hills that separated it from Warrendale and Lime Acres. Lena Marshall had a flair for planning and her village remains one of the Northern Cape's delights. Every house has a view and there is space on every side. The only drawback in the original plan was the siting of the airstrip, which aimed at the centre of Owendale like an arrow approaching its target. Each day De Witt flew to Owendale from Kuruman. As they heard him landing, Owendale housewives raced to rescue washing from their lines for otherwise it would have been coated in dust.

The Milk Run

One of the prides of Hotazel village is the mine manager's residence, a two-storied mansion based on Britain's 'house of the year' of 1959. Mike Wilson's wife spotted the design in a magazine and S A Manganese's directors agreed to build it for her. Her husband was still responsible for all the company's mines and to reach them had the services of a twin-engined Piper Comanche. His 'milk run' to Lohatlha paralleled Associated Manganese's regular route between Beeshoek and Black Rock. The old Rapide had been retired in 1957 and Associated Manganese men now used a De Havilland Beaver.

The little Beaver provided a fine view of the many mines now operating on the manganese belt. Rust-red dust clouds marked the position of iron ore handling plants at Beeshoek and Manganore. Gloucester and Lohatlha boasted deep canyons where manganese had been stripped way to expose ancient cliffs of limestone. Sishen's iron ore mine was an expanding hole in the flat veld around it and to the north lay the abandoned workings of Smartt manganese mine. Associated Manganese was developing Devon and Perth next door, and National Manganese had opened Langdon Annex.

Perhaps the most remarkable sight was Black Rock kopje, which from the air looked like a giant blackened tooth with a gaping cavity reaching to its roots. Most of Black Rock's workings were underground, but at Hotazel to the south all were exposed to view. Giant scrapers had removed the sand cover, huge excavators were biting into limestone overburden, and beneath the white and yellow was the black of manganese. Even that was not the final goal, for S A Manganese's purpose in opening Hotazel was to reach a lower ore body containing manganese suitable for smelting ferro-manganese.

Before opening Hotazel, Mike Wilson and a colleague had travelled widely to inspect open-cast techniques used in North America and Europe. In the United States they had been out of luck, for at the time of their visit miners were on strike. But they did see iron ore workings in Canada and Sweden. Hotazel was to be mined along similar lines, each layer of rock stepped back in a series of benches to provide access to the lowest parts of the ore body without risking rockfalls from above. Each bench was up to 20 metres high and a strict 60 metres wide.

An account of typical open-cast mining methods is included in an unpublished draught of S A Manganese's official history. 'With most open-cast mines the mining engineer first collects all the data he can on the ore body, then weighs them against the amount of overburden he has to remove to reach it,' says the draught. 'He has to calculate the optimum slope angle—the degree of incline from the surface to the ore body, not so steep that the overburden will fall in and bury the mine, not so shallow that he is removing too much overburden and wasting potential profits.

'He is left with the overall stripping ratio—the ideal balance between overburden and ore body which will influence all operations down the mine. So much for the preliminary calculations. With the overall stripping ratio settled, the mining engineer can plan the successive "benches" which eat into the overburden like steps. These benches are horizontal or nearly so, and their main purpose is to act as catchnets when the levels immediately above them are blasted.'[6] Ideally, benches keep pace with one another and are blasted in succession.

'The rock falls on to the flat surface of the bench,' continues the draft, 'and is easily scooped up by power shovels or front-end loaders, and transferred to trucks which carry it to the waste tip. The width of a bench is termed the "lead", which again is calculated exactly; and so are the vertical "longwalls" between benches, which are also the working faces though the blasting holes are drilled from above.'[6] In most cases these holes are overdrilled by ten per cent to make sure no hump is left on the bench as a result of uneven blasting.

At Hotazel, S A Manganese's engineers made allowance for seven separate benches and for an incline roadway that spiralled from bottom to top. The highest bench consisted of fine-grained Kalahari sand cover that was removed by a bucket wheel excavator, a series of scoops mounted on an endless belt that revolved on a swivelling boom. Sand was transferred to a conveyor belt that transported it to a distant dune. Under the sand was a deep layer of limestone, and below that the upper manganese ore body which contained too much iron for Amcor's purposes so was reserved for export.

The upper ore body was seven metres thick. Underneath it were 27 metres of banded ironstone that were more than a match for S A Manganese's drills and seriously slowed the mine's productivity. The low-iron manganese needed by Amcor lay under the banded ironstone, and to Mike Wilson's disgust there were blobs of ironstone within the ore body that destroyed its consistency and greatly reduced its value. Amcor complained, and S A Manganese was forced to look for yet another source of low-iron manganese. Fortunately the company still had options over 18 farms, and the most promising of these were Mamatwan and Goold which lay south of Smartt.

As a vital preliminary to any mining, S A Manganese ordered a full exploration of Mamatwan with diamond drills. By coincidence, at the same time Associated Manganese was opening a mine on Adams, the farm next door. Adams's ore was the same as Mamatwan's and S A Manganese watched closely as the rival company removed sand and limestone to expose the manganese beneath. Before long S A Manganese was ready to follow suit and began mining an area next to Mamatwan's boundary with Adams. Only a pillar separated the two operations, as prescribed in mining regulations.

The attraction of the ore body mined on Adams and Mamatwan was its high ratio of manganese to iron. The actual percentage of manganese in the ore was relatively low. 'When first explored Mamatwan's ore body had been dismissed as hopeless,' says S A Manganese's draught history. 'Leslie Boardman had persuaded the owner of the farm, an elderly man named Duvenhage, to grant S A Manganese an option—not so much because he thought the farm would make a mine as that he considered it valuable insurance.'[6] Duvenhage had been more sanguine, forecasting that Mamatwan would be the biggest mine of all.

The prediction was coming true. The exploratory drilling programme had covered only a small part of Mamatwan, enough to meet immediate requirements. It would have astonished S A Manganese to learn that later drilling would reveal an ore body stretching for at least 40 kilometres and possibly much further. 'The main part of the ore body is on average 19 metres thick,' says S A Manganese's history, 'solid manganese with only very tiny intrusions to disturb the effect. Visiting geologists and mining men shake their heads in wonder, for in mining terms Mamatwan is near-perfect.'[6]

Beneath the main ore body was a shallow layer of banded ironstone, and beneath that a metre or two of higher grade manganese that was to be mined separately. Adams mine's share of the ore body was limited, not more than half of a bubble-shaped extrusion that crept into surrounding formations like a peninsula. S A Manganese mined its half of the bubble, then tackled the isthmus of manganese that led to the flat veld beyond a high kopje of ironstone. On top of the kopje S A Manganese established a blasting platform that commanded a bird's eye view of the whole of Mamatwan and several neighbouring farms as well.

'From the height of the control box activity in the huge hole seems to move at the pace of the snail,' says the S A Manganese draught. 'The great trucks look like toys from that height, labouring up the graded access roads with 50 tons of waste rock or 35 of manganese. Men are like matchsticks, power shovels like novelty nutcrackers, drilling rigs like marker pegs. Even the noise is barely audible—though down in the mine it is so loud you can barely hear yourself speak. The sun shines nearly all the year. Mamatwan can be Hotazel too, though there is often a pleasant breeze.'[6]

In its early days, Mamatwan was worked in two shifts. White miners drove or were bussed from Hotazel but their leading hands and labourers lived in a hostel close to the open pit. Some were assigned to removing the overburden with power shovels and the larger trucks; others tackled the ore body with front-end loaders, a more crucial task in that those concerned always had to remember what the customer wanted. The shift-boss told his miners what grades he needed, and each of them had to act as his own geologist.

A handful of those at Mamatwan manned the drilling rigs that produced lines of holes along the edge of benches to be blasted. When a hole was finished it was marked with white paint and left like that until needed. Then a miner filled each hole with nitrate solution, connected up his fuses and wired them to the blasting point on top of the hill. Mamatwan blasted twice a day, at 12 noon and four o'clock in the afternoon. At blasting time all personnel had to clear the mine, and the miner took up his station behind the control cabin.

'Red flags fly,' records the S A Manganese draught history, 'and when all is ready the miner connects his wires, and . . . marvel!!! A great black cloud bounces into the air, thick black dust and hundreds of tons of broken rock spinning high above the mine and for a moment poised in mid-air before it falls back towards the ground. And only then comes the bang, a shock even when you are expecting it, somehow remote from the cloud which you have seen go up in silence.'[6] Gradually the debris settled, and when the red flags came down Mamatwan's relentless progress could resume.

Crocodile Crush

While James de Kock and his labourers were clearing the site of Ulco during 1935, a thunderstorm struck and they took refuge in a cave. As De Kock's daughter Lydia Swartz tells the story, 'all of a sudden they heard strange cries that sounded like "Oh God! Oh God!" They didn't know what it could be until there was a rush of bodies and a whole troop of baboons came running at them and scrambled through their legs to escape. I don't know who were more frightened, the baboons or the men. I do know that every one of them ran away and my father was left by himself.'[7]

Ulco's baboons seem to take a dim view of the miners' invasion of their territory. Charles Langeveld reports that when quarrying began, the baboons liked to perch on the cliffs and pelt rocks at those working below. But the miners were at Ulco to stay, and so were the baboons. Gradually the two groups came to respect one another. Baboons became frequent visitors to the mine hostel and to the location as well. On one occasion a baboon found his way into the room where the labourers' beer was kept and drank himself into a stupor.

'By the time the hostel manager found him, he was dead drunk and glassy-eyed,' recorded Lu Matter. 'They locked him in a storeroom and kept him there till he was sober. Then they let him go with a stern warning.'[8] The baboon troop remains one of Ulco's special attractions, and another is the visits of high-jumping kudus found all through the district. Quite frequently, kudus approach the hostel and location and some jump the high fence guarding the quarry. A favourite haunt of the kudus is 'the kloof', a gorge cutting into the Ghaap Plateau that has been set aside as a private nature reserve.

In the 1960s there were constant modifications at Ulco as managers experimented with new methods. One new 'toy' that delighted visitors was a heavy breaker's ball used in the quarry. Before, rocks too large to be loaded into lorries had been broken up by mud blasting. With the new method, a crane swung the breaker's ball against rocks and smashed them in a fraction of the time. Another of Ulco's spectacles was the daily blast, when a succession of dynamite cartridges exploded one after another along the line of the cliff and rock tumbled to destruction.

Limestone ready for loading was scooped up by mechanical shovels and dropped into the old reinforced semi-trailers acquired in 1948. The semi-trailers' pans took heavy punishment and were replaced as necessary, but under Charles Langeveld's care their chassis were as good as new. The trailers' horses parked them beside a jaw crusher, where a derrick hooked on to a pan's outside rim and tipped its load sideways. Rock cascaded into the mouth of the jaw crusher and its steel plates chewed the limestone into small lumps. Black workers knew such crushers as 'crocodiles'.

In earlier days, rock intended for the cement factory came from one part of the quarry while limestone intended for the limeworks came from another. Now the quarry was more sophisticated and high and low grades of limestone were produced together. From the crusher, the broken rock dropped on to a conveyor belt that carried it past a line of hand-sorters. Low-grade stone was left on the belt and proceeded on to storage silos attached to the cement factory. But high-grade lumps were picked out by the sorters and dropped down chutes to be classified by size and fed to the limeworks.

'By high-grade limestone, we mean rock with a calcium carbonate content of 95 per cent or higher,' says Theo Cloete, a former assistant production manager at Ulco. 'The limeworks need 40 per cent of the rock we produce, the cement factory takes the remainder. Different parts of the quarry hold different grades of limestone but we organise our quarrying programme so that we maintain a 40–60 ratio. In the lime kilns, the high-grade stone is mixed with anthracite and we aim to burn off all its carbon dioxide. We're left with lime and we sell it unslaked or hydrated.'[9]

At Buxton and Lime Acres, Northern Lime had no use for low-grade limestone and consigned it to dumps. The Buxton deposit was nearing exhaustion but Lime Acres was going from strength to strength in spite of a serious setback. In opening Lime Acres, Northern Lime had believed that its limestone beds were virtually free of impurities, but in reality they were interrupted by beds of chert and dolomite. 'Our ore body was turning out to be a Dagwood sandwich,' says John Wotherspoon, now quarry manager at Northern Lime. 'Some layers we wanted, others we had to discard as useless.'[10]

Lime Acres quarrymen reconciled themselves to having to remove large tonnages of waste. 'We settled down to a ratio of 1,6 tons of waste to each ton of high-grade limestone,' says Wotherspoon. 'Our operation was less profitable than expected, but the rising demand for lime soon made up the difference. The ore body dipped at a gentle angle and we decided to work it in benches. We had drilling rigs and mechanical shovels and two fleets of trucks. One fleet consisted of side-tipping lorries that carried high-grade limestone to the crushers; the other carried waste to our dumps.'[10]

An interesting picture of operations at Lime Acres comes from a booklet put out by Northern Lime, which explains that to make one ton of lime, 2,1 tons of closely graded limestone are fed to the kilns. 'Due to wastage in the crushing and screening process, one ton of graded limestone requires 1,5 tons of run-of-quarry limestone,' says the booklet. 'To obtain one ton of run-of-quarry limestone, it is necessary to remove 1,4 tons of overburden. Each ton of lime sold therefore calls for 7,5 tons to be quarried.'[11] Following crushing, the limestone is screened into four sizes.

The four grades are stored on four stockpiles. When required, explains the booklet, 'stone is removed from the stockpiles by means of belt conveyors operating in an underground recovery tunnel'.[11] Some of the limestone is loaded straight into rail trucks for despatch to customers. The remainder is fed to the kilns. Lime Acres's first rotary kiln was commissioned in 1954, its second and third in 1956, a fourth in 1968. Numbers five, six and seven came into use during 1972, 1977 and 1979, and number eight during 1980. Each kiln is all but horizontal, a lengthy tube with one end a few metres higher than the other.

At Lime Acres, says the booklet, 'limestone is accurately measured into the kiln at the feed end. Due to the rotating motion and the slope, the limestone gradually works its way down the kiln, cascading and uniformly absorbing heat as it does so. It takes about 2,5 hours for material to pass through a kiln.'[11] At Ulco and Buxton, limestone was burnt or 'calcined' in vertical kilns and normally needed two *days* to pass from top to bottom. Apart from the speed advantage, Northern Lime's rotary kilns scored in that they could be 'tuned' to produce particular grades of lime.

'The heat source is pulverised coal,' continues the booklet. 'Approximately 0,34 tons of coal are required to produce one ton of lime. In the hottest zone of the kiln the temperature reaches around 1 200 °C. After its discharge from the kilns, the lime passes through coolers before being elevated into storage silos. From the silos some 80 per cent of the lime is conveyed to the loading plant where screening and loading into railway trucks takes place. The balance of the lime passes to a grinding plant where it is reduced by a hammermill and emerges as ground lime.

'The calcining process is a continuous one and the kilns run 24 hours a day, seven days a week. Runs average about 30 days, although periods of two months are not uncommon. Kiln stoppages are caused occasionally by refractory failures or mechanical problems, but the most common cause is ash ring, a deposition on the refractory lining caused by the ash in the coal combining with the lime dust.'[11] Most of the ground lime produced by the hammermills is loaded out in rail tank wagons, but a small proportion serves as feed for the hydrating plant.

'In the hydrator plant,' says the booklet, 'unslaked lime is reacted with water under closely controlled conditions, to produce calcium hydroxide, or hydrated lime, in dry powder form. The hydrated lime then passes through an air separator which removes coarse particles. The fine powder is pumped to a silo from which it is loaded into rail tank wagons or packed into paper sacks.'[11] John Wotherspoon points out that unslaked lime travelling in rail trucks must be well protected from rainfall. 'If it isn't,' he says, 'the lime will react and twist the truck into a tangle of metal.'[10]

Limestone is classified as an industrial mineral, and so is salt which in the Northern Cape has a long history. As early as 1805 Hinrich Lichtenstein noticed a large saltpan south of the Orange River, quite possibly the one now exploited by Sulpura saltworks. Several other pans exist in the region and there are many more in Gordonia north of Upington. The largest of all is the Loch Marie deposit of Gordonia which has a circumference of 24 kilometres. At Loch Marie, the pan is covered by a crust of salt a metre thick and underneath is a concentrate of brine.

At Sulpura and elsewhere, salt producers 'mine' by pumping brine into large paddocks each walled with salt. The Northern Cape's everlasting sunshine evaporates water from the brine and leaves salt of remarkable purity. Reports published in the 1940s estimated that the Northern Cape produced 80 per cent of all the salt mined in South Africa and that is still the case today.

Treasure Trove Diamonds was a company registered in Kimberley and active on the Sover diamond fissure. Treasure Trove had been founded during the 1920s to work alluvial claims on the Lichtenburg fields and had bought claims at Sover after individual diggers had reached 'blue ground' too hard to be worked with picks and shovels. Then in 1961 a group of Kimberley shareholders rebelled against the directors and after a series of stormy meetings won control of the company. Their plan was to sell the Sover workings and use the money to reopen the old West End pipe at Postmasburg.

The rebel shareholders elected a new board of directors and put Sover on the market. They called for tenders, and among those who responded was Danie de Bruin of Bellsbank. 'I put in a tender for R101 000,' says De Bruin. 'I thought the mine was worth R100 000 and the extra R1 000 would clinch it for me. There were plenty of diamonds at Sover but Treasure Trove had been robbed blind. I heard that a fellow who'd been managing the mine for them left with the wherewithal to buy hotels and farms in the Transvaal. No wonder the shareholders were so dissatisfied.'[12]

Cash in hand, Treasure Trove descended on Postmasburg. West End was half-full of water, but before pumping it out the directors decided to sink a shaft beside the open hole and probe the kimberlite with a crosscut. As manager they appointed Obie Oberholzer, who when the shaft reached a depth of 130 metres called in Dirk Bleeker as part-time surveyor. 'I was still working for Associated Manganese as mine captain at Beeshoek,' says Bleeker. 'But I was glad to help out in the evenings after finishing work. Oberholzer and I went down the mine and he held my tape measure for me.'[13]

The crosscut was being driven only a few metres below the bottom of West End's open pit. Oberholzer realised that the rock might cave in and dump millions of litres of water into the workings. 'He cut the hanging wall in an inverted V-shape,' remembers Bleeker. 'That minimised the chance of a rockburst.'[13] Fortunately all went well and the crosscut was completed. Sample washes showed that the kimberlite was payable and the company pumped out the water. On the bottom were picks, shovels, old cocopans and a skeleton.

By mid-1964 Treasure Trove was ready to go into production and the directors were confident. An article in the Johannesburg *Star* quoted 'Mr V Markantonis, a director of the company', who said that 'a considerable amount of automation will be employed at the new mine—especially in the security measures. The ore will not be touched from the time it is mined to the time the diamonds are recovered.'[14] A high security fence was being put up around West End's perimeter, and a headgear was being erected to hoist skips of kimberlite from workings far below.

Postmasburg had been starved of diamond fever for three decades but it was currently receiving a double dose. The West End aside, Thorny Fincham's Finsch kimberlite pipe was a success and the great De Beers Consolidated Mines of Kimberley was taking an interest in it. 'At first they hadn't bothered with us,' says Brahm Papendorf. 'One geologist said there was so much banded ironstone about that there couldn't possibly be much kimberlite. If we were finding a lot of diamonds, then we must be salting the pipe—bringing them in from other sources. But every month we found more.

'De Beers began sending senior chaps to see us. Eventually they asked us to give them an option to prospect. That was in 1962. They said they might want to buy the pipe, but it would depend on what they found. They brought in two great boring machines that punched holes 1,5 metres across and used them to sink 78 prospect pits over a systematic grid. They also sank five proper prospect shafts and brought in a diamond drill to follow the rim of the pipe and see if the sides were vertical. All this kept them busy for about nine months.

'As part of the prospecting agreement De Beers took a large tonnage of our kimberlite to Kimberley and washed it to see if it was payable. In the end they were satisfied that Finsch was something special and told us: "Come to the Kimberley Club." They had a big feast for us, and they said they wanted to buy. Fincham, Schwabel and I were there and so were the De Beers general manager and mine secretary and a lot of other big shots including some of the directors—I don't remember exactly who. The waiters treated us like kings and there was one at my shoulder all through the meal.

'At one stage we three partners had some idea of what we wanted for the pipe, but as yet nobody from De Beers had mentioned a price. That soon changed. Negotiations began at De Beers head office in Stockdale Street in Kimberley, in the old board room there. De Beers had two very tough negotiators—it was impossible to win any concessions from them. The negotiations took several days, but every so often there was a break and the De Beers people took us into a long room that was filled with drink from end to end. There were wonderful snacks too, caviar, salmon, everything.'[15]

Papendorf says that he and Schwabel were not keen to sell the Finsch pipe to De Beers and wanted to mine it themselves. 'But Fincham insisted,' he says. 'He had the majority shareholding and there was nothing we could do.'[15] Papendorf received ten per cent of the cash price and he and his wife moved to Johannesburg where they live today. Willie Schwabel received 35 per cent and he and his wife went to Cape Town. Fincham's share was R2,5 million and after a few years in Postmasburg he bought back The Grange near Hopetown, the farm his father lost after floods had ruined his salt mine.

During 1964 De Beers opened the Finsch pipe and erected a treatment and recovery plant beside it. The mine was to be an open pit with its benches stepped in 13–metre intervals. Blasting holes were drilled on the rims of the benches, 15 metres deep and at a slight angle to the vertical. After a blast, explained a De Beers publication, 'the broken ore is fed by either a mechanical shovel or front-end loaders into a fleet of dump trucks which carry it to the treatment plant. Another fleet of dump trucks is removing country rock from the sidewalls.

'At the treatment plant the ore is first screened, crushed to below 3,5 cm and then passed to the washing plant which concentrates the heavier materials, including diamonds, and rejects the waste. The crushed materials are mixed with a muddy liquid ("puddle") in a series of washing pans and agitated by rakes. The density of the puddle causes the lighter materials to float off, while the diamonds and other heavier concentrates sink to the bottom, are drawn off and fed into storage bins in the recovery section. The lighter materials are either re-circulated through the pans or passed to a tailings dump, according to size.

'In the recovery section the concentrates pass through a magnetic separator, which removes any remaining pieces of banded ironstone, and are then screened and passed to one of two sink and float circuits, which use a ferro-silicon suspension media to control the density of the mixture. The plus-0,7 cm concentrates are passed to a heavy media cone, the smaller sizes to a heavy media cyclone. The light materials again float off and pass to the tailings dump as waste, while the heavier concentrates are drawn off for treatment in attrition mills, which remove fine coatings of foreign matter adhering to the diamonds.

'The concentrates are sized before passing through rotating drums containing an adhesive reagent which coats the surfaces of most of the refractory diamonds (*which have a natural surface coating that prevents them from sticking to grease belts*). The concentrates then pass to grease-coated belts, to which the diamonds and some concentrates stick. The larger concentrates from the grease belts are finally scrutinised by colour-sorting machines to remove further waste, while the smaller sizes are fed into mills which grind away much of the softer materials, thus reducing the volume of the concentrates.

'Tailings flowing over the grease belts pass through optical separators to recover any refractory diamonds which have not stuck to the grease belts. The concentrates from the sorting machines, the mills and the optical separators are then collected and sent to the central diamond sorting office in Kimberley. Approximately 25 per cent of the Finsch diamonds are of gem quality, the rest consisting of near-gem and industrial stones.'[16]

At West End, Treasure Trove was spending hundreds of thousands. At Finsch, De Beers was investing tens of millions. But rather than originate a brand new township for miners and those working in the plant, De Beers preferred to expand Northern Lime's village of Lime Acres which lay only two kilometres away. Northern Lime's streets were named after farms; De Beers's were named after gemstones like Ruby, Opal, Sapphire and Emerald. With the population increase came a shopping centre, a new post office and improved recreational facilities including a nine-hole golf course.

For the official opening, in 1967 De Beers flew in crockery, silver and glasses from Johannesburg, together with food, wine, cigars and the catering staff of a Johannesburg hotel. South African Railways' luxurious Blue Train was chartered to carry 100 guests from Johannesburg to Lime Acres and 100 more were flown to Kimberley and joined the train for the last stretch of the journey. Among the guests were De Beers's chairman, Harry Oppenheimer, and his wife, other De Beers dignitaries and the state president-designate, Dr T E Dönges, who was to set off a major blast in the kimberlite.

De Beers had confidence in the future of diamonds, but the tiger's eye industry was in the doldrums. Dawie Voges says former employees of his were responsible. 'Men who'd been mining for me decided to try exporting reject tiger's eye at very low prices,' he says. 'The buyers in Germany and the United States were only too pleased to buy it, but then they turned round and complained when we asked higher prices for better quality stone. That was in the 1950s, and I went to the government and asked them to do something about it.'[17]

At the time the government declined, but persistent lobbying over the next decade convinced them that a valuable resource was being wasted. During 1967 South Africa's minister of mines set up an 'Interdepartmental Committee on Tiger's-Eye and Related Varieties.' Among other responsibilities, it was to report on 'whether it is desirable to control or regulate the mining and marketing, including the export or import of such semi-precious stones and, if so, the steps whereby this end may be best served'. To find out, the committee visited workings near Griquatown, Niekerkshoop and Prieska.

'Until now,' the committee reported, 'tiger's eye of gem quality has been found on 25 farms in the divisions of Prieska and Hay, and mining operations are being conducted more or less regularly, but often intermittently, on about 12 of these farms. As the tiger's eye mining industry is still completely unorganised and also because of the way in which the mining is usually carried out, it is very difficult to obtain reliable statistics, but from what the committee could establish there are only about 12 whites and a maximum of about 200 coloureds (contractors and labourers) engaged. . . .

'The mining of tiger's eye is undertaken mainly by coloured contractors under arrangements with the owners of the mineral rights or their nominees, in terms of which a royalty or other form of consideration is payable. The equipment used by these coloured contractors is limited to picks, shovels, crowbars, iron wedges and hammers, which are used to break away the rock, extract the tiger's eye, and hand-cob and prepare the crude pieces so obtained to sizes and qualities which in their opinion have the best market value. A considerable quantity of usable tiger's eye is lost in the process through excessive breakage, cracking or splintering.'[18]

Crude tiger's eye was being shipped to 12 countries and in particular to Japan, West Germany, the United States and Hong Kong. 'From one ton of crude tiger's eye exported from the Republic at from R200 to R700 per ton,' reported the committee, 'tumbled and polished tiger's eye stones to the value of between R60 000 and R70 000 can be manufactured overseas. The loss suffered by the country through the export of tiger's eye in the crude instead of the processed form is therefore considerable, even if the quoted figures are 50 per cent in error.

'It is therefore the committee's considered opinion that the entire processing or manufacturing of South Africa's crude tiger's eye reserves should now be set as the ultimate object, and that as a first—and the most important—step in that direction the export of crude tiger's eye from South Africa should be controlled forthwith by means of a permit system, and should be totally prohibited as soon as possible thereafter.'[18] That recommendation and others were made to the minister of mines, and before very long the South African parliament passed legislation that implemented nearly all of them.

CHAPTER NINE 1968–1978

Copper Bottom

EDWIN BEECROFT was a geologist famous for two reasons. One was his discovery of copper deposits in South West Africa. The other was his marriage to Cecilia Wessels, South Africa's most accomplished soprano. By the middle 1960s Beecroft was in his eighties and had retired to Cape Town where he enjoyed regular games of golf and bowls. Growing international tensions convinced him that South Africa needed yet more domestic sources of strategic metals, especially copper. Traditional suppliers like Zaïre and Zambia were no longer reliable.

At the outset of Beecroft's career, geologists looking for minerals had roamed the veld with a hammer and a sample bag. By the middle 1960s they were more likely to be armed with a magnetometer and supported by aerial surveys. A few of them were becoming interested in the potential of colour photographs taken from satellites. With the help of special filters, geophysicists analysed photographs of the variations in rock formations and tried to pinpoint new deposits of minerals. A friend of Beecroft's living in London came across satellite photographs of the Northern Cape.

The photographs suggested there was a substantial deposit of copper south of the Orange River, so Beecroft's friend let him know. As Beecroft well knew, years earlier copper had been mined at Areachap north of Upington and in Namaqualand to the west. But the possibility of copper in the Karoo had not occurred to him. He asked a Transvaal geologist to visit the Chamber of Mines in Johannesburg on his behalf to look for information on the region. The geologist unearthed a reference to an old report on the farm Vogelstruisbult south-west of Prieska, the one now owned by Charlie Marais.

The report was not available in Johannesburg, and Beecroft began a lengthy correspondence in hopes of tracking it down. He mentioned his quest to a bowls partner in Cape Town, a lawyer named Chris Hutchings. To his astonishment, Hutchings already knew the name Vogelstruisbult and explained that his father had been involved there. In the early 1890s his father had travelled through the Northern Cape in search of minerals, and after the South African War had grubstaked a prospector named Chenoweth who in 1907 had worked on Vogelstruisbult.

It may be that Chenoweth was the 'tramp' recalled by Charlie Marais's mother. His results were apparently positive, and it may be that the 'man called Samowit' who visited Vogelstruisbult during 1908 was also working for Hutchings. But nothing more was done until 1912 when prospector Bleloch arrived on the scene. As Hutchings explained to Beecroft, Bleloch had been his father's brother-in-law. Bleloch and his men bored holes and dug several prospecting trenches. Hutchings asked a mining engineer named Blenkensop to produce an independent report on their activities.

Blenkensop spotted a 'hardcap'—today called a gossam—on surface which had copper mineral stainings in it and he assumed there was copper sulphide beneath. Ron Middleton, a geologist who has made a close study of Vogelstruisbult, writes: 'Blenkensop reasoned that sufficient money could be made by selling oxide copper from surface workings to generate capital for a more substantial mining effort. It is known now that he would have been mistaken in his expectations because the copper is nearly all leached away by the acid generated by the massive sulphides in the upper portions of the ore body.'[1]

According to Charlie Marais, the men working for Bleloch disappeared on the eve of World War I. He believes they were German nationals and must have fled to South West Africa. Meanwhile, Hutchings was preparing to visit Europe in search of finance for a copper mine. He arrived in London after the outbreak of war and found that nobody was interested in his proposition. The work of nearly 25 years had been in vain. He returned to South Africa and the Vogelstruisbult papers were put away in a suitcase.

Hutchings's father died a few years later and his son and daughter-in-law went through his papers. Chris Hutchings admitted that he saw little point in keeping the documents concerning Vogelstruisbult but his wife told him he would be wrong to burn them. He kept them in their suitcase and stored them in his attic, where they remained for nearly 50 years. Then Hutchings met Beecroft, who accompanied him home to look at the papers. Beecroft soon uncovered the Blenkensop report and found it was even fuller than he had hoped.

37. A labourer peers down the collar built to top the Hutchings shaft at Prieska Copper Mines. Around it are the foundations laid for the shaft's 85 m headgear.

Anglovaal

38. A miner and his team prepare to drill a development round down Prieska Copper Mines at Copperton.

Anglovaal

39. Senior underground staff and a party of black miners celebrate the first intersection of the ore body at Prieska Copper Mines.

Anglovaal

The Hutchings papers gave Vogelstruisbult's postal address and named Charlie Marais's father. Beecroft wrote to Charlie Marais and asked for permission to visit the farm. 'I remember him as a very tall man, well dressed and correct,' says Marais. 'Even though he was nearly 90 years old we walked all over the farm and I showed him the workings left by the old prospectors.'[2] Chris Hutchings was interested too, and he, Beecroft and a fellow lawyer named Boehmke formed a syndicate and persuaded Charlie Marais to grant them prospecting rights.

The three partners could not develop Vogelstruisbult by themselves so contacted mining houses in Johannesburg. Mike Hearn, Anglovaal's consulting geologist, recalls that the syndicate approached Anglovaal with a proposition during 1965 or 1966. 'At that time we were unable to proceed with it,' he says, 'owing to staff shortages and as our prospecting budget was fully committed. At the end of 1967 it was again submitted, having, I understand, been in the meantime declined by several companies.'[3]

This time the approach was made by Boehmke, who mentioned the prospect to the managing director of one of Anglovaal's industrial companies. The matter came to the attention of Slip Menell, Anglovaal's chairman. The upshot was that early in 1968 Beecroft revisited Vogelstruisbult, this time accompanied by Anglovaal's Ron Middleton. The two geologists examined the old prospect pits, and as a result of their findings Mike Hearn recommended that Anglovaal should invest in a three-hole drilling programme.

So it was that during November 1968 the Boart Drilling Company sent a rig to Vogelstruisbult in the charge of Hector Blunden. Hearn and Middleton were to visit the drillsite at regular intervals to monitor progress and mark off new boreholes as necessary. 'Usually a geologist plans the hole to intersect the target below the present known water table,'[1] explains Middleton, who wrote a doctoral thesis on the exploration of Vogelstruisbult and has since been working in Brazil. In 1968 the water table on the farm was plus or minus 35 metres from the surface.

The geologists could not have known that millions of years ago the water table had dropped to about 100 metres below surface, causing the massive sulphides to be leached out to that depth. According to Middleton, the residue was a 'soggy mess' which was virtually impossible to recover with diamond core drilling. 'The result,' he says, 'was that we had perfect recovery of rock core in the inclined boreholes until we entered the critical ore zone and then lost nearly all the core over some ten metres, the width of the ore body.'[1]

At the time, of course, no one could be sure that an ore body existed. The first two boreholes encountered the 'soggy mess' but both yielded slight traces of copper. The results were not very encouraging, so Mike Hearn advised Anglovaal to attempt an intersection further to the north.

This almost led to the delaying of the discovery of the Prieska ore body as the borehole failed to reveal any sort of mineralisation. Months later, it was realised that the ore body has the shape of a parallelogram and the drill had missed it.

There was still enough money left for one more attempt, so Hearn sited the fourth hole some 400 metres south of the best showings to cut the suspected ore zone at a depth of about 130 metres. Middleton takes up the story: 'During one of my routine visits to the drillsite Hector Blunden looked rather strange. I had already seen and logged V1 and V2 and wanted to see the last core of V3 which I had not yet logged. "Forget V3," said Hector. "You had better look at V4." I wanted to be systematic but he was already getting the men to lay out the boxes of V4.

'Hector said with unconcealed excitement: "I don't know much about geology but this is going to take some beating!" One did not have to be a genius to see the massive sulphide—all 13 metres of it—an incredible intersection by any standards—without any core loss. On closer examination I could see that there were significant quantities of copper (chalcopyrite) and zinc (sphalerite) minerals in the iron sulphide or pyrite which is a "barren" mineral. We excitedly discussed the intersection for some time. "The ore cuts like butter," explained Hector.

'After siting a new hole to the south (he had already drilled well into the rather distinctive footwall) we packed the massive sulphide intersection into four small reinforced cardboard core boxes. They weighed a "ton" but I knew that Anglovaal would not be concerned about paying the baggage excess for my flight from Kimberley back to Johannesburg. I requested Hector to await telephone instructions about moving the rig to the next site as a new budget would have to be approved by Anglovaal Proposition Committee.'[1] Not surprisingly, the decision was quickly made.

From then on everything went smoothly and efficiently. Under Mike Hearn's guidance, Anglovaal proceeded with a drilling programme which hit ore with virtually every hole. A prospect winze was sunk and named 'Marais Shaft,' and beside it Anglovaal built a pilot separation plant that was to experiment with methods of treating the ore to produce copper and zinc concentrates. A larger prospect shaft was named after Beecroft and there were plans to honour Hutchings and Boehmke in the same way.

Hutchings shaft was to be used to hoist ore, and to top it Anglovaal commissioned a massive concrete headgear that for a time was the tallest structure in the entire Cape Province. The headgear had to be built in a continuous operation, and construction workers poured concrete around the clock to make sure the tower went up without a crack. It grew at the rate of four metres per day and the entire job took 17 days. The completed headgear was 86 m high.

The construction company responsible for the headgear ,also built a residential township three kilometres from the mine complex. The township was named Copperton, and the mine manager and assistant manager and their families were the first to move in. Charlie Marais and his wife still occupied their farmhouse, less than half a kilometre from the Hutchings headgear. Anglovaal had offered to help them move but they preferred to stay where they were. Indeed, Charlie Marais felt a proprietorial interest in all that happened and watched progress from a deckchair on his lawn.

Of course, most of the progress was hidden from sight. Hutchings shaft was being sunk to a final depth of nearly 900 metres and engineers were to install a giant crusher at the bottom. All ore from the mine would gravitate down to the crusher and would be broken into smaller lumps before being hoisted to the surface. Of the three support shafts, Boehmke was small and designed for ventilation, while Marais and Beecroft were being used to hoist rock blasted in the course of developing underground drives and ore passes.

All these features could be found in scores of other mines in Southern Africa, but one aspect of Prieska Copper Mines was revolutionary. Miners were excavating a system of 'decline roadways' within the mine, gently sloping access tunnels that would allow self-propelled load–haul–dump machines ('scoop trams') to travel from the surface to loading stations all through the workings. Each machine was long, low and powerful. At one end was a giant scoop, at the other a massive engine that helped to balance it. The driver sat halfway along, facing sideways so that he could steer in both directions.

Load–haul–dump machines had been used with great success in base metals mines of Europe and North America, but in the Northern Cape there had been nothing like them. Each machine ran on four huge tyres and was equipped with powerful headlights to give the driver a clear view. His job was to scoop ore at the working face, haul it clear and dump it into rock passes which fed cocopan-like trucks serving the main ore pass. Drivers needed considerable skill and the mining company took great care in selecting them. Each underwent a comprehensive course at a driving school on the surface.

To obtain ore, Anglovaal resorted to a mining method not previously attempted in the Northern Cape. Known as 'sub-level open stoping', it has been likened to slicing bread. 'You drill holes from a tunnel,' says Corrie van der Walt, Prieska's ventilation engineer. 'Then you create a big hole and blast vertical slices of ore into the hole. The ore falls to the bottom of the stope and filters into a loading station below, and that's where the scoop trams load it up. Eventually your stopes are hundreds of metres high and when the caving reaches the surface you're left with a spectacular sinkhole.'[4]

On surface, Anglovaal erected a large concentrates flotation plant. In the early days a fleet of lorries carried concentrates to Prieska and the Cape Provincial Administration built an expensive tarred road. South African Railways laid a spur line connecting with Prieska station. Part of the mine's production was railed to Walvis Bay on the coast of South West Africa, then shipped to West Germany. The rest went to a copper smelter in Namaqualand. A pipeline was laid to bring water from the Orange River and Escom provided a power link.

Ore in Bulk

Since the time of Manganese Corporation in the 1930s, Northern Cape ore destined for export had been railed all the way across South Africa to be shipped from Durban. At first the system worked well enough, but tonnages steadily increased and placed a severe strain on the railways. Ore trains congested the routes and the weight of their trucks damaged rails. During the 1960s S A Manganese had persuaded South African Railways to develop sophisticated ore-handling facilities at Port Elizabeth. As a result much of the ore was diverted to new routes and efficiency was greatly improved.

A Johannesburg consortium wanted to go still further. With an eye to Japan's growing demand for South African ore, the consortium asked the government to approve an offshore bulk ore-loading terminal close to Port Elizabeth, sheltered by St Croix island. A prominent member of the consortium was Peter Wilhelmi of Consolidated African Mines which was stepping up its manganese exports. For a time it seemed the St Croix scheme had a strong chance of success. Iscor had realised that Sishen contained far more iron ore than was needed by its own steelworks and was preparing to export.

Iscor's idea had first been mooted in the 1960s, and stemmed from a transport scheme dreamed up by Amcor. There were large deposits of magnetite iron ore near Mafeking, and Amcor wanted to grind them to powder, mix them with water and pump them by pipeline to domestic steelworks and perhaps to Natal for export. The scheme was dropped when it was found that the iron ore contained haematite that would require separate processing. But in the meantime Iscor took a fresh look at Sishen and examined the prospects of crushing and piping its haematite or even of carrying it by conveyor belt.

Neither scheme was practical, so Iscor turned to the railways. Its idea was to introduce block ore trains up to two kilometres long and pulled by up to six locomotives. Such trains had been used with success in North America but would be new to South Africa. Natal was not a practical destination because of congestion. Port Elizabeth was a likely contender, but Iscor had reservations about the quality of the rail track and about wave action off St Croix. Reviewing all its options, Iscor decided it would be better to develop a new rail route to Saldanha Bay north of Cape Town.

Centuries earlier, Saldanha Bay had been a favourite haven for Portuguese mariners on passage to and from the Orient. Dutch settlers of the seventeenth century had preferred Table Bay to the south and since that time Saldanha Bay had been little used. Even so, it was ranked as one of the world's great natural harbours and its considerable depth made it perfect as a bulk loading terminal. Iscor commissioned engineers to choose a route down the escarpment edging the inland plateau, the only serious obstacle between Sishen and the sea. Prospective customers were lined up and construction could begin.

The Sishen–Saldanha scheme was to cost many hundreds of millions. Iscor divided the work into some 70 segments and invited engineering firms to tender for contracts. Some were to lay sections of the rail track, build bridges or hole a tunnel. Others were to develop facilities at Saldanha Bay or new plant and a new town at Sishen, where a special export mine was being developed. The new railway was to be 861 km long and would be electrified all the way. It was to be controlled by computer and built to the same gauge as the national system. Construction began in 1973.

The line was to be ready for use by 1976 and would be operated by Iscor. At least, that was Iscor's original plan, but during April 1977 control of the line was given to South African Railways so that it could be used as a multipurpose line in the national interest. Meanwhile, the population at Sishen was expanding rapidly and much of it was being accommodated in the new Kathu township sited about 20 km from Sishen village. There was no room for expansion in the old township, and in any case there was iron ore under the site and Iscor realised that one day it might want to mine there.

The original open pit at Sishen was now known as 'South Mine' and continued to produce iron ore for Iscor's South African steelworks. Iscor had also acquired Lylyveld from Amcor and employed outside contractors to mine haematite for a steelworks in Natal. But the main focus of attention was 'North Mine' which was to supply ore for export. North Mine and South Mine were to work separate sections of the same ore body and were to be administered independently. Their ore was to be treated in separate plants and was to be loaded aboard separate trains using separate sets of tracks.

'In the beginning there was a lot of rivalry between the two mines,' says Jan Kotze, who remained at South though Mike Pauer went to North and took charge of transport. 'The export mine started with much bigger equipment than ours and the tonnage of waste and ore they were moving was bigger too. Of course, that didn't mean they were more efficient. But all their operations were planned by computer in Iscor's head office and we sometimes felt a little neglected. Mind you, whenever there was a chance we commandeered their equipment and made use of it for as long as we could.'[5]

When North Mine started, Mike Pauer's transport fleet consisted of 136-ton dump trucks. It was soon reinforced by 150-ton giants imported from the United States. The trucks were to carry both waste and ore and to load them Iscor introduced the largest mechanical shovels yet seen in South Africa and a number of powerful front-end loaders to support them. Both waste and ore were to be blasted in benches and holes were drilled by mammoth rotary drills mounted on caterpillar tracks. The holes were drilled in a grid, then charged with jelly-like 'slurry' explosive mixed in a tank truck.

North Mine's plans called for a stripping ratio of one ton of waste to one ton of ore. Waste was carried up ramps to dumps sited beyond the limits of the ore body. The dumps were to be built in lifts of 20 metres with straight sides and flat tops, and trucks drove to the end and emptied their cargo down the slopes. Today the dumps look like fingers stretching across the flat veld beneath them. With the waste out of the way, trucks carried ore to an enormous gyratory crusher that was the pivot of the mine's operations. The crusher was the largest in Africa and one of the largest in the world.

Mike Pauer's trucks reversed to the rim of the crusher, tipped their pans and shrouded themselves in dust as 136 tons of ore cascaded into the pit. The crusher looked like a huge ball inserted in the neck of a deep funnel. The ball was mounted on a strong pivot which gyrated slowly and squeezed both ball and pivot towards the steel liner of the funnel. Rocks slipped between the pivot and the liner and were compressed until they cracked. The pieces slipped into a shaft below the crusher and were ready for their journey through the ore-handling plant.

Sishen's giant crusher is still in use, but since 1978 it has been fed by a fleet of 150-ton dump-trucks that dwarf the 35-tonners used at Sishen in the early days. Excavators and drilling rigs are bigger too, and so are the blast-holes drilled for explosives. Tonnages handled at Sishen have increased in leaps and bounds and today the mine is one of the four largest in the world. Even so, the basic mining sequence remains much as it was in the early days and so does the ore-treatment programme of crushing, washing, screening, beneficiating, stacking, blending and loading into rail trucks.

North Mine ore falling through the gyratory crusher has a maximum measurement of 250 mm. It is promptly fed to a secondary cone crusher that crushes it into lumps no larger than 160 mm across. A conveyor belt then delivers it to tertiary crushers that reduce it to less than 90 mm. Next it is conveyed to a stack ready for the washing and screening plant, where high-pressure water-sprays wash off mud and other sediments, which are pumped to a slimes dam. Meanwhile the ore is screened into four different sizes and stacked before entering the beneficiation or upgrading plant.

The two larger sizes of ore lumps—8 to 25 mm and the coarse 25 to 90 mm—are fed into a 'heavy-medium separation' (HMS) plant filled with a suspension of ferro-silicon in water. Heavy lumps of iron ore sink to the bottom while lighter materials float and are skimmed off as waste. The two smaller sizes of ore—0,21 to 5 mm and 5 to 8 mm—are fed into cyclone units that spin the lumps and concentrate the iron ore. Where required, the beneficiated ore can be crushed into smaller lumps. Then it is transferred to ore beds, one for lumps and one for 'fine ore' ready for blending.

North Mine and its plant are programmed by computer, but that still leaves some latitude for its supervisors and miners. A control tower has been established on a prominent kopje and provides a view of operations all through the mine and in parts of South Mine too. Shovels, loaders and indeed all vehicles entering the mine are fitted with two-way radios. The trucks are equipped with individual transmitters that beam signals to a sensor connected with the computer. Immediately the computer flashes a number on to a display board and the driver is directed to an unattended shovel.

Giant trucks like Sishen's have been introduced to Northern Lime's quarry at Lime Acres. Indeed, the two mines pool a mechanical adviser provided by the American suppliers. Northern Lime's John Wotherspoon says that 'driving one of those huge machines is like trying to fly an aircraft carrier. You have no sensation of the roadway below and there's a 30-metre blind spot immediately in front of you.'[6] To make sure they are not run over by mistake, Sishen drivers in small runabouts fly red pennants at the top of five-metre masts.

Nothern Lime's 150-ton trucks carry only waste for they are too large to fit the top of the quarry's gyratory crusher. 'Apart from size, there's a big difference between our crusher and Sishen's,' says John Wotherspoon. 'Limestone is so soft that we expect our crusher liner to last ten years. Sishen ore is so hard that they're lucky if a liner lasts three months.'[6] On one occasion a Northern Lime driver muddled his gears and reversed his truck into the crusher. Fortunately the truck was caught on a long hook used to free rocks that become stuck, and the driver was not hurt.

Northern Lime closed its Buxton quarry in 1977 and today draws nearly all its product from Lime Acres. The company supplies about 60 per cent of the South African market while Union Lime supplies nearly all the rest. Increased industrial demand has encouraged Union Lime to step up production at Ulco and open a quarry at Danielskuil, on the farm

Ouplaas. The new quarry mines primary limestone only ten kilometres from Lime Acres and uses similar methods but on a smaller scale. Those who work there live in Danielskuil, and Ouplaas quarry and limeworks have been in production since 1975.

The Ouplaas quarry works with front-end loaders and 35-ton trucks. The limeworks began with two rotary kilns and by 1979 two more kilns were under construction. 'Unfortunately there's a geological fault where the kilns were supposed to be,' said Ouplaas's manager, Eugene Richards. 'A construction firm from Johannesburg was contracted to drive piles and create a steady foundation, but their machines became stuck in mud. Because Danielskuil's water table is quite high, the holes were flooded with muddy water 30 metres deep and they had to bring in divers to rescue their equipment.'[7]

Special Status

Since 1978 three large sections of the Northern Cape have been part of the Republic of Bophuthatswana, one of the former South African 'homelands' that have opted for independence from the mother country. Bophuthatswana's capital is Mafikeng, the old Mafeking, and it includes four more 'islands' of territory in the Transvaal and Orange Free State. More than twice as many Tswana live in Bophuthatswana as in Botswana and they provide all but a small proportion of the labour force on Northern Cape mines. Other workers are drawn from Transkei, Ciskei and homelands of the Sotho.

In earlier days, mines sent their own recruiters to visit tribal chiefs and ask them for labourers. Today much of the work is done by recruiting agencies, and labourers are invited to sign contracts to work for the mine for six months, nine months or a year. The recruits travel to the mine by bus or train, and on arrival they are given quarters in the mine hostel. They are taken to see the kitchens, beerhall, clinic, clothes-washing facilities and other features, and hostel police lecture them on dos and don'ts and explain to them how they are to draw their pay.

Before starting work, the recruits are given medical examinations and at some mines they are required to take aptitude tests. As many recruits cannot read, the tests require them to match colours, shapes and sizes. Those who fare best in the aptitude tests are seen as potential drivers and machine operators. Some may already have driving licences, but even so they must undergo further tests to check their suitability. At several mines, including Wessels and Copperton, potential drivers undergo the tests set for would-be bus drivers by Johannesburg's Public Transport Commission.

The recruits selected as drivers are given special training, and at mines like Mamatwan they start on relatively simple machines and are gradually promoted to more sophisticated (and more expensive) models. Other recruits work out their contracts as loaders, sorters, cooks, handymen or whatever other roles are available. At the termination of his contract the recruit returns home. He is paid a bonus if he signs a new contract and returns to the mine within 30 days, and there are chances of promotion as he gains experience. Ultimately he may be appointed a 'leading hand' or 'bossboy'.

'Leading hands' have special status on the mines and may be provided with married quarters where they can live with their families. In terms of labour legislation, only three per cent of a mine's black work force may be given permanent housing. The legislation does not apply to coloured miners and other workers who on several mines have villages of their own. In the Cape Province but not elsewhere, coloureds may hold blasting certificates and can therefore qualify as miners. Like their white counterparts, they take charge of a gang and have a leading hand as lieutenant.

Many of the coloureds employed on Northern Cape mines are skilled artisans who work on surface or underground as required, not least in ore recovery and treatment plants. A significant number work at Finsch diamond mine, which has acquired a large new diamond recovery plant that has more than doubled its production capability. To feed it, Finsch is mining more kimberlite from its open pit and the hole is now more than 250 metres deep. From an aesthetic viewpoint Finsch's concentric benches make it one of the most satisfying mines in Southern Africa.

Finsch mine has progressed from strength to strength, but during the 1970s its neighbour at Postmasburg returned to obscurity. After a decade of only moderate returns, Treasure Trove gave up on diamonds and began crushing stone instead. West End's equipment was sold and the open pit has filled with water. Near Boetsap, Roelof Versluis has been working the old Frank Smith pipe by means of a shaft and conveyor belt. Fred Flanagan, the manager at Smith's, reports that relatively few diamonds are recovered there but those found are of good quality.

At Finsch, most diamonds are recovered in enclosed X-ray machines and are hidden from view. At Smith's, the concentrates are washed over old-fashioned grease tables and diamonds are in plain sight. Each table consists of three steps sloping downwards at a sharp angle. The top step is coated with fresh grease, a smooth mixture of petrolatum and white wax, while the lower steps are smeared with used grease that has been boiled. Water and concentrates cascade over the table from the top and the table vibrates. Diamonds stick to the grease and are removed with tweezers.

Grease tables are in use at the three mines on the Sover fissure not far from Smith's and at Bellsbank too, though Danie de Bruin has also invested in X-ray machines. On the alluvial fields, diggers continue to hand-sort washes rinsed in sieves and flipped upside down on to their sorting-tables. Josias Pretorius, the mining commissioner at Barkly West, says there are fewer than 60 full-time diggers in the Northern Cape. They are scattered over about 40 proclaimed public diggings, but the majority work claims in the Barkly West district.

Most of the older diggers remain loyal to traditional working methods. They use picks, shovels, a crane with a bucket, a rotary pan and a sorting-table. Perhaps they have a trommel, perhaps they have a dummy. But since 1970 they have been joined by a new breed of diggers, younger men prepared to invest in heavy earth-moving equipment and sophisticated washing and screening plants. The newcomers process as much ground in a day as the long-established diggers work in a month. They too are gamblers but they are playing for higher stakes.

Before a newcomer is allowed to peg any claims, he must first qualify for a digger's certificate. He earns it by entering a two-year partnership with an established digger. He registers the partnership at the office of the mining commissioner in Barkly West, and both claims inspectors and the CID diamond branch keep an eye on him. At the end of the two-year partnership he applies for his certificate, and if it is granted he can peg claims on public diggings and apply for prospecting licences to search for diamonds on land not yet proclaimed.

Diggers with stones to sell traditionally take them to Barkly West on a Saturday morning. In the past, they had a wide choice of buyers. Today the number is much diminished. Arthur Bosman is a licensed buyer who lives in Lichtenburg and travels to Barkly West each weekend. He carries pocket-sized diamond scales, tweezers, a diamond shovel, a magnifying loupe, white paper, a pocket calculator and a diamond broker's book in which he must record all transactions. He also carries cash and a gun. He occupies an empty office above a bank that contains a desk and three chairs.

'When a digger offers me a stone, I must weigh it and assess its colour and quality,' says Bosman. 'I check the colour by placing it on a sheet of white paper and I use my loupe to look for flaws. Weighing the stone is critical and takes a long time. When I'm satisfied I consult a chart of diamond prices based on value per carat and bring out my calculator. Diggers know what they want for a particular stone but they expect the buyer to name a price. Then they can accept it or reject it. If they accept, they like to be paid in cash.'[8]

Before he so much as glances at a stone, Bosman asks to see the digger's certificate. 'It's the law,' he explains. 'The CID is very tough.'[8] As a buyer he must file a monthly report on his transactions and diggers must file reports on both transactions and finds. Illicit Diamond Buying or IDB has been a problem since the early days, chiefly because it encourages labourers to steal from their employers. Danie de Bruin says that years ago a crooked syndicate asked him to act as a front for them, pretending to find stones that they supplied and registering them as his own.

Eric Cockcroft, formerly general works manager at Ulco, tells of an old labourer who stole several large diamonds and saved them for a rainy day. 'Years later, he approached one of our miners and asked him to use the diamonds to buy a farm,' says Cockcroft. 'He suggested the two of them could retire to it. Our man took the diamonds and hid them but his nerves got the better of him. After three days he gave them back. The old labourer thought for a day or two and took his diamonds to someone living in Delportshoop. This man accepted the stones, gave the man a hiding and chased him away.'[9]

To catch offenders, the CID sometimes employs diamond traps who sell diamonds to IDB suspects and allow detectives to catch them red-handed. Micky Gaw of Ulco recalls one such venture that went wrong. 'The intended victim was well known for IDB but always escaped,' says Gaw. 'On this occasion he arranged to meet the trap beside the Vaal. As soon as he accepted the diamonds the detectives pounded. But he quickly slipped the stones into a bag on the end of a fishing line and dropped them into the water. A friend of his across the river reeled in the bag and they got away with it.'[10]

Anyone convicted of IDB is fined heavily, and the same goes for those convicted of offences involving unprocessed tiger's eye. A revised Tiger's Eye Control Act passed in 1977 made it illegal to deal in more than two kilograms of raw tiger's eye without a permit obtained from the Department of Mines. The act also made it illegal to transport raw tiger's eye further than the nearest railway station. Among the first to be convicted under the new legislation was the mine secretary of Koegas–Westerberg asbestos mine, who was caught selling seven tons of tiger's eye in South West Africa.

Tiger's eye suppliers say it will take time for the new legislation to prove its worth. So much tiger's eye has been smuggled out of the country illegally that possible export markets have been saturated. Ultimately overseas buyers will have to depend on stone processed by South African cutters, among them firms established in Griquatown and near Taung which is now within Bophuthatswana. The Taung works was established to quarry champagne-coloured marble on a farm 47 km to the west. The marble deposit was 13 km long and wire saws cut the stone into huge blocks that are lifted out by crane.

At least two other gemstones are mined in the Northern Cape. Jasper is quarried in the Niekerkshoop area by means of picks and shovels. The rock must not be blasted for fear of cracks, and even hammers can do irreparable damage. Some of the jasper is coral red, some is brecciated, and it is not dissimilar to a form of chalcedony that Dawie Voges quarries on a farm in the Langeberg. 'A German professor saw it when he visited us in Griquatown in the 1950s,' says Voges. 'He took a sample to have it analysed, found it was something new and had it registered as vogesite.'[11]

Serving the World

The mining industry as a whole offers few opportunities for women, but asbestos mines are an honourable exception. In the early days women stamped and cobbed fibre for their menfolk or for mining companies, and today several mines employ shifts of women to hand-sort fibre from waste. Unlike males who are accommodated on the premises, the women are bussed to work from their home villages in Bophuthatswana. Those at KCB's Whitebank mill are issued with headphones connected to a central sound system and listen to music while they work. According to KCB, it means they concentrate more.

Whitebank's ore body is rich but patchy, and the company has opened five separate mines to work it. At one of them, White Kloof West, KCB has sunk an incline shaft and uses load–haul–dumpers. 'We find they're ideal so long as the asbestos seams are high enough and the footwall isn't too steep,' says Gert van Tonder, KCB's mine overseer. 'A disadvantage is that we can't sort as we go, but we eliminate much of the waste by preblasting waste cuts from panels on the working face. Besides removing waste, we find we're using less explosives to drop the fibre.'[12]

White Kloof's ore body dips and folds, and in some areas of the mine KCB prefers to use wheelbarrows. Both barrows and LHDs tip fibre into ore passes which carry it to the main haulage. There, the fibre is funnelled into trains of cocopans hauled by electric locomotives that pull them to bins at the bottom of the shaft. The fibre is released into measuring flasks, dropped into skips and hoisted to the surface. Much the same happens at the twin mines opened by Gefco at Coretsi in Bophuthatswana, except that in the stopes Gefco has spurned wheelbarrows in favour of scraper winches.

About 90 per cent of the Northern Cape's asbestos is sold to make asbestos cement, so the mines' fortunes depend on the construction industry. 'When there's a slump, we're hit doubly hard,' said Doug Todd. 'Our regular customers retrench, and we face competition from Canada and Russia which dump asbestos on the market at bargain prices. We're also affected by boycotts imposed on blue asbestos by countries that consider it a health hazard.'[13] Bags of Northern Cape asbestos are railed to South Africa's ports, and from there are shipped to destinations all over the world.

Copper concentrates from Copperton go to West Germany by way of Port Elizabeth, except for the small proportion sent to the copper smelter in Namaqualand. Most of Copperton's zinc concentrates go to a zinc refinery in the Transvaal though a small proportion is sent to West Germany. Finsch's diamonds go to Kimberley and then the world, and lime goes to gold refineries, plastics manufacturers and half-a-dozen other industries. Manganese and iron ore go to Japan and Europe and more manganese is sent to the United States, while only a small proportion is sold on the home market.

Everywhere mines have been mechanising in hopes of greater productivity, not least those of Associated Manganese where the centre of gravity has been moving northwards. Gloucester is still working but Beeshoek, Adams, Devon and Perth have been phased out. Most of the company's ore comes from Black Rock and a clutch of new mechanised mines on neighbouring farms. Even Black Rock went trackless in the early 1970s. 'That was a difficult conversion,' says Associated Manganese's Rudolf Vertue. 'We developed roadways underground but had to lower vehicles down the main shaft.'[14]

All Associated Manganese's northern mines use front-end loaders and dump-trucks rather than load–haul–dumpers. Until 1979 upper levels at Black Rock were still being mined with cocopans—'just as at Gloucester but with a roof on top,' says Vertue. 'Belgravia mine began like that too.'[14] Now the cocopans have gone and Belgravia has a decline roadway though ore is hoisted to the surface in skips. That is the pattern at Black Rock too, but at Gloria mine opened in 1977 and at Nchwaning opened more recently the ore is carried up a long incline shaft on a conveyor belt.

Mechanisation has affected southern manganese mines too. Gloucester and Lohatlha have dispensed with cocopans and now rely on excavators and dump-trucks. The same was true of Beeshoek, Manganore and the CAM mines too though all have closed. Hand-sorting at Gloucester and Lohatlha now involves one grade rather than nine and wheelbarrows are disappearing in favour of conveyor belts. The only link between today's miner and his predecessors is his kaia, still built along traditional lines with a couch and a cooking-place and a tank of water alongside.

To the north, the great pit of S A Manganese's Mamatwan grows ever larger. The pit is in the shape of a fan and its benches expand outwards in a giant semicircle at the rate of 20 metres a year. A new control tower has been installed, even higher than the original one, and waste rock is being used to backfill sections of the open pit and improve roadways leading to the ore-treatment plant. Even conservative estimates suggest Mamatwan has enough ore to keep the mine in business for 200 years.

Mamatwan originally complemented Hotazel, but Hotazel closed down in 1978 because it was so difficult to mine. 'There was still ore, but it was contaminated with banded ironstone,' says Peter Townsend, manager of S A Manganese's northern mines. 'There was a bit of a dip in the market in the late 1970s, and in any case we were opening a new underground mine at Wessels near Black Rock which was designed to take Hotazel's place.'[15] In 1981 S A Manganese reopened sections of Hotazel for the sake of pockets of high-grade ore, but the operations are spasmodic and low-key and the once-great mine is nearly deserted.

The ore at Wessels was detected by Leslie Boardman in the early 1950s, but the subsequent drilling programme was too shallow to reach the ore body. S A Manganese left Wessels alone until 1965 when a fresh geophysical survey yielded promising returns. A three-year drilling programme covered Wessels and the neighbouring farms Dikgathlong and Diaboghomo and revealed three separate high-grade ore bodies. The top one was about 320 metres down, the bottom one 100 metres below it. No manganese company had mined so deep before but S A Manganese needed the ore.

Plans for the new mine called for a vertical shaft to hoist ore and a decline roadway for vehicles. The vertical shaft was sunk by outside contractors, the decline by S A Manganese's own miners who worked around the clock to meet a tight deadline. When they hit gravel there were problems with flooding from fissures below the water table. Normally mines block such fissures with cement, but the gravel was too soft to hold it and S A Manganese had to install pumps. The company thought the fissures would eventually dry out, but that has not happened.

Wessels began producing in 1973 and before long it was the largest underground manganese mine in the world. S A Manganese and Associated Manganese co-operated in laying a spur rail line connecting Wessels and Black Rock with the main line at Hotazel. At first S A Manganese tried to work Wessels with load–haul–dumpers but they were not a success. 'The manganese was too heavy for them,' says Peter Townsend. 'We had trouble with their transmissions and gears. Instead we brought in front-end loaders and dump-trucks and we have found them much more efficient.'[15]

The mine currently produces two grades of ore. High-grade 'WI' accounts for about 80 per cent of the total and lower-grade 'L4' is much like the ore produced at Lohatlha. 'To avoid mixing the two grades, we extract them by different routes and treat them in separate plants,' says Peter Townsend. 'L4 is hoisted up the main shaft, then railed to our old plant at Hotazel. W1 is treated at Wessels and is carried up to surface on a cable belt—a reinforced conveyor that came into operation in 1979. We sank a new incline for the cable belt and there's a new roadway beside it.'[15]

The cable belt and the roadway have to negotiate a hairpin bend on their way to the surface and they are major engineering achievements. Meanwhile, S A Manganese's strategy at Wessels has been to tunnel drives all through the ore body—veins and arteries that run all the way toWessels's boundaries. With the drives developed, miners can stope out the ore body as required but will leave substantial pillars to hold up the hanging wall. There are also plans to develop another ore body found above the original ones.

S A Manganese and Associated Manganese account for nearly all South Africa's manganese mining but they are not the only producers. Close to Hotazel, Benny Struck's National Manganese continues to mine Langdon Annex, though on a very small scale. 'In the past we had miners from all over, but now there are only 80 labourers and two of us to look after them,' says Gideon Hoon, the manager at Langdon Annex. 'We drill and blast the ore and private contractors carry it to our sort floor. Our sorters separate the ore from the waste and stack it ready for despatch to Hotazel station.'[16]

During 1976, the giant Anglo American Corporation of South Africa decided to develop a manganese mine on Middelplaats, the farm neighbouring Mamatwan. Like De Beers, Anglo American was headed by Harry Oppenheimer but it had had little previous involvement in the Northern Cape. Anglo American was primarily interested in gold, diamonds and coal but its 'new mining business' division believed there were profits in manganese. A subsidiary company had bought options on Middelplaats in 1969 and also information about a drilling programme carried out by an American company.

'Anglo appeared on the scene rather late,' says Vin Oliver, a veteran of Zambia's Copperbelt who was the first manager at Middelplaats. 'Associated Manganese and S A Manganese had tied up all the farms that had manganese outcropping on the surface and we had no alternative but to go underground. On Middelplaats the ore body dips at a shallow angle and in the middle of the farm it lies about 400 metres below the surface. We bought Middelplaats outright and in designing the mine we counted on a production life of 30 years.'[17]

Like Wessels, Middelplaats was provided with a vertical shaft sunk by outside contractors and an incline service ramp for vehicles. The vertical shaft goes down 489 metres and is topped by a concrete headgear. Work on the shaft was completed in 1979. The 'service ramp' stretches 2 500 metres. On the way to the ore body it is routed in a series of long straight stretches, but at deeper levels it winds round and round the vertical shaft until at the bottom the two are united. Halfway down and near the ore body the shafts are connected by crosscuts.

Middelplaats's mining operations are not merely mechanised but mobilised too. There is not a hand-held jackhammer to be seen. Drilling is carried out by five hydraulic drill rigs, self-propelled platforms each carrying two drilling booms that operate in the glare of powerful arc-lights. A sixth rig drives roofbolts into the hanging wall to lessen chances of a rockfall. Six front-end loaders clean the working faces after each blast and tip manganese into five dump-trucks which carry it to the nearest ore pass. Miners charging holes with explosives use four scissors liftcars.

The mine's rock-handling level is just below the orebody, 400 metres down. Middelplaats tackles the orebody with a 'room and pillar' technique originally developed in collieries: parallel 'rooms' are driven through the orebody, then connected by crosscuts so that only pillars are left. The orebody is up to 14 metres high and at first the mine took only a cut from the top. The ore remaining in the footwall is removed by horizontal benching—just like vertical benching except the blastholes are drilled horizontally.

When a dump-truck tips its load into an ore pass, the ore drops to a big jaw crusher deep underground. Then it falls down another ore pass that feeds a conveyor belt which in turn fills a measuring flask in the shaft. The measuring flask empties into a skip and the ore is hoisted to the surface and tipped into a large bin beside the headgear. From there it is fed to the treatment plant where it is screened, washed, crushed again if required, and conveyed to stockpiles where it is stored until needed for railing.

Middelplaats's orebody is an underground extension of Mamatwan's and is relatively expensive to extract, but the mine was well planned and quickly earned a share of the world market. In 1982 the Anglo American Corporation sold the mine to S A Manganese, or rather Samancor, as the company has been known since its merger with Amcor.

CHAPTER TEN SINCE 1978

Savings Schemes

BESIDE THE ROAD between Bellsbank and the Sover diamond fissure stands the rusting framework of an oil-drilling rig. It belongs to Danie de Bruin, who bought it during the 1960s. 'There was oil fever all over South Africa, not because we had it but because we didn't,' says De Bruin. 'I thought I'd drill a hole and take pot luck. The hole went through sand, then shale, then lava, then the deeper formations. A geologist said I was crazy. With so much volcanic kimberlite about, any oil in the region would have been burnt up long ago.'[1]

De Bruin's hole produced no oil and he was not inclined to try again. Professional geophysicists searching elsewhere in South Africa fared no better. With no domestic sources, South Africa was seriously affected when oil producers of the Middle East raised their prices or cut off supplies altogether. Fortunately South Africa's scientists had already developed an economic means of producing oil from coal. Besides, it was rumoured that South Africa was obtaining Middle East oil in exchange for gold. Even so, the rising cost of fuel had serious implications for the whole economy.

In the Northern Cape, there was an early response at Ulco. Union Lime had introduced new mechanical horses to tow the old side-tipping semitrailers and general works manager Eric Cockcroft took a fresh look at them. 'It occurred to me that we could couple semitrailers together so that each horse could pull two at a time,' says Cockcroft. 'There was a problem with steep gradients in the shale pit but the horses coped and we have saved a great deal of fuel. All the other parts of our operation are electrified except for a couple of small diesel locomotives on our rail spur.'[2]

Ulco has been connected to Escom's national power grid since the 1940s, and there is scarcely a mine in the Northern Cape that is isolated from it. The line arranged by Doug Todd zigzags through the heart of the region and extends to Black Rock and Hotazel. Newer lines connect Hotazel with Sishen and Kuruman with Lime Acres, and in the 1960s Escom erected a line to serve Prieska, Koegas and Upington. Without it Anglovaal would not have developed Copperton, and because of Copperton Escom has erected lines all over Bushmanland.

Escom power is relatively cheap whereas in the late 1970s the cost of diesel fuel rose rapidly. All over the Northern Cape, mines looked for ways to electrify their operations and reduce their dependence on diesel. At Mamatwan, trucks carrying manganese to the treatment plant were making return journeys of nearly five kilometres. S A Manganese installed a huge crusher in the heart of the pit, connected to the treatment plant by an electrically-powered conveyor system stretching more than two kilometres. The trucks' journeys were cut by 80 per cent, and besides saving fuel they saved time.

Mamatwan's excavators are powered by electricity, and the mine may decide to electrify the trucks too. There are two main methods to choose from. In one, cables trail on the ground and are connected to vehicles by drums that work like self-winding tape measures. In the other, vehicles are connected to overhead cables by pick-up arms, rather like trolley-buses. At Sishen, Iscor has introduced a sophisticated 'trolley assist' overhead system to help specially adapted trucks ascend the steep ramp leading to the waste dumps.

Sishen's system was the first of its kind to be seen in South Africa, and the first in the world to be applied to 150-ton trucks. The system consists of parallel cables strung from tall pylons over a distance of very nearly three kilometres. As a truck approaches the bottom of the ramp, its driver raises twin pantographs or pick-up rigs that make contact with the cables. The electrical power boosts the efforts of the diesel engine, and the truck climbs the ramp at nearly twice the speed and much more economically than if it was running on diesel alone.

Another innovation at Sishen is a semi-mobile crushing station, an immense piece of equipment that can be raised by a crawler jack and moved forward to keep pace with the working face. The crusher is designed to keep three shovels and a dozen trucks busy around the clock, shifting not ore but waste overburden that must be removed to expose the ore body. Once crushed, the waste is transported to the dumps by conveyor belt. The conveyancing system reduces operating costs by one-quarter, reduces diesel fuel consumption, man hours and truck use, and last but not least increases production.

40. New surface plant and a handsome headgear dominate the landscape at the Finsch diamond mine.

De Beers Consolidated Mines

41. The concentric benches of the Finsch mine follow the contours of the great pipe of kimberlite that reaches far into the earth.

De Beers Consolidated Mines

42. Sheltered conveyor belts link the tall structures that comprise the mill at Pomfret asbestos mine.

General Mining Union Corporation

43. The Northern Cape's asbestos industry is proud of its progress towards dust-free mills—a far cry from the old days.

General Mining Union Corporation

Northern Lime is introducing an in-pit crushing system not unlike Sishen's, and the Lime Acres quarry is an ideal candidate for a 'trolley assist' conveyancing system. Conveyors are already in use in several underground manganese mines including Wessels, Gloria and Middelplaats. Several underground mines have considered electrifying their trackless vehicles by means of wind-up cables. Besides saving on fuel, the step would help underground ventilation and reduce noise levels. The noisiest operation of all is drilling holes for blasting, and it may be possible to electrify drills.

At Finsch, the high cost of fuel prompted De Beers to go underground much earlier than planned. The open pit was being worked with diesel trucks, but underground workings could be electrified. De Beers's own staff sank a decline roadway leading to a spiral ramp adjoining the kimberlite pipe, while outside contractors using an immense six-leg jumbo drilling boom sank a vertical shaft which would be used to haul out kimberlite.

Both shafts were sunk in the country rock that surrounds the pipe. De Beers meant to connect them with the kimberlite by a network of horizontal drives, then raise a narrow slot from the drive to pierce the bottom of the open pit and function as an ore pass. Miners would blast away the neat benches in the pit and allow the kimberlite to fall to the levels below, but as yet it has not happened. Fortunately for De Beers the fuel problem is no longer so serious, and the open pit is being taken to its intended depth of about 376 metres.

Finsch, Sishen, Mamatwan and Northern Lime have enormous reserves to work with and in mining terms their potential is unlimited. Wessels, Gloria, Nchwaning and Middelplaats are set for long careers as well. But not all mines are so fortunate. The Northern Cape's casualty list already includes famous names like West End, Bretby and Buxton. Perhaps the saddest of all, in 1978 Cape Asbestos closed Koegas–Westerberg after a career that dated from 1890. Ironically, the decision came less than five years after Koegas was linked with the Escom power grid. There was nothing left to mine.

The demise of Koegas–Westerberg heralded major rationalisations in the Northern Cape's asbestos industry. At the beginning of 1981 there were three main participants: Cape Asbestos, which was part of the Barlow Rand financial group, Gefco, which was controlled by Federale Mynbou and its partner General Mining; and KCB, which belonged to the Swiss company Asbesco. KCB had taken control of DCBA of Owendale, and in March 1981 DCBA became a dormant company as KCB took over the administration of its mines and closed all but one.

During winter 1981, Barlow Rand negotiated with Asbesco with a view to taking over KCB. The two sides reached agreement at the end of September, and on October 1 KCB became a Rand Mines subsidiary.

That same day it was announced that Federale Mynbou was taking over all Barlow Rand's asbestos interests, including KCB. 'It was a great surprise for us all,' says Fanie Nieuwoudt who at the time worked for KCB. 'One day we were competing with Gefco, and the next we were working with them on the same side.'[3]

Under the new arrangements, KCB's mines on Whitebank and an old DCBA property, Klipfontein north of Danielskuil, were to be managed by Gefco. Its administrative staff was merged with Gefco's and the company now functions as a Gefco subsidiary. Gefco continued to mine at Coretsi and retained offices in Kuruman, though Gefco's office in Johannesburg took over the administration of Pomfret. The new-look Gefco had four operating mines in the Northern Cape, and with all competition removed its only major administrative headache was transport.

As if asbestos mines were jinxed, all Gefco's properties were far from railheads. Klipfontein's trucks had to make a round trip of more than 100 km to deliver bags of asbestos to Lime Acres station, and those travelling between Kuruman and Hotazel went even further. For many years the mines of Kuruman have urged South African Railways to give them a line, and late in 1982 it was announced that a line was being planned. With diesel fuel so expensive, not only Kuruman's mines but also agricultural and business concerns would benefit.

A new line to Kuruman would almost certainly be electrified, like the present main line from Kimberley to Hotazel. The Sishen–Saldanha line is fully electrified too, but the Kimberley–Douglas, Kimberley–Vryburg and Kimberley–Upington lines are not. Nor are the spur lines serving Ulco, Ouplaas and Middelplaats. Ulco has long used diesel engines and Ouplaas has followed suit. For two years Middelplaats used diesel engines too, but to save on diesel the mine has replaced them with three beautiful coal-burning locomotives retired by South African Railways.

Work and Play

Jumbo Harris founded Ammosal rugby club in the 1950s. By the late 1960s it was one of the top clubs in South Africa. In 1969, 1970 and 1971 the club fielded three Springboks—Joggie Viljoen, Piet Visagie and Piet van Deventer. Many Ammosal players made regular appearances for Griqualand West in Currie Cup matches, and there were seven of them in the Griquas side that won the cup in 1970. In 1980, the Griquas team that came closer to beating the touring British Lions than any other provincial side included no fewer than 12 of the men from Ammosal.

Gefco used to have its own rugby club too, the pride of Jack Duvenhage who in those days worked for Gefco but in 1973 succeeded Jumbo Harris at Beeshoek. 'That was poetic justice,' said Doug Todd.

'At Gefco Jack was convinced that Jumbo Harris was stealing our best men. Each year there were local derbies between Gefco and Ammosal and they were real grudge matches.'[4] Gefco, Ammosal, Postmasburg and Kuruman used to compete for the Van Druten Cup and eventually S A Manganese raised a team as well.

Copperton has three separate rugby clubs, one for whites, one for coloureds and one for blacks. The three are keen rivals and regularly play and practise with one another. Ulco has a keen club too, and for many years one of its major assets was a pair of identical twins, the sons of Blackie and Lydia Swartz. 'Visiting teams used to marvel at the player who seemed to be everywhere at once,' says Eric Cockcroft. 'It gave them the feeling they were up against something bigger than they were.'[2]

Gert van Tonder, KCB's underground manager at the mines on Whitebank, used to be captain of the Transvaal Currie Cup team but says that today he is more interested in golf. Syd Brownrigg would have approved, for his antidote to Ammosal rugby fever was a round each Sunday morning. Brownrigg laid out the first nine holes of Beeshoek's course in 1937 and later added nine more. To this day the ninth hole at Beeshoek is known as 'Brownrigg's folly' for it takes the form of a circular kraal surrounded by high banks.

Hotazel's original golf course was wiped out by floods of the middle 1970s and has been replaced by a miniature course at the centre of the village. There are courses at Black Rock, Kuruman, Lime Acres, Kathu and Copperton, and at Postmasburg a herd of springbok grazes on the fairways. At Owendale, golfing enthusiasts built a three-hole course next to the village. 'We launched it with a bang,' said DCBA's Gert Kotze. 'A team from KCB came down and we played nine holes in the morning and nine in the afternoon. To make it more interesting we changed the pars on every round.'[5]

At Ulco, golfers began with a single hole and played it again and again. The course was extended to three holes and ultimately to nine, but Lu Matter forbade golfers to destroy Ulco's precious trees. 'The swarthaak was thick, and if you lost a ball in it that was that,' says Eric Cockcroft. 'One day there was a tournament and I heard a voice coming out of the swarthaak: "Caddy, where are you, caddy?" The caddy called back: "Over here, boss." "What are you doing, caddy?" "Looking for the ball, boss." "Well, you can forget the ball, caddy. Come and look for me."'[2]

Tennis, bowls, badminton and jukskei are firm favourites at many mines. Several have squash courts, some have a shooting range, and all have swimming-pools. Among black employees the favourite sport is soccer and every weekend there are matches between neighbouring mines. Associated Manganese's black teams call themselves 'Assmang' but practise with their Ammosal counterparts. KCB's Whitebank has a fine pitch but the best facilities of all are at Sishen. There, Iscor's coaches are producing black athletes of international calibre.

In most cases mine sports clubs are autonomous but affiliated to the mine recreation club, which is necessarily the centre of mine social life. At Beeshoek, the club is built around a large hall that was originally the mine powerhouse. At one end of the hall is a spacious stage. At the other is a 'rogues' gallery' of Associated Manganese personalities painted by a visiting signwriter during the early 1960s. Photographs and trophies hang on the walls and up above are the flags of the world's rugby-playing nations, not forgetting Uruguay and Japan.

A story told at Lohatlha recalls an elaborate hoax arranged by a former club manager. Each Saturday afternoon there was a large attendance at the club, and to entertain both drinkers and snooker-players the manager played radio music. One Saturday he concealed a tape recorder under the bar counter and connected it to the radio. When he switched over, the 'radio' broadcast an urgent message reporting that Russia had dropped bombs on London and New York and that the whole world was at war. More details would be given later and all should stay calm. Of course, there was pandemonium.

The days of radio have given way to nights of television. The main casualty has been attendance at recreation club film nights. 'Here at Lime Acres we still run two different films each week,' says Northern Lime's John Wotherspoon. 'But no matter how good they are, only a few people turn up.'[6] Copperton has a full-scale drive-in which used to be popular, but since television arrived in 1979 it has been all but deserted. There has been more interest in films at the outdoor cinemas that are a feature of every mine hostel. Patrons are happy to sit on the ground.

The size and atmosphere of Northern Cape mine villages vary greatly but most of them contain a primary school, a clinic with at least one registered nurse and an interdenominational church. Other features are a post office and a store or two, a garage and filling station and a guest house for official visitors from head office or elsewhere. Apart from the recreation club, the focus of social life is the mine manager's house, but usually the liveliest area is the single quarters where young bachelors live. Older bachelors and married couples have flats or houses provided by the mine.

Close to each village are quarters for coloured and black families and hostel complexes for black contract workers. At mines like Wessels or Mamatwan there are hostel complexes but no accommodation for whites apart from the hostel manager. The most modern complexes are at Finsch and the Sesheng black township near Sishen. At Sesheng, black workers are accommodated in three-bedroom flats that include bathrooms, commonrooms and verandahs. At Finsch, rooms are grouped in blocks centred on a lounge and separate dining room. The most attractive married quarters for blacks are at Ulco.

Sesheng, Ulco and several other villages have primary schools linked to black married quarters and some have a coloured school too. Sishen has a full-scale black hospital and Sishen doctors regularly visit other mine communities. Serious cases can be driven or flown to major hospitals in Kimberley or Klerksdorp. The healthy gravitate to large communal dining rooms or the recreation halls that are the centre of hostel social life. The halls sell traditional millet beer, malt and spirits but most Tswana patrons seem to prefer wine.

Tswana have adopted more features of European lifestyle than most black Africans, as was shown by an incident at Middelplaats. The management built an oval arena like those on gold mines to serve as a badminton court and outdoor cinema and also to accommodate tribal dancing. 'We even laid a gravel floor so that the Tswana could stamp their feet,' says Vin Oliver, who was mine manager at the time. 'I thought they'd be delighted. Instead they hooted with laughter. Tswana don't like tribal dancing. They're keen on *ballroom* dancing, so now we've laid a concrete floor and they invite partners from the district.'[7]

Good Neighbours

Ten years out of twelve, the Kalahari and indeed all the Northern Cape are nearly bone dry, except for the flow of major rivers that draw their water from sources far away. Little rain falls, and lesser rivers and streams appear virtually empty. Water abounds beneath the surface, as can be seen at the Eye of Kuruman and Kathu springs, but that is the result of drastic changes in the weather pattern which occur every 12 years or so. That is when the drought is broken and the Northern Cape receives cataclysmic rains.

In 1973, for instance, there were sudden downpours around Black Rock and Wessels where S A Manganese men were sinking their decline shaft. Water poured in from the surface and trapped heavy equipment. The miners rigged pumps but they were soon choked by mud, and eventually the decline was flooded for 300 metres. To make matters worse, the Gamagara River broke its banks and Wessels was isolated from Hotazel. Work at Wessels was stopped for a month, but in the meantime the miners improvised rafts and lashed their pumps on to them, then nursed them day and night until the shaft was dry again.

In planning Prieska Copper Mines, Anglovaal consulted a local farmer whose family had kept rainfall records since 1903. 'That gave us an idea of the floods we might expect,' says Copperton's Corrie van der Walt. 'Our engineers designed a system of dykes and canals to protect the shaft openings and prevent water from entering the underground workings.

The system was supposed to be a match for the highest floods in 100 years. Unfortunately for us, while it was still under construction Nature decided to let loose and gave us the heaviest rainfall in 150 years.'[8]

The rains came in 1974 and more than 150 mm fell in less than five hours. Luckily for Copperton the dykes held and the shafts were saved, but the mine offices were under water and the hostel was marooned. The same floods hit the Bellsbank diamond fissure, and some sections have not yet been pumped dry. Near Danielskuil, a dry pan about five kilometres long was flooded and for years served as a boating lake. Within Danielskuil, springs appeared on low-lying land and a lake formed around houses that had to be abandoned.

The raising of the water table helps to replenish boreholes, but it is ironic that the Northern Cape's climate swings so wildly from drought to flood and back to drought. Charlie Marais of Copperton forecasts that the spread of Escom powerlines and water pipelines will make all the difference. 'Already farmers on the Orange and Harts rivers are irrigating land to grow crops,' he says. 'Before long we'll be pumping water all through the Kalahari and Bushmanland. The one is perfect cattle country, the other is ideal for sheep, and with water they'll be a Land of Milk and Honey.'[9]

Charlie Marais and his wife still live in their old homestead close to Copperton's Hutchings headgear and insist they are happy, in spite of earth tremors each afternoon as blasting takes place far below. 'After ten years we're used to it,'[9] says Marais. He continues to farm large flocks of merinos and angoras and says the mine's presence has been a great help to him. Quite apart from financial rewards, he now has a tar road and a railway spur almost to his door and his farm is served by Escom power and water pumped from the mine.

Jacobus Thiart's farm is near Black Rock where mining started when he was small. 'In some ways I regret the arrival of the mines,' he says. 'Some farmers sold their land to mining companies years ago and now they've spent all their money and are left with nothing. Others have taken jobs at mines during hard times and their wives have become accustomed to easy living, so they're not really farming people any more. But against that the mines have opened up our region with new roads and a railway, and because of them our telephone service has improved and we have television.'[10]

Of course, farmers who have gone mining are complemented by miners who go farming. Many miners who have moved to the Northern Cape from other parts of South Africa have invested in small farms where they raise cattle or sheep and spend their weekends. Even those who have no farm of their own can see farming all around them, for in many cases mines have leased grazing rights to the original owners. At Sishen, Iscor runs its own farm to provide families with milk, meat and other products. Not far away, Iscor has developed a 1 000 ha nature reserve in Kathu Forest.

Sishen's reserve holds zebra, eland, red hartebeest, springbok and other species of buck, but its special prides are two white rhinos that take pleasure in buffeting any structures that annoy them. There are also some Indian water buffalo and a group of camels that like to feed near the main road and regularly astonish passers-by. Attached to the reserve is a picnic area and two fishing ponds that are favourite rendezvous for Sishenites with something to celebrate.

The world over, mining companies have become conscious of environmental concerns and must guard against pollution of land, water and air and in some cases against noise. In the Northern Cape, there are few complaints that mines are ruining the landscape: on the contrary, in several cases they are making it more interesting. The manganese mines of Postmasburg have opened deep limestone canyons that are fascinating to explore. Northern Lime's worked-out quarries are filling with water and could be developed as a recreational area, and so could the old Postmas mine near Postmasburg.

There are plans to create a mining museum at Manganore, which still has its endless rope haulage and cocopans on the rails, just as they were when mining stopped. An even better site for the museum would be the West End mine in Postmasburg, but it is not safe. Not only are there rockfalls, but Jan Jacobs the caretaker insists that a snake-like monster lurks in the water. According to Jacobs, the monster bleats like a kid to attract the unwary to the edge of the hole. They lose their balance and fall into the water, and the monster gobbles them up.

One of the biggest problems facing Northern Cape mines is dust, especially when the wind blows. At Ulco, both houses and trees have a permanent coating of white lime dust and the same is true of Northern Lime's hostel at Lime Acres. Lohatlha used to suffer from dust too, but a tree-planting programme has improved matters. Northern Lime is rehabilitating worked-out areas of its quarries by covering them with topsoil removed from newer workings. The topsoil contains seeds, and before long the treated areas sprout indigenous vegetation.

Dust problems are most serious on asbestos mines, because asbestos dust has been blamed for asbestosis, a form of phthisis. According to Doug Todd, South Africa became aware of the danger because of deaths in Europe in the 1940s and 1950s. 'The people affected were former shipworkers who'd had the job of spraying asbestos cladding on to ships' boilers,' he explained. 'They'd spent half their lives wrapped in clouds of asbestos dust, so it wasn't surprising that some of them caught phthisis. The disease develops slowly and years went by before any of them died, but doctors said asbestosis was the cause and there was a public outcry in many countries.

'Here in South Africa, health officials and the asbestos industry worked hard to counter risks in our mills and our mines. We developed new milling machines that reduced dust to a minimum and packed fibre in specially secure bales that would not be opened until they reached their destination. Down in the mines the asbestos was kept wet and ventilation was much improved. As a result of these measures asbestosis is becoming rare, and the asbestos industry as a whole is well on its way to redeeming its good name.'[4]

The Big Blast

From Copperton in the south to Pomfret in the north there are at least 70 distinct mine sites in the Northern Cape, nearly half of them still active. They range from the Stone Age workings at Gatkoppies to salt pan operations in Gordonia; from part-time jasper quarries near Griquatown to the sophisticated underground mines of the northern manganese belt. Many of the mine sites are little known even to people living in the vicinity, but at least one is known to mining men everywhere. Sishen's iron ore complex has become famous as one of the great mines of the world.

Part of Sishen's fame comes from the scale of its operations. Late in 1982 its mining and processing activities covered an area of 11 square kilometres, and its excavators and trucks worked around the clock to remove massive tonnages of ore and waste rock. 'Visitors assure us that in terms of the tonnages we move we must be in the front rank of the world's hard rock mines,' says Chris Swart, mine manager at Sishen. 'We're more cautious about it—there are mines as big as Sishen in Australia and America. But they work all through the week whereas we close down on Sundays, so in capacity Sishen probably is the biggest.'[11]

Sishen is organised on the grand scale, and the mine is matched by the arrangements on the 861 km rail line between Sishen and Saldanha. Ore trains are up to 2,3 km long and include up to 210 wagons able to carry 17 800 tons of ore. Most are pulled by three electric units and the journey to the sea takes 18 hours. There have been surprisingly few mishaps on the single-track line, though in 1982 28 trucks were derailed on the bridge over the Olifants River in the Western Cape and ended up in the water after falling 56 metres.

Nobody was hurt in the accident, and Sishen itself has a remarkable safety record. During nine months in 1981 Sishen's 5 000-odd employees worked 9,8 million man-hours without a time-losing accident. 'We were disappointed not to reach the 10 million mark, but 9,8 million man-hours is a huge achievement,' says Chris Swart. 'In South Africa we're second only to a mine in the Eastern Transvaal.'[11]

44. Part of the iron-ore processing plant at Sishen's North Mine.

Iscor

45. Pick-up arms connect Sishen's 150-ton trucks with an overhead pantograph that provides supplementary power to help them ascend uphill ramps.

Iscor

46. The dusty expanse of Sishen, one of the largest iron-ore mines in the world.

Iscor

47. The executive committee of the Northern Cape Mine Managers Association, 1982: (*front, from left*) Tony Cox (Middelplaats), Johan Pretorius (Samancor southern section), John Walls (Finsch, chairman), Peter Townsend (Samancor northern section); (*back, from left*) Frans Knox (Gefco), Chris Swart (Sishen), Rod Burnham (Finsch, honorary secretary).

Northern Cape Mine Managers Association

48. The benches of the Mamatwan manganese mine cut deep into the wide, sandy plains of the Kalahari.

Samancor

Iscor issued a special Sishen tie to commemorate the 9,8 million man-hours and the mine's employees wear it with pride. They take equal pleasure in recalling the day in April 1981 when Sishen set a new world record with a single blast. The mine was expanding westwards across the natural boundary of the old national road between Kuruman and Postmasburg. When a new road was built along the mine's eastern boundary, Sishen's pit superintendents were ready to explode a 2 660 m working face along the pit's edge in what was probably the biggest non-nuclear blast in history.

The working face ran parallel with the old road, and blasting crews drilled no fewer than 2 662 blast-holes each averaging 14,5 m in depth (adding up to 38,6 km) and 380 mm in diameter. The charging of the holes began weeks ahead of the day scheduled for the blast: each was charged with an average of 912 kg of explosives, amounting to a total of 2 427 tons. Each hole was equipped with two booster charges, connected by double lines of detonating cord which taken together stretched for 60 km. The cords were linked to 64 km of trunk lines, making a total of 124 km of detonating cord.

On blasting day, Sishen men and their guests took up position on a ridge about two kilometres from the working face and watched intently as shift foreman Bill Coleman pressed the detonating button. A salvo of explosions lasting 13 seconds rippled along the working face from left to right, each one accompanied by a neat plume of smoke and a dull thud as more than seven million tons of rock were lifted into the air and deposited in a long pile of rubble. As far as Sishen men can ascertain, the previous world record had been set in Australia with a blast of four million tons.

Among those who watched the great explosion were representatives of many other Northern Cape mines, brought together under the auspices of the Northern Cape Mine Managers' Association which was founded in the 1960s as an informal discussion group. Today its membership includes not only mine managers but also mine secretaries, engineers, geologists, mine captains and others. The association is part social club, part lobbying group and its officials are equipped to speak for the industry in dealings with the national governments, South African Railways and other bodies. Since its foundation, the Association's office-bearers have been:

	Chairman	*Vice-chairman*	*Hon Secretary*
1966	P C B Wentzel		
1967	N E Dougans	C N Blore	E J Millar
1968	J N Grobler	B Lowther	E J Millar
1969	B Lowther	S C Watson	C J Sargeant
1970	S C Watson	M R Oberholzer	A G Coreejes
1971	M R Oberholzer	F G Claughton	G H Kruger

(continues overleaf)

	Chairman	Vice-chairman	Hon Secretary
1972	F G Claughton	H S Botha	J H Every
1973	H S Botha	W B Parker	C J Sargeant
1974	D C Duffy	S C Watson	F Grieve
1975	S C Watson	F Gast	C F Heyns
1976	A D Ochse	J J Duvenhage	C F Heyns
1977	T D Brown	W B Parker	C F Heyns
1978	W B Parker	J S Oelofse	G E Smith
1979	P A Townsend	V H Oliver	G E Smith
1980	V H Oliver	H Kruger	G E Smith
1981	P J Pretorius	H Kruger	P Badenhorst
1982	J W Walls	J A Cox	R F Burnham

At regular intervals the association convenes at a Northern Cape mine which plays host for the day. Someone gives a talk on the mine and the visit includes tours of the workings, a tour of the surface plant and more than likely a round of golf. Once a year a strong party of managers flies to another region of South Africa or Namibia and tours mines on the invitations of sister associations. Periodically the sister associations return thc compliment.

Contacts like these help Northern Cape mines to keep abreast of developments elsewhere, and so does the recruitment of mine personnel from other parts of the country. Not all the newcomers are impressed with what they find, but Ulco's Dirk Jordaan has some encouragement for them. 'My wife and I are from the Western Transvaal,' he says. 'When we first came here a farmer told us: "In the Northern Cape you only cry twice—first when you arrive because you don't want to stay, and second when you leave because you can't bear to go." That's exactly how it is.'[12]

Author's Acknowledgements

THE AUTHOR thanks Allen Robinson of Johannesburg for permission to quote from his manuscript history of the Cape Asbestos Company; Nora Pascoe of Aynho, United Kingdom, for permission to quote from Harold Pascoe's article *Asbestos Fever* and from her own poems and letters; and Rev Humphrey Thompson of the Danielskuil district for permission to quote from his autobiography, *Distant Horizons*.

More than 150 Northern Cape mining men contributed information for the book in the course of interviews. I cannot name them all, but I am particularly grateful to such veterans as Willie Bam of Postmasburg, Faan Riekert of Kuruman, Mollie Franke of Port Shepstone and Charles Langeveld of Barkly West. Doug Todd of Johannesburg, an expert on the asbestos industry, died while the book was in preparation, and so did Syd Brownrigg who was an important pioneer of the manganese industry, and Lu Matter, formerly manager at Ulco.

Outsiders who provided information included Peter Beaumont of the McGregor Memorial Museum, Kimberley; Muriel Macey, Africana specialist at Kimberley Public Library; and the directors and staffs of the South African Library, Cape Town, the Cape Archives, Cape Town, and the Africana Museum, Johannesburg.

Those most closely concerned with the evolution of this book have been the successive chairmen and committee members of the Northern Cape Mine Managers' Association. The successive chairmen have been Peter Townsend, manager of the northern section of S A Manganese Amcor; Vin Oliver, former manager of Middelplaats mine and now in Zimbabwe; Johan Pretorius, manager of the southern section of S A Manganese Amcor; and John Walls, manager of Finsch mine.

Select Bibliography

BABE, JEROME: *The South African Diamond Fields* (New York, David Wesley, 1872)

BEET, GEORGE: *The Grand Old Days of the Diamond Fields* (Cape Town, Maskew Miller, c 1931)

BORCHERDS, PETRUS: *An Auto Biographical Memoir* (Cape Town, A S Robertson, 1861)

BURCHELL, WILLIAM: *Travels in the Interior of Southern Africa* (London, Longman Hurst, 1822)

CAMPBELL, JOHN: *Journal of Travels in South Africa* (London, Religious Tract Society, 1835)

CORNELL, FRED: *The Glamour of Prospecting* (London, Fisher Unwin, 1920)

DART, RAYMOND, *ed*: *Africa's Place in the Human Story* (Johannesburg, South African Broadcasting Corporation, *c* 1954)

DE VILLIERS, JOHN, *comp*: *The Manganese Deposits of the Union of South Africa* (Pretoria, Government Printer, 1960)

DEPARTMENT OF MINES: *Report of the Interdepartmental Committee on Tiger's Eye and Related Varieties* (Pretoria, Government Printer, 1968)

HALL, A L: *Asbestos in the Union of South Africa—Geological Survey Memoir 12* (Pretoria, Government Printing and Stationery Office, 1918)

KITTO, THOMAS: *Report on the Diamond Fields of Griqualand West* (Kimberley, Government of Griqualand West, 1879)

LICHTENSTEIN, HINRICH (trans A Plumptre): *Travels in Southern Africa* (London, Henry Colburn, 1815)

MOFFAT, ROBERT: *Missionary Labours and Scenes in Southern Africa* (London, John Snow, 1842)

PAYTON, CHARLES: *The Diamond Diggings of South Africa* (London, Horace Cox, 1972)

SOMERVILLE, WILLIAM: *Narrative of his Journey to the Eastern Cape Frontier and to Lattakoe* (Cape Town, Van Riebeeck Society, 1979)

S A MANGANESE AMCOR: *Kalahari Wealth* (Cape Town, Purnell, 1976)

THOMPSON, HUMPHREY: *Distant Horizons* (Kimberley, the author, 1976)

WAGNER, P A: *The Diamond Fields of Southern Africa* (Johannesburg, Transvaal Leader, 1914)

WYBERGH, W J: *The Limestone Resources of the Union* (Pretoria, Government Printing and Stationery Office, 1918–20)

References

Introduction (pp 1–4)

1 Piet Ludick, interviewed in Ulco, August 1980

Chapter One (pp 5–18)

1 Peter Beaumont, interviewed in Kimberley, August 1980
2 Peter Beaumont and Adrian Boshier, *Report on Test Excavations in a Prehistoric Pigment Mine near Postmasburg, Northern Cape* (South African Archaeological Bulletin 29)
3 William Somerville, *Narrative of his Journey to the Eastern Cape Frontier and Lattakoe*
4 Petrus Borcherds, *An Auto Biographical Memoir*
5 Hinrich Lichtenstein, *Travels in Southern Africa*
6 William Burchell, *Travels in the Interior of Southern Africa*
7 E J Dunn, *Through Bushmanland* (Cape Monthly Magazine, December 1872)
8 John Campbell, *Journal of Travels in South Africa*
9 Robert Moffat, *Missionary Scenes and Labours in Southern Africa*

Chapter Two (pp 19–38)

1 Jerome Babe, *The South African Diamond Fields*
2 *Rules and Regulations for the Vaal-River Diamond-Fields* (copy in South African Library, Cape Town)
3 Charles Payton, *The Diamond Diggings of South Africa*
4 George Stow, *Griqualand West* (Cape Monthly Magazine, August 1872)
5 Thomas Kitto, *Report on the Diamond Fields of Griqualand West*
6 *Diamond Fields Advertiser*, October 11, 1884
7 *Diamond Fields Advertiser*, May 29, 1886
8 *Diamond Fields Advertiser*, April 10, 1886
9 *Cape Times*, February 13, 1926
10 Quoted in Allen Robinson, *A History of the Activities of the Cape Asbestos Company in the North Western Cape (unpublished manuscript)*
11 Thomas Shone to Johannesburg, 1943 (copy in Postmasburg Public Library)
12 Daniel Ludick, interviewed in Delportshoop, August 1980.
13 *Report of the Inspector of Claims, Barkly West, for the year 1908* (copy in Kimberley Public Library)
14 Charlie Marais, interviewed in Copperton, July 1980
15 Fred Cornell, *The Glamour of Prospecting*

Chapter Three (pp 39–51)

1 *Asbestos in the Union of South Africa—Geological Survey Memoir 12*
2 *Cape Times*, February 13, 1926
3 Daniel Ludick, interviewed in Delportshoop, August 1980
4 Hans van der Walt, interviewed in Postmasburg, September 1980
5 Willie Bam, interviewed in Postmasburg, August 1980
6 W J Wybergh, *The Limestone Resources of the Union*
7 Raymond Dart, *The Proto-Human Inhabitants of Southern Africa* (radio talk included in *Africa's Place in the Human Story*)

Chapter Four (pp 52–69)

1 Hans van Staden, interviewed in Sishen, August 1980
2 Chalon St Quentin, interviewed in Vryburg, September 1980
3 John Stewart, interviewed in Pomfret, September 1980.
4 quoted in De Beers Consolidated Mines, *The History of Finsch Mine* (unpublished manuscript)
5 Molly Shone, interviewed in Postmasburg, July 1975
6 quoted in first draught of S A Manganese Amcor, *Kalahari Wealth* (unpublished manuscript)
7 Pieter Vertue, interviewed in Beeshoek, July 1980
8 Hans van der Walt, interviewed in Postmasburg, September 1980
9 Alwyn Vorster, interviewed in Postmasburg, September 1980
10 Willie Bam, interviewed in Postmasburg, August 1980
11 Syd Brownrigg, interviewed in Johannesburg, September 1980
12 Syd Brownrigg, *Manganisation* (Anglovaler magazine)
13 Gene Stanton, interviewed in Lohatlha, August 1980
14 Mangancsc Corporation, *Annual Report 1931*
15 Terry Shone, interviewed in Postmasburg, August 1980
16 Alwin Austin, interviewed in Lime Acres, August 1980
17 Humphrey Thompson, *Distant Horizons*
18 Faan Riekert, interviewed in Kuruman, August 1980
19 Nora Pascoe to Mollie Franke, 1979

Chapter Five (pp 70–89)

1 Manganese Corporation, *Annual Report 1934*
2 Syd Brownrigg, interviewed in Johannesburg, September 1980
3 quoted in S A Manganese Amcor, *Kalahari Wealth*
4 George Stow, *Griqualand West* (Cape Monthly Magazine, August 1872)
5 A B Robertson, *History of Union Lime* (unpublished paper)
6 Elsie Lowther, interviewed in Cape Town, September 1980
7 Piet Ludick, interviewed in Ulco, July 1980
8 Charles Langeveld, interviewed in Ulco, July 1980
9 Koekie Daniels, interviewed at Longlands, August 1980
10 Dawie Voges, interviewed in Kuruman, September 1980
11 Andries Estebeth, interviewed in Prieska, July 1980
12 Louw Markram, interviewed in Kuruman, August 1980
13 Harold Pascoe, *Asbestos Fever* (photocopied typescript)
14 Nora Pascoe to Mollie Franke, 1979
15 Nora Pascoe, *Folds, Seams and Patches* (photocopied typescript)
16 quoted in De Beers Consolidated Mines, *The History of Finsch Mine* (unpublished manuscript)
17 Piet Coetzee, interviewed in Postmasburg, August 1980
18 Kiewiet Reinecke, interviewed at Nchwaning, August 1980

Chapter Six (pp 90–108)

1 Frik Scholtz, interviewed in Owendale, August 1980
2 Hans van Staden, interviewed in Sishen, August 1980
3 Mike Pauer, interviewed in Sishen, August 1980
4 *Iscor News*, December 1952
5 Jan Kotze, interviewed in Sishen, August 1980
6 Pieter Vertue, interviewed in Beeshoek, July 1980
7 Percy van der Walt, interviewed in Black Rock, August 1980

8 Henry Maritz, interviewed in Black Rock, August 1980
9 Dan Koorzen, interviewed in Lohatlha, July 1980
10 Willie Bam, interviewed in Postmasburg, August 1980
11 Flippie Badenhorst, interviewed in Lohatlha, July 1980
12 Lydia Swartz, interviewed in Ulco, August 1980
13 Charles Langeveld, interviewed in Ulco, August 1980
14 *Northern Cape Bulletin*, September 1949
15 Eric Cockcroft, interviewed in Ulco, August 1980
16 Alwin Austin, interviewed in Lime Acres, August 1980
17 Stan Hoelson, interviewed in Lime Acres, August 1980
18 John Wotherspoon, interviewed in Lime Acres, August 1980
19 Doug Todd, interviewed in Kuruman, August 1980
20 Sarel de Witt, interviewed in Kuruman, August 1980
21 Faan Riekert, interviewed in Kuruman, August 1980
22 Sarel de Witt, interviewed in Kuruman, August 1980

Chapter Seven (pp 109–124)

1 Manie Pyper, interviewed in Pomfret, September 1980
2 Pieter Vertue, interviewed in Beeshoek, July 1980
3 S A Manganese Amcor, *Kalahari Wealth*
4 Danie de Bruin, interviewed at Bellsbank, August 1980
5 *Diamond News*, December 1954
6 Pietman Selzer, interviewed in Delportshoop, August 1980
7 Faan Deetlefs, interviewed at Frank Smith Mine, August 1980
8 Jan Krieg, interviewed at Sover, August 1980
9 Syd Brownrigg, interviewed in Johannesburg, September 1980
10 Brahm Papendorf, interviewed in Johannesburg, September 1980
11 Doug Todd, interviewed in Kuruman, August 1980
12 Mollie Franke, interviewed in Kuruman, August 1980
13 Marthinus Uys, interviewed in Danielskuil, August 1980
14 Elsie Lowther, interviewed in Cape Town, September 1980
15 Lu Matter in letter to the author, October 1980
16 Mike Pauer, interviewed in Sishen, August 1980
17 Dirk Bleeker, interviewed in Beeshoek, July 1980

Chapter Eight (pp 125–140)

1 Sarel de Witt, interviewed in Kuruman, August 1980
2 Corrie Pieterse, interviewed in Owendale, August 1980
3 Harold Pascoe, *Asbestos Fever* (photocopied typescript)
4 Simon Spies, interviewed in Kuruman, August 1980
5 Nora Pascoe in letter to Mollie Franke, 1979
6 quoted from unpublished draught of S A Manganese Amcor, *Kalahari Wealth*
7 Lydia Swartz, interviewed in Ulco, August 1980
8 Lu Matter in letter to the author, October 1980
9 Theo Cloete, interviewed in Ulco, July 1980
10 John Wotherspoon, interviewed in Lime Acres, August 1980
11 Northern Lime Company (brochure)
12 Danie de Bruin, interviewed at Bellsbank, August 1980
13 Dirk Bleeker, interviewed in Beeshoek, August 1980
14 *The Star*, May 4, 1963
15 Brahm Papendorf, interviewed in Johannesburg, September 1980

16 De Beers Consolidated Mines, *Finsch Diamond Mine*
17 Dawie Voges, interviewed in Kuruman, August 1980
18 *Report of the Interdepartmental Committee on Tiger's Eye and Related Varieties*

Chapter Nine (pp 141–158)

1 Ron Middleton in letter to the author, October 1980
2 Charlie Marais, interviewed in Copperton, July 1980
3 Mike Hearn in letter to the author, October 1980
4 Corrie van der Walt, interviewed in Copperton, July 1980
5 Jan Kotze, interviewed in Sishen, August 1980
6 John Wotherspoon, interviewed in Lime Acres, August 1980
7 Eugene Richards, interviewed in Danielskuil, August 1980
8 Arthur Bosman, interviewed in Barkly West, August 1980
9 Eric Cockcroft, interviewed in Ulco, July 1980
10 Micky Gaw, interviewed in Ulco, August 1980
11 Dawie Voges, interviewed in Kuruman, August 1980
12 Gert van Tonder, interviewed in Kuruman, August 1980
13 Doug Todd, interviewed in Kuruman, August 1980
14 Rudolf Vertue, interviewed in Black Rock, August 1980
15 Peter Townsend, interviewed in Hotazel, August 1980
16 Gideon Hoon, interviewed at National Manganese, August 1980
17 Vin Oliver, interviewed at Middelplaats, August 1980

Chapter Ten (pp 159–170)

1 Danie de Bruin, interviewed at Bellsbank, August 1980
2 Eric Cockcroft, interviewed in Ulco, July 1980
3 Fanie Nieuwoudt, interviewed in Kuruman, October 1982
4 Doug Todd, interviewed in Kuruman, August 1980
5 Gert Kotze, interviewed in Owendale, August 1980
6 John Wotherspoon, interviewed in Lime Acres, August 1980
7 Vin Oliver, interviewed at Middelplaats, August 1980
8 Corrie van der Walt, interviewed in Copperton, July 1980
9 Charlie Marais, interviewed in Copperton, July 1980
10 Jacobus Thiart, interviewed near Black Rock, August 1980
11 Chris Swart, interviewed in Sishen, October 1982
12 Dirk Jordaan, interviewed in Ulco, October 1982

Index

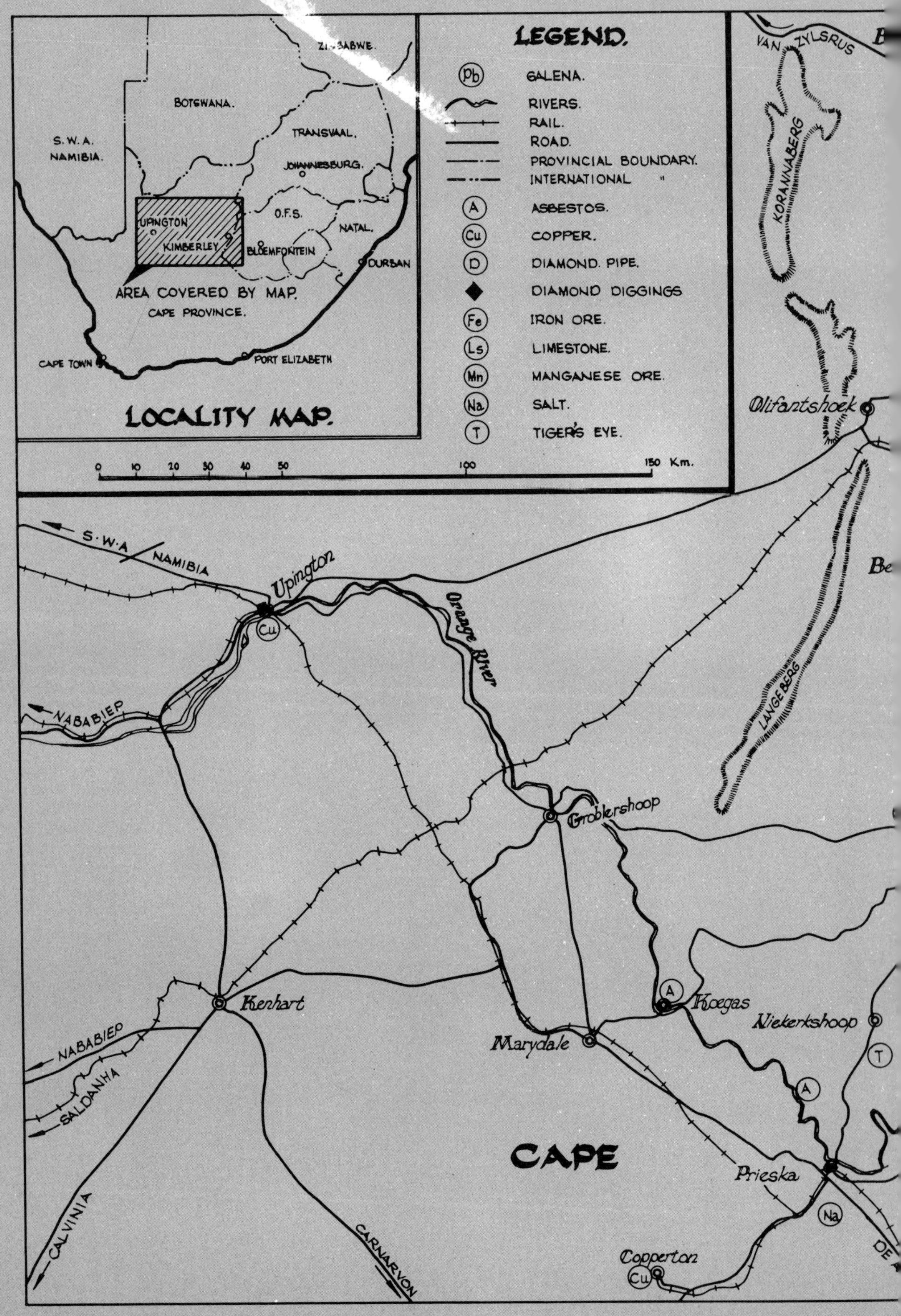
LEGEND.
GALENA.
RIVERS.
RAIL.
ROAD.
PROVINCIAL BOUNDARY.
INTERNATIONAL "
ASBESTOS.
COPPER.
DIAMOND. PIPE.
DIAMOND DIGGINGS
IRON ORE.
LIMESTONE.
MANGANESE ORE.
SALT.
TIGER'S EYE.
0 10 20 30 40 50 100 150 Km.
BOTSWANA.
S.W.A. NAMIBIA.
TRANSVAAL.
JOHANNESBURG.
UPINGTON
KIMBERLEY
O.F.S.
NATAL.
BLOEMFONTEIN
DURBAN
AREA COVERED BY MAP.
CAPE PROVINCE.
CAPE TOWN
PORT ELIZABETH
LOCALITY MAP.
VAN ZYLSRUS
KORANNABERG
Olifantshoek
LANGEBERG
S.W.A NAMIBIA
Upington
Orange River
NABABIEP
Groblershoop
Kenhart
Koegas
Marydale
Niekerkshoop
SALDANHA
CAPE
Prieska
Copperton
CALVINIA
CARNARVON